DATE DUE

DEC 0 9 2011		
AUG 0 8 2012		

GAYLORD   #3522PI   Printed in USA

ON THE ROSEBUD SIOUX RESERVATION IN SOUTH DAKOTA

Photo by Paul Conklin

American Indians
and
Federal Aid

STUDIES IN SOCIAL ECONOMICS

American Indians
and
Federal Aid

Alan L. Sorkin

THE BROOKINGS INSTITUTION
Washington, D.C.

ISBN 0-8157-8044-3

Library of Congress Catalog Card Number 78-150957

THE BROOKINGS INSTITUTION is an independent organization devoted to non-partisan research, education, and publication in economics, government, foreign policy, and the social sciences generally. Its principal purposes are to aid in the development of sound public policies and to promote public understanding of issues of national importance.

The Institution was founded on December 8, 1927, to merge the activities of the Institute for Government Research, founded in 1916, the Institute of Economics, founded in 1922, and the Robert Brookings Graduate School of Economics and Government, founded in 1924.

The general administration of the Institution is the responsibility of a Board of Trustees charged with maintaining the independence of the staff and fostering the most favorable conditions for creative research and education. The immediate direction of the policies, program, and staff of the Institution is vested in the President, assisted by an advisory committee of the officers and staff.

In publishing a study, the Institution presents it as a competent treatment of a subject worthy of public consideration. The interpretations and conclusions in such publications are those of the author or authors and do not necessarily reflect the views of the other staff members, officers, or trustees of the Brookings Institution.

Foreword

Of all nonwhite ethnic groups, American Indians are in the least favorable economic position. Living on a reservation that is far removed from the mainstream of American life, the Indian is often torn between a desire to remain on the reservation, preserving his tribal culture despite limited economic opportunity, and a desire to break away for a chance at greater economic benefits in an alien environment.

To develop the economic potential of the reservation and to ease the burden of adjustment for those Indians who want to relocate, the federal government conducts a variety of assistance programs. The purpose of this study is to describe and evaluate those programs, and to identify their strengths and weaknesses. It concludes with an estimate of the additional funds needed to make the federal effort more effective.

The author appreciates the generous assistance of several Indian leaders who provided essential information: Robert Lewis, governor of the Zuñi Tribe; Robert Jim, chairman of the Yakima Tribal Council; Emmett York, chairman of the Mississippi Choctaw Tribal Council; and Enos Poorbear, chairman of the Oglala Sioux Tribal Council. He also wishes to thank the Bureau of Indian Affairs for providing unpublished materials that were basic to the analysis. He is particularly grateful to Joseph Lasalle of the Employment Assistance Branch, L. Madison Coombs of the Division of Education, Gordon Evans of the Division of Industrial Development and Tourism, and above all to former Commissioner of

Indian Affairs Robert L. Bennett, who played a central role in arranging the author's trips to thirteen reservations.

For comments and helpful suggestions on the manuscript, the author is grateful to several present and former Brookings staff members—Henry J. Aaron, Wilfred Lewis, Jr., Alice M. Rivlin, and James Gaither—and to the members of his reading committee—Carl K. Eicher, Peter P. Dorner, Calvin A. Kent, and Edwin S. Mills. He also expresses his sincere thanks to Joseph A. Pechman, Brookings' director of Economic Studies, for his encouragement and counsel while the study was in progress. Evelyn P. Fisher checked the statistical material for accuracy, Frances M. Shattuck edited the manuscript, and Joan C. Culver prepared the index.

This volume is the eighth of the Brookings Studies in Social Economics, a program of research and education on selected topics in the fields of health, education, social security, and welfare. It was financed by the William H. Donner Foundation, which has a continuing interest in finding solutions to some of the pressing economic and social problems facing today's Indian. The views expressed are those of the author and should not be attributed to the Donner Foundation or to the trustees, officers, or staff members of the Brookings Institution.

KERMIT GORDON
President

January 1971
Washington, D.C.

Contents

CHAPTER I

The Reservation Indian

Some half million American Indians live in the United States. They belong to several hundred tribes, with many separate languages and cultures. There are Indians in every state, but a large majority are on or near reservations, in sparsely settled portions of states west of the Mississippi River, living with their own tribes according to their inherited customs. The only reservations of any size east of the Mississippi are in Wisconsin, Florida, and North Carolina, with much smaller ones in Michigan and Mississippi. Some Indians choose to live off the reservations, frequently in large cities, following the ways of the whites and assimilating to various degrees into the dominant society. This book is concerned chiefly with the Indians on or adjacent to reservations, who are served by the U.S. Bureau of Indian Affairs.

A General View

An Indian reservation can be characterized as an open-air slum. It has a feeling of emptiness and isolation. There are miles and miles of dirt or gravel roads without any signs of human life. The scattered Indian communities are made up of scores of tarpaper shacks or log cabins with one tiny window and a stovepipe sticking out of a roof that is weighted down with pieces of metal and automobile tires. These dwellings, each of them home for six or seven persons, often have no electricity or running water—sometimes not even an outhouse. The front yards are frequently littered with

1

abandoned, broken-down automobiles that are too expensive to repair and too much trouble to junk.

The largest settlement on the reservation contains the offices of the Bureau of Indian Affairs and the hospital operated by the U.S. Public Health Service. The large modern homes of the government employees are in shocking contrast to the shacks of the Indians they are supposed to be helping. The stores in the town are small but fairly modern. Very few Indians are employed in them, and few are Indian owned or managed.

The walls and shelves of the reservation trading post are lined with silver and turquoise articles as well as family treasures pawned by Indians who will never save enough money to reclaim them. Most of the items for sale have no price tags. What better way to keep the Indian rug weaver or silversmith who sells to the trader from learning the real value of his work?

The number of unemployed is striking. Everywhere there seem to be dozens of Indians standing or sitting around doing nothing. With so much time on their hands, many pass the day drinking in bars just outside the reservation.

Indians are in general a stoic people. They have learned to accept in silence the burdens of suffering brought by white domination. They wait hours to see the Indian service doctor or to meet with a Bureau of Indian Affairs official to discuss payment of income from Indian lands leased to whites. The Indians seldom complain about the wait or the lack of chairs or the indifference with which they are treated by white officials.

The "generation gap" among Indian people is at least as wide as that between young and old non-Indians. On the Navajo Reservation the older men still wear their hair in braids and the women wear heavy thick skirts down to their ankles. The younger people dress in much the same manner as non-Indians, the boys mostly in dungarees, many of the girls in short dresses. While older Navajos carry on traditional sheep raising, the younger people are leaving the reservation in larger and larger numbers for the major cities on the West Coast.

However, the difference in outlook does not cause the young to disrespect or resent the authority of the old. At a tribal council meeting at Laguna Pueblo, some older members could speak only

Laguna and many younger members spoke only English. Interpreters translated from one language to another. The tribal chairman listened carefully to all points of view, allowing the discussion to continue until a common position was reached by virtually all present. Only then was the issue put to a vote. While such legislative procedure is time-consuming, who is to say that in the long run it may not be the most efficient.

There is no typical reservation: each one is unique, but all have some aspects in common. Some of the significant characteristics of reservations and their inhabitants—observed during nearly seven weeks of travel to thirteen of the major reservations in the United States (see Table 1-1)—are described in this book. The picture is depressing, but it is the background against which federal programs to improve the lot of reservation Indians must be examined.

History of Government Programs

No single definition distinguishes an American Indian from a non-Indian. The U.S. Bureau of the Census has followed varying practices in identifying Indians. In 1960, when the census takers were

TABLE I-I

Reservations Visited, 1968

Reservation	State	Date
Mississippi Choctaw	Mississippi	April 1–6
Creek	Oklahoma	June 10–13
Osage	Oklahoma	June 14–16
Laguna Pueblo	New Mexico	June 17–19
Zuñi Pueblo	New Mexico	June 20–22
Navajo	New Mexico Arizona	June 23–27
Papago	Arizona	June 28–30
Yakima	Washington	July 1–3
Blackfeet	Montana	July 4–8
Crow	Montana	July 9–10
Standing Rock	North Dakota South Dakota	July 11–14
Pine Ridge	South Dakota	July 15–16
Rosebud	South Dakota	July 17–19

TABLE I-2

Total American Indian Population (Including Alaskan Natives),
Selected Years, 1890–1965

Year	American Indians[a]	Alaskan natives[b]	Total
1890	248,300	25,400	273,700
1900	237,200	29,500	266,700
1910	265,700	25,300	291,000
1920	244,400	26,600	271,000
1930	332,400	30,000	362,400
1940	360,500[c]	32,500	393,000
1950	421,600[c]	33,900	455,500
1960	509,100[d]	43,100	552,200
1965 (est.)	555,000[e]	45,000[e]	600,000

Sources: U.S. Public Health Service, *Indian Health Highlights* (June 1966), p. x. Data for 1890–1960 are U.S. Bureau of the Census decennial enumerations.
a. Excludes Alaskan Indians.
b. Includes Indians, Eskimos, and Aleuts.
c. Adjustments were made for underenumeration in 1940 and 1950. In these censuses, owing to the procedures used, many Indians of mixed racial backgrounds were not identified as Indians. The self-enumeration procedures used in the 1960 census resulted in a larger proportion of such persons being listed as Indians.
d. Includes Hawaii.
e. Public Health Service, Division of Indian Health, mid-decade estimate based on post–census year projections.

instructed to let the individual indicate his racial identity, 524,000 identified themselves as Indians. That number is double the 1890 figure (when Indians were first enumerated in the decennial census), and it is still increasing (Table 1-2). The U.S. Bureau of Indian Affairs (BIA) counts only those who are eligible for its services: those living on or near reservations (in Oklahoma, former reservations are included). The bureau estimated that in 1962 367,000 Indians on or adjacent to reservations were receiving its services—this included 38,000 in Alaska. By September 1968 the number had risen to 452,000 (including 55,000 in Alaska). This service population lived in twenty-five so-called reservation states. In 1968 about 86 percent of the total were in eight states—Arizona, New Mexico, Oklahoma, Alaska, South Dakota, Montana, Washington, and North Dakota—and 68 percent of the total were in the first four.[1]

Reservations are tribally owned lands, ranging from less than

[1] U.S. Bureau of Indian Affairs, "U.S. Indian Population (1962) and Land (1963)" (November 1963; processed), pp. 5, 6; and "Estimates of the Indian Population Served by the Bureau of Indian Affairs: September 1968" (March 1969; processed).

one acre (Strawberry Valley Rancheria in California) to about 25,000 square miles (the Navajo Reservation, with an estimated 120,000 Indians occupying an area embracing parts of Arizona, New Mexico, and Utah, a tract about the size of West Virginia). Over 200 of these units are technically reservations, but in this volume "reservation" refers to the 160 largest. Most of them were established before 1871 by treaties between the United States and the Indians as the white man moved west in his search for more land; others were founded later by federal statutes, presidential orders, or agreements approved by Congress. Indians living on reservations have almost all the freedoms other Americans possess; restrictions are placed only on tribal funds and property.

Secretary of War Henry Knox was given responsibility for Indian affairs in 1789, but territorial governors retained some authority over Indian agents. The office of superintendent of Indian trade was established in 1806 and abolished in 1822. Two years later Secretary of War John C. Calhoun ordered the creation of the Bureau of Indian Affairs. Congress created the position of commissioner of Indian affairs in 1832 and a Department of Indian Affairs in 1834, both of which were transferred to the Department of the Interior upon its establishment in 1849.[2] The commissioner is a presidential appointee responsible to the secretary of the interior.

The Bureau of Indian Affairs provides many of the services that non-Indians receive from state and local government. Each of its functions, such as social services, education, and industrial development, is the responsibility of an assistant commissioner. Reservation programs have been administered by ten area directors, but beginning in 1971, this position will be abolished. The functions the area directors have performed will be taken over by sixty-three field administrators, in the hope that they will be able to form a closer working relationship with tribal leaders.

From the 1880s until 1934 the federal government put strong pressure on Indian tribes to discard their traditional customs and act like white men. The General Allotment Act of 1887 (the Dawes Act), which remained the instrument of federal Indian pol-

[2] Laurence F. Schmeckebier, *The Office of Indian Affairs: Its History, Activities and Organization* (Johns Hopkins Press for Institute for Government Research, 1927), pp. 26–28, 43.

icy for thirty years, permitted the breaking up of tribal or reservation land into individual allotments if the President believed the land could thereby be advantageously employed. Each head of a family was eligible for 80 acres of agricultural land or 160 acres of grazing land.[3]

The deed to the land was retained by the federal government for twenty-five years, or longer if the President thought an extension necessary. At the end of this period the title to the land was given to the Indian along with his citizenship. Lands not allotted to individual Indians were declared surplus and opened up to homesteading. It was believed that pressuring Indians to become individual farm operators would accelerate their assimilation into the dominant culture and help to make them productive members of the community.

Because many Indians had little interest in agriculture and their farms were too small to yield an adequate income, numerous allotments were sold at low prices. By 1933, 91 million acres, two-thirds of the Indian land base, had passed into non-Indian hands.[4]

In 1934 the Dawes Act was repealed and replaced by the Indian Reorganization Act (the Wheeler-Howard Act). This law, reflecting the belief that "the tribal Indian remains the self-reliant and self-supporting Indian," provided for strengthening tribal governments and stated new economic policies. The trust period on Indian land was continued indefinitely, and those lands remaining unsold after allotment were returned to the tribes. The act authorized the establishment of a revolving loan fund to provide credit for agricultural and industrial enterprises.

Also, during the 1930s the education of children in their home environment became more common as many small day schools were built on the reservations.

Many Indian lands are still held in trust by the federal government. The erroneous belief thus persists that Indians are wards of the federal government. Since 1924 all Indians have been citizens of the United States and have the right to vote in state and federal

[3] Theodore H. Haas, "The Legal Aspects of Indian Affairs from 1887 to 1957," in George E. Simpson and J. Milton Yinger (eds.), *American Indians and American Life, Annals of the American Academy of Political and Social Science*, Vol. 311 (May 1957), p. 13.

[4] *Ibid.*

elections as well as the responsibility to serve in the armed forces. Indians must pay the same taxes as non-Indians except that trust property and income derived from it are exempt from taxation.

Federal agencies (principally the Bureau of Indian Affairs) spend about $500 million annually to provide services to reservation Indians. The variety of programs has greatly increased since the Second World War, but there has been no economic evaluation of any of them, although some have been in effect since the nineteenth century. While the present programs suffer from internal weaknesses and in many cases from underfunding, in general they give Indians more freedom to decide where they will raise their families (on or off reservation) than did any programs in earlier years.[5] The federal government should not, by its policies, either encourage or discourage Indians' leaving the reservations. Expectations and desires for self-fulfillment vary so greatly among tribes and among their members that programs must be devised to give the individual Indian a choice about where he earns his livelihood.

The Meriam report over forty years ago took the position that "the work with and for the Indians must give consideration to the desires of the individual Indians. He who wishes to merge into the social and economic life of the prevailing civilization of this country should be given all practicable aid and advice in making the necessary adjustments. He who wants to remain an Indian and live according to his old culture should be aided in doing so."[6]

The recent history of federal and state governmental relations with reservation Indians shows a progressive elimination of restrictions. In 1938 seven states refused to let Indians vote; however, by 1948, all seven had removed their restrictions. The Indian Claims Commission Act of 1946 finally permitted Indian tribes to sue the federal government. Unfair dealings in lands have been the major charge in such suits. Another restriction on reservation Indians,

---

[5] During the early and mid-1950s, there was great pressure for terminating federal responsibility for Indian reservations, and programs for reservation development were temporarily suspended. After the disastrous results of forced termination of two important tribes became known, the pressure subsided, and reservation development programs were reinstituted. Termination is discussed more fully in Chap. 7.

[6] *The Problem of Indian Administration*, Report of a Survey made at the request of Honorable Hubert Work, Secretary of the Interior, and submitted to him, Feb. 21, 1928 (Johns Hopkins Press for Institute for Government Research, 1928), p. 88.

imposed in 1802, authorized the President to regulate the selling of alcoholic beverages among the tribes. That authority, broadened and strengthened over the years, ultimately (by act of July 23, 1892, as amended in 1938) prohibited the sale or gift of liquor to Indians. The validity of the Indian liquor law was upheld by the Supreme Court on several occasions by a broad interpretation of Congress's power to regulate commerce with Indian tribes. However, by 1953, Indians were treated just the same as non-Indians when off the reservation (except where state laws singled them out) and were granted the right of local option for their reservations.[7]

One major restriction on reservation Indians remains. Congress has imposed limitations on their disposal of trust or restricted property. Administrative or congressional approval is required for the sale of such property or the expenditure of certain trust funds. Unless this restriction is eliminated (with appropriate safeguards), the Indians will continue to be denied full citizenship rights and will remain in a sense a dependent people.

Income

The vast majority of American Indians live in abject poverty; in 1964, 74 percent of reservation families earned less than $3,000 a year (the poverty threshold).[8] While their income rose considerably more between 1939 and 1964 than that of the total population, it was only 30 percent of the latter in 1964, as shown in Table 1-3.[9]

The table also shows a widening income gap between reserva-

[7] Haas, "Legal Aspects of Indian Affairs," pp. 16–17.

[8] Task Force on Indian Housing, "Indian Housing: Need, Alternatives, Priorities and Program Recommendations," Bureau of Indian Affairs (December 1966; processed). The figure of $3,000 annual money income for a family of four was used in 1964 by the Council of Economic Advisers to measure the extent of poverty. *Economic Report of the President, January 1964*, p. 58.

[9] Although impossible to measure, the standard of living may not differ as much between Indians living on and off reservations or between reservation Indians and non-Indians as the income levels indicate. Reservation Indians receive free medical services if they are of one-fourth or more Indian blood, while non-reservation Indians and non-Indians are not generally entitled to such services. Many reservation Indians are living rent free on allotted land, while off-reservation Indians or non-Indians may be paying rent. Reservation Indians pay no state income tax, and no federal income tax on income derived from trust property. Finally, these data do not include income in kind, which would be higher for reservation Indians.

TABLE I-3

Median Income of Indian, Nonwhite, and All Males,
Selected Years, 1939–64ᵃ

(In 1964 dollars)

Year	Indians			Non-whites	All males
	All	Non-reservation	Reservation		
1939	n.a.	n.a.	500	925	2,300
1944	n.a.	n.a.	660	1,600	2,900
1949	950	1,040	825	1,925	3,475
1959	1,925	2,570	1,475	2,950	5,050
1964	n.a.	n.a.	1,800	3,426	6,283
Percentage increase, 1939–64			260	270	173

Sources: Nonwhites and all males, 1964, from U.S. Bureau of the Census, *Current Population Reports*, Series P-60, No. 47, "Income in 1964 of Families and Persons in the United States" (1965), pp. 41, 51. Other figures are estimated from data in the following publications:

U.S. Bureau of Indian Affairs, "Reservation Income, 1939" (1939; unpublished), Table LV, p. 2;

Bureau of the Census, *Sixteenth Census of the United States: 1940*, Vol. 3, *The Labor Force*, Pt. 1, *United States Summary* (1943), Table 71, p. 116, and *Educational Attainment by Economic Characteristics and Marital Status* (1947), Table 31, p. 161;

U.S. Census of Population: 1950, Vol. 4, *Special Reports*, Pt. 3, Chap. B, *Nonwhite Population by Race* (1953), Table 10, p. 32, and Table 21, p. 72, and Vol. 4, Pt. 1, Chap. B, *Occupational Characteristics* (1956), Table 19, p. 183, and Table 21, p. 215;

U.S. Census of Population: 1960, *Subject Reports, Nonwhite Population by Race*, Final Report PC(2)-1C (1963), Table 33, p. 104, and *Occupational Characteristics*, Final Report PC(2)-7A (1963), Table 25, p. 296, and Table 26, p. 316;

Bureau of Indian Affairs, "Selected Data on Indian Reservations Eligible for Designation under Public Works and Economic Development Act" (December 1966; processed);

Bureau of the Census, *Current Population Reports*, Series P-60, No. 5, "Income of Families and Persons in the United States: 1947" (1949), p. 29, and No. 7, "Income of Families and Persons in the United States: 1949" (1951), p. 35.

n.a. Not available.

a. Data include all males and all sources of income, whether earned or unearned.

tion and non-reservation Indians. In 1949 the median income of Indians on reservations was 80 percent of that of those living elsewhere; in 1959 the figure had dropped to 60 percent. The increased disparity results from the migration of many relatively well educated and highly skilled Indians to major urban centers during the 1950s. In the metropolitan areas better-paying jobs, more commensurate with their level of ability, were available, while the reservation economy remained comparatively stagnant.

From 1939 to 1964, the median income of reservation Indian males averaged about half that of nonwhite males, which rose slightly faster than that of reservation Indians during this period (Table 1-3). By 1959 the median income of non-reservation Indians was nearly that of nonwhites.

The sources of income for reservation Indians have changed

TABLE 1-4

Median Family Income, Selected Reservations, 1964

Reservation	State	Median family income
Fort Apache	Arizona	$1,310
Hopi	Arizona	1,140
Papago	Arizona	900[a]
Salt River	Arizona	2,325
Fort Hall	Idaho	2,235
Leech Lake	Minnesota	2,039
Choctaw	Mississippi	900
Crow	Montana	1,100
Northern Cheyenne	Montana	3,600
Zuñi	New Mexico	2,126
Fort Berthold	North Dakota	1,544
Turtle Mountain	North Dakota	2,228
Pine Ridge	South Dakota	1,335
Rosebud	South Dakota	900

Source: Bureau of Indian Affairs, "Indian Reservations Eligible for . . . Public Works."
a. 1962 data.

fundamentally: in 1939, 38 percent came from wages, 26 percent from agriculture, 8 percent from arts and crafts, and 28 percent was unearned.[10] In 1964, an estimated 75 percent of total income was derived from wages, with 10 percent from agriculture, 5 percent from arts and crafts, and 10 percent unearned.[11]

There is great variation in income among reservations. Median family income in 1964 varied from a low of $900 on the Rosebud and Choctaw Reservations to $3,600 on the Northern Cheyenne Reservation (Table 1-4). Even within a state the variation is sizable. In Montana median income on the Crow Reservation was less than one-third of that on the Northern Cheyenne Reservation; in Arizona, median income on the Papago and Hopi Reservations was less than half that on the Salt River Reservation.

There has been little change in the rank of the states by individual Indian income; the states that were highest or lowest in 1950 generally were the same in 1960. The rank correlation coefficient of relative state income levels in 1960 as compared with those in

[10] Bureau of Indian Affairs, "Reservation Income, 1939" (1939; processed), Table 2, p. 1. Data are not available for non-reservation Indians.

[11] This estimate is based on unpublished income and employment surveys conducted by the Bureau of Indian Affairs on the Navajo, Papago, Crow, Standing Rock, Pine Ridge, and Rosebud Reservations.

1950 is 0.82. If New York is excluded, Indian incomes in 1960 were highest in the West Coast states of California and Oregon (Table 1-5). These states experienced a rapid growth in manufacturing and services during the decade, and Indians migrated to the urban areas to take advantage of job opportunities and increased incomes. Between 1950 and 1960 median incomes increased by $1,698 in California, $1,534 in Oregon, and $1,091 in Washington.

Incomes grew by about $300 in Mississippi and North Carolina in those years because Indians there have remained in unremunerative agricultural occupations. In Mississippi many Choctaws (the principal tribe) earn as little as $300 a year as sharecroppers.[12]

TABLE 1-5

Median Income of Male Indians, Selected States, 1950 and 1960

State	Median income (dollars)		Absolute increase (dollars)	Percentage increase
	1950[a]	1960		
Arizona	539	1,358	819	152
California	996	2,694	1,698	170
Idaho	500	1,304	804	161
Michigan	866	2,076	1,210	140
Minnesota	619	1,398	779	126
Mississippi	341	650[b]	309	91
Montana	681	1,368	687	101
Nebraska	746	1,589	843	113
Nevada	865	1,748	883	102
New Mexico	661	1,703	1,042	158
New York	1,401	3,497	2,096	150
North Carolina	628	950[b]	322	51
North Dakota	552	1,278	726	132
Oklahoma	730	1,538	808	111
Oregon	724	2,258	1,534	212
South Dakota	597	900[b]	303	51
Texas	830	2,017	1,187	143
Utah	520	1,596	1,076	207
Washington	909	2,000	1,091	120
Wisconsin	650	1,961	1,311	202
Wyoming	515	1,220	705	137

Sources: Bureau of the Census, *1950 Census, Nonwhite Population by Race*, Table 21, pp. 72–75; *1960 Census, Nonwhite Population by Race*, Table 56, pp. 234–39.

a. Includes all persons fourteen years old and over. Due to budget limitations, virtually all reservation Indians included in the 1950 income estimates were male.

b. Estimated by author.

[12] Income data furnished by Robert Murray, director, RCA Corporation Training Center, Philadelphia, Miss.

The low income of South Dakota Indians is caused by the steady decline of agriculture on reservation and non-reservation land and the absence of industry to provide substitute employment. The state ranks forty-fifth in industrialization, and some of the reservations there have the highest Indian unemployment rates in the nation.

Employment

The strikingly low levels of Indian income are associated with unemployment rates several times those of non-Indians (Table 1-6). While the rate for all males fell 64 percent between 1940 and 1960, the rate for all Indians rose 16 percent. The increase is chiefly a result of the great exodus of Indians from agriculture in search of better paid employment. Since most of them lack training and education, they are restricted to unskilled occupations

TABLE 1-6

Unemployment Rates, Indian, Nonwhite, and All Males, Selected Years, 1940–67[a]

(In percent)

| | | Indians | | | |
| | | Non-reservation | Reservation[b] | Non-whites | All males |
Year	All				
1940	32.9	n.a.	n.a.	18.0	14.8
1950	n.a.	15.1	n.a.	9.6	5.9
1958	n.a.	n.a.	43.5	13.8	6.8
1959	n.a.	n.a.	48.2	11.5	5.3
1960	38.2	12.1	51.3	10.7	5.4
1961	n.a.	n.a.	49.5	12.8	6.4
1962	n.a.	n.a.	43.4	10.9	5.2
1965	n.a.	n.a.	41.9	7.4	4.0
1966	n.a.	n.a.	41.9	6.3	3.2
1967	n.a.	n.a.	37.3	6.0	3.1

Sources: Nonwhites and all males, 1950–67, *Manpower Report of the President, 1968*, p. 237. Other figures based on information in Bureau of the Census, *1940 Census, Characteristics of the Nonwhite Population by Race* (1943), Table 25, p. 82, and *The Labor Force*, Table 4, p. 18; *1950 Census, Nonwhite Population by Race*, Table 10, p. 32; *1960 Census, Nonwhite Population by Race*, Table 33, p. 104; *Indian Unemployment Survey*, Pt. 1, *Questionnaire Returns*, A Memorandum and Accompanying Information from the Chairman, House Committee on Interior and Insular Affairs, 88 Cong. 1 sess. (1963); Bureau of Indian Affairs (December 1966 and December 1967; unpublished tabulations).

n.a. Not available.

a. Data for Indians in all years and for nonwhites and all males in 1940 include those fourteen years old and over; all other data include males sixteen years old and over.

b. Estimates for reservation Indians are seasonally adjusted, using as a basis monthly fluctuations contained in *Indian Unemployment Survey*.

with high rates of unemployment—particularly on reservations where there has been little industrialization.

That the Indian unemployment rate is far above acceptable levels[13] is apparent in a comparison with the rate for males during the Great Depression, which reached 25 percent in 1933. In the early 1960s the male unemployment rate on reservations was almost double that rate. Furthermore, the rate among Indians seems relatively insensitive to the movements of the business cycle. While there was a decrease of 52 percent in the national male unemployment rate between 1961 and 1967 (a period of increasing prosperity) and 53 percent in the rate for nonwhites, the decrease for reservation Indians was only 25 percent.

Although the data are fragmentary, it appears that non-reservation Indians have unemployment rates about 15 percent higher than Negroes. Since both populations are highly urbanized and have roughly similar income and employment situations, it is not surprising that many of the reservation Indians newly arrived in cities have adjustment problems very like those of southern Negroes who migrate to a northern urban center.

On some reservations more than half of all males in the labor force are unemployed (Table 1-7). Variations among reservations are more a function of off-reservation employment opportunities than of differences in levels of reservation development. The problem is aggravated by a birthrate from two to two and one-half times the national average. High birthrates coupled with swiftly declining death rates have added increasing population pressure to the already overburdened reservation economies.[14] On most res-

[13] Some of the discrepancy between reservation Indian and non-Indian unemployment rates is a matter of definition. While the Department of Labor considers as unemployed only those willing and able to work who are not employed, the Bureau of Indian Affairs counts as unemployed all those not working, with the exception of the sick, infirm, students, and housewives. Thus the Bureau of Indian Affairs considers an individual who is able but unwilling to work as unemployed, while the Department of Labor does not include him in the labor force. Although the size of the "able but unwilling to work" segment of the reservation population cannot be quantified, subjective reports from Bureau of Indian Affairs superintendents contained in a 1962 unemployment survey indicate that it is small. *Indian Unemployment Survey*, Pt. 1, *Questionnaire Returns*, A Memorandum and Accompanying Information from the Chairman, House Committee on Interior and Insular Affairs, 88 Cong. 1 sess. (1963).

[14] U.S. Public Health Service, *Indian Health Highlights* (June 1966), p. 7. Material from this publication and from a 1966 task force report on Indian housing indicates that an estimated 10,000 Indians leave the reservations each year (net migration).

TABLE 1-7

Unemployment Rates, Selected Reservations, Indian Males, 1966

Reservation	State	Unemployment rate (percent)
Fort Apache	Arizona	50
Gila River	Arizona	55
Navajo	Arizona, New Mexico, Utah	39
San Carlos	Arizona	74
Fort Hall	Idaho	56
Leech Lake	Minnesota	31
Blackfeet	Montana	39
Northern Cheyenne	Montana	24
Pyramid Lake	Nevada	42
Fort Berthold	North Dakota	79
Turtle Mountain	North Dakota	65
Pine Ridge	South Dakota	32
Cheyenne River	South Dakota	40
Colville	Washington	20

Source: Bureau of Indian Affairs, "Indian Reservations Eligible for . . . Public Works."

ervations the chief employer is the Bureau of Indian Affairs. For example, in 1966 it employed 30 percent of all permanently employed Indians on the Papago Reservation. An additional 17 percent were employed (most as practical nurses or hospital orderlies) by the Public Health Service in the reservation hospital.[15]

Because a relatively high proportion of reservation Indians are still engaged in agriculture or other outside work, fluctuation in unemployment levels during the year is extreme. The sole survey on seasonal unemployment, for 1962,[16] indicates that in the peak month, January, unemployment is 58 percent higher than in August, the lowest month (Table 1-8). In the two-month period March to May there is a 30 percent decline, while the September to November period brings an increase of almost 40 percent. As agricultural employment continues to decline and industrializa-

Many migrate under the bureau's relocation or adult vocational training programs. However, even with this migration, there is still an increase in the reservation population of 0.9 percent a year.

[15] Papago Agency, "Survey of Income and Employment, Papago Reservation, Calendar Year 1966" (n.d.; processed), p. 9. The Indian hospital, operated by the Public Health Service, is usually the second largest employer of reservation Indians.

[16] *Indian Unemployment Survey.*

TABLE 1-8

Monthly Fluctuations in Unemployment, Selected Reservations,
Fiscal Year 1962

Month	Number unemployed[a]	Percent of annual average
1961		
July	12,394	74
August	12,336	74
September	13,244	79
October	15,815	94
November	18,184	109
December	20,908	125
1962		
January	21,358	128
February	21,076	126
March	20,401	122
April	17,734	106
May	14,259	85
June	13,179	79
Annual average	16,741	100

Source: Computed from data in *Indian Unemployment Survey.*
a. Data are for reservations containing about 60 percent of the labor force.

tion increases, seasonal fluctuations in unemployment may become smaller.

Labor Force Participation

Indian poverty is also associated with low levels of labor force participation, for several reasons (Table 1-9). The high rate of unemployment has discouraged some potential workers from actively searching for jobs; hence, they are not classified as members of the labor force.[17] A significant number have leased their allotted lands to non-Indians and are subsisting solely on the income from them. Many Indian children start school at eight or nine years of age and

[17] The data on labor force participation were collected by the Bureau of the Census, using the Department of Labor's definition of labor force participation. A small segment of those considered as not in the labor force by the Bureau of the Census (those able but unwilling to work) would be classified as unemployed members of the labor force by the Bureau of Indian Affairs.

TABLE 1-9

Labor Force Participation Rates, Indian and All Males,
by Age Groups, 1940, 1950, 1960

(*In percent*)

Age group	Indian			All males		
	1940	1950	1960	1940	1950	1960
14–24	n.a.	44.4	40.9	57.7	59.1	57.1
25–44	n.a.	80.6	78.0	95.0	93.3	95.2
45 and over	n.a.	63.0	57.9	77.0	75.3	72.0
Total	70.0	63.0	59.5	79.0	79.0	77.4

Sources: *1940 Census, Characteristics of the Nonwhite Population by Race*, Table 25, p. 82, and *The Labor Force*, Table 5, p. 19; *1950 Census, Nonwhite Population by Race*, Table 10, p. 32, and Vol. 4, Pt. 5, Chap. B, *Education* (1953), Table 9, p. 73; *1960 Census, Nonwhite Population by Race*, Table 38, p. 129, and *Educational Attainment*, Final Report PC(2)-5B (1963), Table 4, p. 54.
n.a. Not available.

do not leave until eighteen or twenty, so the disparity between Indian and non-Indian labor force participation rates in the age bracket fourteen to twenty-four is greater than it would be if Indians began school at six and graduated at seventeen.[18]

Part of the disparity in participation rates between Indians and non-Indians (especially for the prime working ages) stems from the poor health of the Indians. In the mid-1960s the incidence rate for tuberculosis was seven times as high for reservation Indians as for non-Indians; for hepatitis, more than eight times; and for syphilis, twice as great.[19]

Educational Attainment

The low economic status of the American Indian is closely related to his educational attainment. The median level of schooling of the Indian male in 1960 was about the same as the 1940 level of all males (Table 1-10). Although the median level of Indians increased by nearly three years from 1940 to 1960, in 1960 the percentage of Indians attending college was only about one-third that

[18] On most Indian reservations, school attendance is compulsory until either the age of eighteen or graduation from high school. Also, as an increasing number of Indian children attend college, the labor force participation rate of the group from fourteen to twenty-four should continue to decline.

[19] For further information see Public Health Service, *Indian Health Highlights* (June 1966).

TABLE I-10

Percentage Distribution of Years of School Completed:
Indian, Negro, and All Males, 1940, 1950, 1960

Years of school completed	Indian			Negro			All males		
	1940ᵃ	1950ᵇ	1960ᵇ	1940ᶜ	1950ᵃ	1960ᵇ	1940ᶜ	1950ᵃ	1960ᵃ
0	23.4	14.7	9.6	8.0	7.4	5.0	1.2	2.6	2.4
1–4	19.6	15.1	12.6	32.8	28.7	17.7	5.4	9.3	7.0
5–8	37.8	38.3	37.8	40.5	37.2	36.2	41.7	37.2	32.4
9–11	9.4	15.4	22.8	9.7	11.5	22.7	19.8	16.3	18.7
12	4.8	7.7	11.6	4.5	6.8	12.1	18.2	17.6	21.2
13–15	2.0	2.3	4.0	1.8	2.6	4.0	6.9	6.8	8.6
16 or more	0.7	1.0	1.6	1.1	1.9	2.2	5.7	7.0	9.6
Not reported	2.3	5.4	—	1.8	4.0	—	1.1	3.1	—
Median	5.5	7.3	8.4	5.3	6.4	8.3	8.7	9.0	10.3

Sources: *1940 Census, Characteristics of the Nonwhite Population by Race,* Table 24, p. 80, and *Educational Attainment by Economic Characteristics and Marital Status,* Table 17, p. 75, and Table 18, p. 82; *1950 Census, Nonwhite Population by Race,* Table 10, p. 32, and *Education,* Table 6, p. 54, and Table 9, p. 73; *1960 Census, Nonwhite Population by Race,* Table 9, p. 9, and Table 10, p. 12, and *Educational Attainment,* Table 1, p. 1.
a. Males age twenty-five and over.
b. Males age fourteen and over.
c. Males age eighteen to sixty-four.

of all males, and the percentage of Indians with no schooling or fewer than five years was more than double that of all males. Between 1940 and 1960 the median educational attainment of Indians and Negroes was about the same, while two to three times as many Indians as Negroes had no formal education.

The gap in educational attainment between reservation and non-reservation Indians is significant. In 1960 non-reservation Indian males age fourteen and over had 9.4 years of schooling, compared with 7.9 for those on reservations. One reason for this is that non-reservation Indians start school earlier and live in more urbanized areas, with better opportunities for education. Not until after the Second World War were there enough facilities to permit a majority of reservation Indians to attend high school. Also, as will be discussed in Chapter 2, the more highly educated have migrated from the reservations to major urban centers in search of employment.

Not only has the Indians' relative lack of schooling contributed to the high unemployment rates and low income, but it has probably reinforced their desire to remain on the reservation. Many less educated Indians may believe that they would not be able to compete effectively off the reservation.

Occupational Changes

Partly because of a lack of formal schooling and opportunities for training, a much greater proportion of Indians than of total males are in unskilled jobs (Table 1-11).[20] In 1960 more than one-third of all employed Indians were laborers (farm and nonfarm), compared with one-tenth of the total population, and the percentage of Indians classified as professionals in 1960 was similar to that of the total population in 1940.

The proportions of Indian and Negro males in white-collar occupations were similar in 1940, 1950, and 1960. Blue-collar employment grew more rapidly for Indians, from 23.3 percent in 1940 to 57.6 percent in 1960, than for Negroes, whose rate increased from 38.4 percent to 59.6 percent. Throughout the 1940–60 period the proportion of Indians engaged in agriculture greatly exceeded that of Negroes, although the differences are diminishing.

The most significant occupational change for the Indian has been the rapid decline of agricultural employment. Nearly one-half of all employed Indian males were classified as farmers or farm managers in 1940, but fewer than 10 percent were so classified in 1960. The principal reason was the pressure of competition from non-Indian farmers, whose greater capital resources and technical skill made farming unprofitable for many Indians. The percentage of Indians in the nonfarm laborer classification nearly doubled between 1940 and 1960, while there was a drop in the overall percentage. With the decline in agriculture, many Indian agricultural laborers became laborers in the nonfarm sector of the reservation economy. The rapid expansion in semiskilled employment of Indians arose from the migration during the 1940s and 1950s of younger Indians from the reservations to urban centers in the West.

Those who remain on the reservations have incomes much smaller than those of non-Indians. Male unemployment runs as

[20] Caution should be used in comparing the occupational status of Indians and all males, because the high rate of permanent unemployment on the reservations means that many Indians have no occupation.

TABLE I-II

*Percentage Distribution of Indian, Negro, and All Employed Males,
by Occupation Groups, 1940, 1950, 1960*

Occupation group	Indian			Negro			All males		
	1940	1950	1960	1940	1950	1960	1940	1950	1960
White-collar workers									
Professional and technical	2.2	2.5	4.9	1.8	2.1	3.4	5.6	7.4	10.8
Managers, officials, and proprietors, except farmers	1.4	2.0	2.8	1.3	2.0	1.9	9.8	10.7	11.1
Clerical and sales	2.0	3.1	4.9	2.0	4.3	7.0	12.9	13.0	14.5
Blue-collar workers									
Craftsmen and foremen	5.7	11.0	15.5	4.4	7.8	10.7	14.6	18.8	20.5
Operatives	6.2	13.1	21.9	12.6	21.4	26.7	18.4	20.3	20.9
Laborers except farm and mine	11.4	17.8	20.2	21.4	23.6	22.2	8.8	8.2	7.2
Service workers									
Private household	0.2	0.3	0.3	2.9	1.1	0.8	0.4	0.2	0.1
Other service	2.4	3.6	6.0	12.4	13.5	15.2	6.5	5.9	6.3
Farm workers									
Farmers and managers	46.7	24.2	9.5	21.2	13.6	4.7	14.8	10.5	5.8
Laborers and foremen	21.7	22.4	14.0	19.9	10.5	7.5	8.2	4.9	2.9

Sources: *1940 Census, Characteristics of the Nonwhite Population by Race,* Table 26, pp. 83–84, and *The Labor Force,* Table 62, pp. 88–89; *1950 Census, Nonwhite Population by Race,* Table 10, p. 32, and *Occupational Characteristics,* Table 3, pp. 29–36; *1960 Census, Nonwhite Population by Race,* Table 33, p. 104, and *Occupational Characteristics,* Table 2, pp. 11–20, and Table 3, pp. 21–30. Males not reporting an occupation are excluded from the base used for deriving the percentages. Percentages may not total to 100.0 because of rounding.

high as 50 percent, and the labor force participation rate is lower than that of non-Indians. Lack of education limits Indians to jobs that require little skill or training. Although there has been gradual improvement in conditions, it has been too small and too slow to make much improvement in the economic status of reservation Indians.

Evaluation of Programs

Probably less socioeconomic information exists about the Indian than about any other minority group in the United States. The Bureau of Indian Affairs usually collects only information that is vital for specific federal programs. Since the bureau has placed little emphasis on economic development of the reservations, it has only recently begun to collect data pertinent to development programs.

This study describes some of the federal programs for the reservation Indian on the basis of data available[21] and evaluates the impact of these programs on his economic well-being. Education and job training, as well as agricultural and industrial development, are vital programs provided by the federal government. The government further supplies health and family maintenance services for Indians and supervises the tribal finances of the reservation population. Each of these areas is discussed in the following chapters. Recommendations for improving government policy, stressing the feasible rather than the ideal, are presented in the final chapter.

[21] Lack of detailed information prevents the Bureau of Indian Affairs from formulating programs flexible enough to meet the needs of each tribe and from assessing the effectiveness of present programs at different reservations. Because most of the program data are not available on a reservation or tribal basis, aggregative measures are often used in the evaluations in this book. Such data for all reservation Indians or for a sample of them from many different tribes may indicate a program's overall success or failure; they cannot, however, measure either its effectiveness for a specific tribe or its acceptance by tribal members.

CHAPTER II

Education

For more than three centuries Indian education in the United States was largely under the direction of missionaries.[1] After the United States had won independence, the early treaties made with the tribes provided for Indian education. In 1842 there were 37 Indian schools; by 1881 there were 106. In the belief that the best way to assimilate Indians into the dominant culture was to move children from their home environment, the Bureau of Indian Affairs (BIA) placed most of them in boarding schools it operated, both on and off the reservations.

In 1928 the Meriam report exposed the outmoded teaching methods, primitive housing facilities for the students, staff cruelties toward the Indians, and the requirement that malnourished children work half a day in laundries, dairies, and shops.[2] These disclosures led to some improvements in the boarding schools, largely as the result of increased appropriations by Congress. Also, more children were taught in small day schools in their own communities. The Johnson-O'Malley Act, passed in 1934, authorized contracts with public school districts for the education of Indian children. As a result, in some states with large Indian populations, there are now no federal schools and all of the Indian children at-

[1] For a thorough though somewhat dated history of Indian education, see Evelyn C. Adams, *American Indian Education: Government Schools and Economic Progress* (Columbia University Press, 1946).

[2] *The Problem of Indian Administration*, Report of a Survey made at the request of Honorable Hubert Work, Secretary of the Interior, and submitted to him, Feb. 21, 1928 (Johns Hopkins Press for Institute for Government Research, 1928), esp. Chap. 9.

TABLE 2-1

Annual School Census Report of Indian Children, 1969

Census item	Number	Percent
Enrolled		
Public schools[a]	120,539	63.4
Federal schools[b]	52,471	27.6
Mission and other schools	17,056	9.0
Total, all schools	190,066	100.00
Not enrolled[c]	12,507	
Information not available[d]	7,982	

Source: U.S. Bureau of Indian Affairs, Office of Education, "Statistics Concerning Indian Education, Fisca Year 1969" (Lawrence, Kans.: Haskell Institute, 1969), pp. 7, 11.
   a. Includes 4,089 children who live in federal dormitories and attend public schools.
   b. Of the 52,471 attending federal schools, 16,100 (8.5 percent) are in day schools; 36,263 (19.1 percent) are in boarding schools; and 108 (0.1 percent) receive instruction in hospitals.
   c. Ages five to eighteen only.
   d. Children five to eighteen years of age who reside off the reservation and are recorded at their own agency.

tend public schools.

Despite the stated policy of the Bureau of Indian Affairs to place as many Indian children as possible in public schools, progress in this direction has been slow during the past three decades. In 1969, 28 percent of all reservation Indian children attended federal schools; 9 percent, mission and other private schools; and 63 percent, public schools (Table 2-1). This was not markedly different from the distribution in 1930: roughly 37 percent in federal schools, 11 percent in mission and other schools, and 52 percent in public schools.

Educational Performance of Children

Research indicates that the achievement of Indian students is roughly comparable with that of non-Indians for the first few grades of school. But between the fourth and seventh grades the achievement scores for Indians fall below the national norms and continue a relative decline progressively through high school. A recent study of this so-called crossover effect[3] found that the differ-

   [3] Harry L. Saslow and May J. Harrover, "Research on Psychosocial Adjustment

ences in achievement (as measured by grade level equivalents) between Indian and white students ranged, on the various tests, from 1.7 to 2.1 years for sixth grade students and from 2.7 to 4.0 years for twelfth graders (Appendix Table A-1).[4]

Most of the research on the educational achievement of Indian children has been done by psychologists and educators, and the findings reflect their concepts. Educators stress early preparation, home background, parental support, and classroom procedures, and mental health personnel emphasize psychosocial factors. For example, a study of 105 Oglala Sioux students found that alienation significantly affected achievement, their performance falling each year more than the last.[5] Another study discovered that performance of reservation children improved with increases in (1) the percentage of children speaking English as a preschool language, (2) the educational level of the mother, and (3) the percentage of half-blooded Indians on the reservation. On the other hand, it deteriorated with increases in the percentages of (1) children speaking an Indian dialect as a preschool language, (2) full-blooded Indians, and (3) children having only Indian friends. The influences were stronger at the twelfth grade level than at the fourth.[6]

However, there may be other explanations for Indian children's

of Indian Youth," *American Journal of Psychiatry*, Vol. 125 (August 1968), p. 226. For some recent studies of the crossover effect, see M. V. Zintz, "The Indian Research Study, Final Report" (University of New Mexico, College of Education, 1960; processed); and S. Rosenberg, "Achievement Test Score Results for Albuquerque Indian Regular School Program" (University of New Mexico, College of Education, 1965; processed).

[4] James S. Coleman and others, *Equality of Educational Opportunity*, U.S. Office of Education (1966). Moreover, Indian high school seniors are a select group, since, as discussed in detail below, it appears that at least half of the high school students drop out before graduation, mostly in the ninth and tenth grades.

[5] Bernard Spilka and John F. Bryde, "Alienation and Achievement Among Oglala Sioux Secondary Students" (1966; processed). The negative correlation between alienation (and its components) and scores on the Iowa test of educational achievement increased with grade level, reaching a maximum in the twelfth grade.

[6] Kenneth E. Anderson, E. Gordon Collister, and Carl E. Ladd, *The Educational Achievement of Indian Children*, U.S. Bureau of Indian Affairs (1953), pp. 47, 60. The study compared performance with each factor by their respective ranks within the ten administrative areas of the Bureau of Indian Affairs.

progressive retardation—for instance, poverty. Families with very low incomes have inadequate housing. Many Indian homes are crowded one- or two-room shacks, with no room for study.[7] Many lack electricity, so that studying must be done by candle or kerosene lamp light. As more outside study is required, a student living in such an impoverished environment falls further and further below the national norms. Also, as the Indian child grows older, the fact that his family is poverty-stricken, and that probably his father is unemployed, becomes evident. He may feel that there is little point in studying hard at school if he will merely duplicate the economic circumstances of his parents. Finally, poor families seldom purchase such educationally helpful items as books, magazines, newspapers, or television sets.[8]

Economic circumstances have in the past few years been recognized as an important factor in educational performance. A comparison of Indian family income levels with student achievement levels shows a slight positive association, the effect being somewhat stronger at the twelfth grade than at the eighth grade level (Appendix Table A-2). A further comparison of twelfth graders' performance with income, language capacity, and percentage of Indian blood points up the significance of economic and cultural factors. Income level proves to have a small positive effect on achievement, language factors a decidedly greater positive effect; but a stronger influence, this time negative, is Indian blood.[9]

These findings are somewhat discouraging, for cultural or biological factors, such as the language of the home or the percentage

---

[7] A 1966 study showed that 75 percent of the reservation homes were substandard, with 54 percent beyond repair. Task Force on Indian Housing, "Indian Housing: Need, Alternatives, Priorities and Program Recommendations," Bureau of Indian Affairs (December 1966; processed), p. 10.

[8] On the Navajo Reservation only 33 percent of the families receive a daily newspaper, and only 48 percent own a television set.

[9] Correlation of scores on the total battery of achievement tests for 1966 with income was 0.22; with English as the language of the home, 0.70; with English spoken by the student when he started school, 0.70; and with percentage of Indian blood, —1.00 (this coefficient should be interpreted cautiously because of the small sample size). Computed from data in Willard P. Bass, "An Analysis of Academic Achievement of Indian High School Students in Federal and Public Schools, 1966–67," Bureau of Indian Affairs (January 1968; processed), and U.S. Bureau of the Census, U.S. Census of Population: 1960, Subject Reports, Nonwhite Population by Race, Final Report PC(2)-1C (1963) , pp. 104–07, and Detailed Characteristics, Alaska, Final Report PC(1)-3D (1962), p. 210. Similar results were obtained for the series of tests given in 1950.

of Indian blood, cannot be altered by any federal program. Reservation incomes, however, can be raised by a variety of strategies. It is unfortunate that income is not more closely related to test scores; if it were, reservation development might increase educational achievement.[10]

Although it appears that economic conditions are not the most important factor influencing achievement test scores, it is clear that severe educational retardation (as measured by test scores) has profound economic effects. Employers would undoubtedly consider that a person with eleven years of schooling who performs three years below grade level on achievement tests has the equivalent of an eighth grade education.

Some evidence of this is provided by data on unemployment and earnings of Indians in metropolitan areas. Rates of unemployment there are not so high as on reservations, and unemployment is as much a function of supply as of demand factors. Since Indians score about three years below the norm on achievement tests, their employment and earning capabilities should be compared with those of non-Indians of comparable age who have had three years less formal schooling. Indians twenty-five to thirty-four years of age (the median age is thirty-three) with an average of 10.7 years of school have an unemployment rate of 11.8 percent and a median income of $3,235. The unemployment rate for all males in this age group with 8 years of school and living in central cities is 7.3 percent, median income about $4,000.[11] While this may confirm employer assessments of the low achievement levels of Indians, it also indicates considerable economic discrimination against Indians. Part of the earnings disparity, of course, is attributable to adjustment problems of Indians living in an urban environment, particularly those who grew up on a reservation.

It appears that, at most, only one-half of all reservation Indian students finish high school. One study estimated that fewer than 40 percent of these high school entrants graduate, compared with 60 percent of all American students; another found that in 1963, 77

[10] This assumes that the association between relative income and relative performance on achievement tests implies that raising income over time will raise test scores; that is, that the relations implied by cross-section analysis will also apply in a dynamic situation.

[11] Derived from data in Bureau of the Census, *1960 Census, Subject Reports, Nonwhite Population by Race*, pp. 42, 129, and *Educational Attainment*, Final Report PC(2)-5B (1963), pp. 58, 92.

percent of non-Indian students graduated from high school, compared with 40 percent of reservation Indians. A third study, on the dropout problem on reservations in six northwestern states, found that 48 percent of the Indian students who were eighth graders in 1962 had dropped out by June 1967, compared with 16 percent for non-Indians.[12]

Although the percentage of Indians finishing high school continues to be low, the number of graduates who further their education has increased substantially. According to BIA officials, in 1967 nearly 30 percent of all reservation high school graduates entered college—almost double the rate of ten years earlier. Another 25 percent attended institutions providing advanced vocational training. While only some 250 reservation Indians graduated from four-year colleges and universities in 1967, this was an increase of 100 percent over a five-year period.[13]

Despite such improvement, a large proportion of Indians fail to complete college. The data are sparse, but the available studies show that college dropout rates are much higher for Indians than for non-Indians. For example, an investigation conducted at Southern State Teachers College in South Dakota indicated that of 112 Indian students who attended over a period of thirty-three years, 59 (52 percent) had failed to remain for as long as three quarters.[14] Another survey showed that of 100 Indian students enrolled at the University of New Mexico in 1954 (in all classes), 70 percent were subsequently dropped because of low grades, 20 percent were still enrolled (as of 1958), and 10 percent had obtained degrees.[15]

Though it may not be possible to alter the poverty and cultural environment, which deeply affect children when they are not in school, it should be possible to compensate in some degree for these influences while the children are in school. The educational

[12] Wesley Apker, "A Survey of the Literature Related to Indian Pupil Dropout" (M.Ed. thesis, Washington State University, 1962); Spilka and Bryde, "Alienation and Achievement Among Oglala Sioux Secondary Students"; Alphonse D. Selinger, *The American Indian High School Dropout: The Magnitude of the Problem* (Northwest Regional Educational Laboratory, September 1968).

[13] Interview with L. Madison Coombs, director of educational research, Bureau of Indian Affairs, October 1968; letter from Roderick H. Riley, assistant to the commissioner of Indian affairs, Sept. 17, 1969.

[14] Cited in Saslow and Harrover, "Research on Psychosocial Adjustment," p. 226.

[15] Zintz, "The Indian Research Study."

TABLE 2-2

Accreditation Status of Secondary Federal Indian Schools,
Mission Schools, Public Schools Enrolling Indians,
and Public Schools Enrolling Non-Indians [a]

Type of school	Percent with state accreditation	Percent with regional accreditation
Federal Indian schools	100	38
Public schools enrolling predominantly Indians[b]	100	64
Mission schools[c]	82	6
All Indian schools	96	52
Public schools enrolling predominantly non-Indians	93	75

Sources: Public schools attended by Indians, Leah W. Ramsey, *Directory of Public Secondary Day Schools,* *1958–59*, U.S. Office of Education (1961); mission schools, Diane B. Gertler and Leah W. Ramsey, *Nonpublic Secondary Schools, A Directory, 1960–61*, U.S. Office of Education (1963); federal Indian schools, interview with Bureau of Indian Affairs official, April 1968; public schools attended by non-Indians, James S. Coleman and others, *Equality of Educational Opportunity*, U.S. Office of Education (1966), p. 87; all Indian schools, weighted average of components.

a. Date varies with date of source.

b. Based on a sample of 64 high schools used in Alphonse D. Selinger, *The American Indian High School Dropout: The Magnitude of the Problem* (Northwest Regional Educational Laboratory, September 1968).

c. Based on a sample of seventeen mission high schools.

achievement of reservation Indian children can be raised by high quality education and an adequate remedial education program.

Although there is little agreement among educators and social scientists about the best indexes of school quality, one generally accepted measure is accreditation status. The status of schools attended by Indians and those attended by non-Indians is compared in Table 2-2.[16] While the secondary schools had similar state accreditation, only 52 percent of those with mainly Indian students had the more rigorous regional accreditation, as against 75 percent of all non-Indian public schools. This difference in quality may account for some of the disparity in achievement scores between Indians and non-Indians.

It is not clear why the quality of federal Indian schools falls be-

[16] There are six regional accrediting associations, which consider quality of faculty, library size, student–teacher ratio, curriculum, expenditure per pupil, and other educationally relevant variables in accrediting schools. For further information, see Christian E. Burckell, *The College Blue Book*, 11th Ed., Book 6, *Accreditation and Recognition of Secondary Schools and Institutions of Higher Learning in America* (Yonkers, N.Y.: College Blue Book Publishing Co., 1965), p. 95.

low that of the public schools. According to BIA data, expenditures per pupil in day schools for 1968 were $861. This figure is not only above that for public schools in reservation states but above the national average. Why then is the quality of the federal schools (as measured by their accreditation status) so low? The federal government spends over $100 million a year on Indian education; therefore it is important to have an answer. If federal management of education—especially for disadvantaged children—is to provide a model for the states, the great gap between that ideal and the reality in Indian education, as shown by the data in Table 2-2, will have to be narrowed.

Clearly, the church-affiliated and private schools enrolling Indians are very weak, some of them not even state-accredited. The private schools receive federal government payments for children accepted as pupils when there is no room for them in federal schools; thus the government is in the position of subsidizing inferior schools. However, since most of these are mission schools, the bulk of their funds are provided by church members whose generosity (or lack of it) determines the quality of the schools.

Remedial Education

Aside from the quality of the school environment, the amount of remedial work offered has a profound effect on the educational achievement of Indian children. Many of them need such work, but the Bureau of Indian Affairs provides it for only a few. From 1964 to 1969 an average of only 5,000 students a year were enrolled in remedial summer courses (Appendix Table A-3). Since about 52,000 attend federal schools in the regular term, probably at least 26,000 need remedial summer work.

Remedial courses could be offered to many more students at relatively low cost. Civil service regulations allow bureau teachers only two to three weeks of annual leave. Teachers devote some of their summer working hours to student recreational activities on the reservations, but most of the time they are idle. An expanded remedial program would simply make better use of this pool of instructors already on the payroll. (The students currently enrolled in summer courses are instructed by teachers who receive no extra pay.) Since the teachers and buildings are fixed costs, the marginal cost per pupil should be very low. However, it is possible that adding to the general workload would intensify teacher dissatisfaction and lead to a higher rate of turnover, thereby increasing recruiting expenditures and reducing efficiency.

A useful remedial enrichment project is conducted during the summer months on the Yakima Reservation. Children from the seventh to eleventh grades are taken to a woodland camp, where they receive intensive instruction four hours a day for six weeks. There is one teacher for every ten students. Few textbooks are used; instead, the camp stresses programmed learning. Testing before and after the camp experience showed an average increase in scores (on the California achievement test) of 0.4 year in reading, 0.3 in mathematics, and 0.5 in language skills.[17]

THE ELEMENTARY AND SECONDARY EDUCATION ACT

In 1967 BIA schools received about $5 million through the Indian amendment to Title I of the Elementary and Secondary Education Act of 1965. A large part of the funds have been used for remedial programs, recreational activities, and such enrichment programs as field trips. Evaluation of the program by a private management consulting firm[18] indicated that it is operating smoothly, although there appears to have been some difficulty in recruiting competent staff on some of the more isolated reservations.

The remedial program was effective in some schools and not in others. Tests of 3,045 students before and after remedial instruction[19] showed that some students raised their reading and arithmetic achievement levels by as much as one year after only two or three months' instruction. Others showed no growth (not even that normally expected) with even longer periods of remedial work. In general, the gains in achievement were small and not encouraging

[17] *Indian Education,* Hearings before the Special Subcommittee on Indian Education of the Senate Committee on Labor and Public Welfare, 90 Cong. 1 and 2 sess. (1969), Pt. 5, pp. 2038–46.

[18] ENKI Corporation, "Evaluation Report, Bureau of Indian Affairs Title I Programs, Elementary and Secondary Education Act" (San Fernando, Calif., 1967; processed).

[19] *Ibid.,* Vol. 3, "Detailed Test Data."

(Appendix Table A-4). However, most of the results were reported after the remedial programs had been in operation less than ninety days; it would be extremely optimistic to expect any significant changes in performance in such a short time. Nor does the program evaluation indicate why there was so much variation among schools. Differences in quality of staff and equipment, variations in intensity of instruction, or overall administrative ability are among the more important factors to be considered.

DROPOUTS

Figures on Indian high school students indicate that from 48 percent to 60 percent leave before graduating. Until recently there has been little research on the causes of the high dropout rate. Bryde found, on the basis of personality tests given to Oglala Sioux students, that "dropouts apparently feel more rejected, anxious, depressed, psychasthenic, paranoid, self, socially, and emotionally alienated."[20] A comparison of eighth grade students on the Pine Ridge Reservation who later left school with those who remained showed that dropouts tended to come from more isolated sections of the reservation than graduates. In addition, most dropouts were older on entering the ninth grade than the graduates, and their performance on the Iowa test of educational achievement was significantly poorer.[21]

One analysis of dropouts from nineteen reservations in six states produced rates varying widely, from 25 percent on the Umatilla Reservation in Oregon to 62 percent on the Rosebud Reservation in South Dakota.[22] Three factors seem especially likely to account for these variations. First, family income level is important not only because it reflects the financial ability to educate children, but also because a relatively high standard of living may give a child an incentive to complete school so that he and his family can

[20] John F. Bryde, *The Sioux Indian Student: A Study of Scholastic Failure and Personality Conflict* (n.p., 1966), p. 132.

[21] Donn Knudson, cited by Selinger, *Indian High School Dropout*, p. 3. A survey of the South Dakota secondary school population in 1963–64 showed that 59 percent of Indian dropouts occurred in the ninth grade, compared with 20 percent for non-Indians; *ibid.*

[22] Selinger, *The American Indian High School Dropout*.

someday enjoy the same, or a higher, standard. Second, the educational attainment of the father is a motivating force, for each parent wants at least as much education for his children as he received. Finally, the percentage of the population speaking English is one indication of the degree of Indian culture that is retained. When these three factors and the dropout rate are examined together, differences in family income and levels of educational attainment by males are closely associated with variations in high school dropout rates. Thus, reservations with high family incomes or above-average levels of schooling have lower dropout rates than reservations with low incomes and levels of schooling. (The fact that income level affects the dropout rate but has little influence on achievement test scores is not inconsistent; the survey on dropouts indicated that their achievement scores are almost as high as those of graduates.) Proficiency in English has little effect on the dropout rate.[23]

These results are confirmed by a study of Indian dropouts on the Pine Ridge Reservation, which revealed that 87 percent of the children of families in the lowest economic class of the reservation left school, compared with only 25 percent of the children of families in the upper strata. Again, the dropout rate was not affected by proficiency in English.[24]

Reservations having the lowest family incomes ($1,200 per year

[23] The following multiple regression equation was used to test the variables (figures in parentheses are the standard errors of the estimates):

$$Y = 2087.4 - 0.118X - 8.692Z - 7.57P$$
$$(0.036) \quad (4.85) \quad (11.7)$$

$$r = 0.81 \qquad r^2 = 0.66$$

where Y is the dropout rate, X is median family income, Z is the median level of schooling of males fourteen and over, and P is the proportion of the population speaking English. The income variable is significant at the 0.01 level, while the education variable is significant at the 0.05 level. The percent-speaking-English variable is not significant (when the equation was run with P representing only the portion of the population over forty-five years of age speaking English, the results were unchanged). The simple correlation between the income and dropout variable is -0.76, between the education and dropout variable -0.64. The association between the independent variables, as given by the correlation coefficient, is 0.53; thus, the multicollinearity problem does not appear serious.

[24] Rosalie H. Wax and Murray L. Wax, "Dropout of American Indians at the Secondary Level," in *Indian Education*, Hearings, Pt. 4, pp. 1465, 1467.

or less) not only contain more poverty-stricken families, who are less able to permit their children to remain in school, but provide little opportunity to their residents to use their education. Becker has shown that the demand for education is a function of the rate of return on the investment in it.[25] It is likely that on the low-income reservations the rate of return to education is low and the dropout rate high. Moreover, if the rate of return to education were lower for Indians than for non-Indians, one could expect fewer Indians to complete high school.

In three states—Alaska, South Dakota, and New Mexico—roughly 85 percent of the nonwhites are Indians, Eskimos, or Aleuts. These states contain over one-third of the population under Bureau of Indian Affairs jurisdiction. The income differential between Indian and non-Indian dropouts and graduates in those states in 1960 is apparent in the following table:[26]

Level of schooling (years)	Median annual earnings	
	Nonwhites	Whites
9–11	$3,050	$4,600
12	3,300	5,200

Median earnings of Indian graduates are only $250 more annually than for dropouts, compared with an earnings differential between white graduates and dropouts of $600. Although sufficient data are not available to compute the exact rate of return to Indians for high school graduation, it is undoubtedly very low.[27]

One reason for the small differential between the earnings of graduates and those of dropouts is the low level of economic activity on the reservations. Of the few jobs available many require only unskilled workers and can be handled as easily by a dropout as by a

[25] See Gary S. Becker, *Human Capital* (Columbia University Press for National Bureau of Economic Research, 1964), pp. 90–103.

[26] Estimated from U.S. Bureau of the Census, *1960 Census, Detailed Characteristics, Alaska,* Final Report PC(1)-3D (1962), p. 217, *New Mexico,* PC(1)-33D (1962), p. 285, *South Dakota,* PC(1)-43D (1962), p. 326.

[27] For example, assume that a dropout leaves school two and one-half years before a graduate and earns $700 a year (income estimate based on age earnings profiles). At a 5 percent discount rate, the graduate, with a constant $250 advantage in income, would take ten years to overtake the dropout in total income earned.

graduate. The differential may also reflect the small difference in academic achievement between graduates and dropouts. (See the section above on educational performance.)[28]

On the basis of the limited data presented, low incomes and lack of economic opportunity are important factors affecting the reservation dropout rate (both on an aggregate basis and between reservations). Policies aiding reservation development, through industrialization, public works programs, or some other income-creating activity, might provide incentives for remaining in school and lower the dropout rate. Unless there is a demand for skilled labor or white-collar employment on the reservation, not only will the dropout rate remain agonizingly high, but most of the better educated young people will leave the reservation.

In spite of the fact that only one-half of all reservation Indian students finish high school, the Bureau of Indian Affairs has no program of high school dropout prevention, nor is it clear whether such an effort would represent an efficient use of federal funds.[29] The differential between the earnings of graduates and those of dropouts is probably not large enough to produce benefits equal to the cost of an intensive high school dropout-prevention program. However, if such a program were linked to a program of training and relocation, there might be a considerably higher payoff. Most adult vocational training courses require a high school education, and those who relocate with no training find steady employment difficult without a high school diploma. Potential dropouts who could be persuaded to finish high school and then to enter a training or relocation program would have a much greater opportunity to earn an adequate income than those who dropped out of school on the reservation.[30]

[28] The differential between earnings of graduates and dropouts does not reflect the income advantage the graduate would have over the dropout off the reservation. That possible future migration affects an Indian high school student's decision to remain in school is questionable, however.

[29] In the only published evaluation of a dropout prevention program, Burton A. Weisbrod examined one in St. Louis that had financial support from the Ford Foundation. Using a 5 percent rate of discount, he found the ratio of benefits to costs to be 0.42. "Preventing High School Dropouts," in Robert Dorfman (ed.), *Measuring Benefits of Government Investments* (Brookings Institution, 1965), p. 148.

[30] Training and relocation are described in Chap. 6.

VOCATIONAL EDUCATION

During the years between 1880 and 1940, when a majority of Indian children were educated in federal boarding schools, the emphasis was on vocational skills, including vocational agriculture. After the Second World War, educational policy makers in the Bureau of Indian Affairs decided that vocational courses should be gradually phased out and almost exclusive emphasis placed on academic courses. Between 1957 and 1963 shop courses above the prevocational level were gradually eliminated from all but four high schools operated by the BIA.[31] Moreover, most bureau schools offer few commercial courses, such as shorthand, bookkeeping, or office practice. The sole exception to this generalization is beginning typing (one school visited did not provide even this course).

In addition to this very limited opportunity for vocational training, the course offerings are generally inadequate. Courses tend to be in older, traditional, low-paying occupations, such as shoe repair, dry cleaning, cosmetology, janitorial work, auto mechanics, and welding. There are few courses in electronics parts manufacturing and none in any of the building trades, radio and TV repair, drafting or commercial art, or airplane, refrigerator, or air-conditioning repair. Such courses are given in many vocational schools in metropolitan areas. Also, most of the equipment used in the shops is old and therefore of limited usefulness. The Bureau of Indian Affairs, unable to decide whether to abolish vocational training altogether, apparently has refrained from spending any appreciable amount on new equipment since the late 1950s.

There is no way for a student interested in vocational training to arrange to be sent to the off-reservation boarding schools offering programs. Only students with social problems or severe academic retardation or those who live one and a half miles or more from a school bus route are eligible to attend those schools. Moreover, location or tribal affiliation determines the school to which a

[31] The schools still offering vocational training are Phoenix Indian, Phoenix, Ariz.; Intermountain, Brigham City, Utah; Chilocco Indian, Chilocco, Okla.; and Sherman Institute, Riverside, Calif. In addition, post–high school vocational and commercial training is available at Haskell Institute, Lawrence, Kans.

student is sent. Thus, Intermountain School is exclusively for Navajo students, and Phoenix Indian School is also attended by a high proportion of Navajos. Students usually are sent to the schools offering vocational training if the education officer on the reservation deems it advisable.

Since 1963 the bureau has not formulated any real policy concerning the future of vocational education in its schools. The rationale for severely limiting vocational offerings has been that, since such training is available at the post–high school level through the adult vocational training program (which is discussed in Chapter 6) or at Haskell Institute, it is more efficient for the high schools to concentrate on academic courses. This gives students who wish to attend college enough preparation, and those who desire vocational or commercial training can obtain it after high school.[32] Economic factors appear to have received little consideration (beyond the savings to the government of vocational teachers' salaries or equipment purchased for the shops) when the questionable practice of phasing out vocational courses was decided upon.

Facilities at Haskell Institute or through the adult vocational program have never been adequate to accommodate all who are interested in obtaining training. There are about three times as many applicants to Haskell as there are openings in the first-year class, and in recent years 25 to 30 percent of the applicants for adult vocational training have been turned away for lack of facilities. To complicate the problem, the adult vocational training program is not operated solely for recent high school graduates. Many applications come from older graduates who, being unable to find a job on the reservation, apply for the training and relocation that the program provides.

About half of the vocational courses offered at the post–high school level are similar to those given in vocational high schools or in comprehensive high schools enrolling only non-Indians. Arthur J. Corazzini has concluded that the earnings differential between graduates of post–high school vocational courses and graduates of

[32] Based on interviews at the Bureau of Indian Affairs with L. Madison Coombs and with Anselm Davis, vocational education specialist, Division of Education. However, the conclusion is the author's, not theirs.

vocational high schools is so small that the rate of return to post–
high school vocational education at a 5 percent discount rate is negative, because the opportunity costs (forgone earnings) are greater
than the increment in income earned by postponing vocational education.[33] Postponement of vocational training for two years may
result in a lower lifetime income for many students. Also, students
who receive vocational training in high school tend to earn
more than those who do not (and who fail to go to college). The
former are more likely to obtain industrial employment on or near
the reservation and also have more chance to obtain semiskilled or
skilled jobs if they participate in the relocation program.[34]

As was pointed out earlier, 50 percent of the Indian students fail
to complete high school. They are not eligible for post–high school
vocational training, and for the most part they lack the educational qualifications for the adult vocational training program.
They might have a better chance for permanent employment if
they received some vocational training in school rather than academic courses exclusively.

The Bureau of Indian Affairs has never considered using vocational training as a form of dropout prevention, although many
Indian children, like non-Indians, probably leave school because
of a lack of interest in what is being taught. With industrialization
of the reservations under way and the strong interest in relocation
shown by younger Indians, it may be important to lower the dropout rate. Research in this area is not conclusive. In an evaluation of
vocational training in New York City it was concluded that "recognizing the unfortunate amount of ignorance in this area, it would
still seem a fair judgment that the vocational program in New
York City has demonstrated no overall significant holding power
over potential dropouts."[35] However, Corazzini found that "the
difference between the tracks is clearly the success of the voca-

[33] "When Should Vocational Education Begin?" *Journal of Human Resources,* Vol.
2 (Winter 1967), p. 48. This conclusion applies only if the post–high school vocational
students are taking the same courses as high school vocational students.

[34] Corazzini found, in a study of vocational training in Worcester, Mass., that, for a
wage differential of $360 between vocational high school graduates and those taking
the general course, at a 5 percent rate of discount the extra costs of the vocational
program could be recovered in eleven years. See Arthur J. Corazzini, "The Decision to
Invest in Vocational Education: An Analysis of Costs and Benefits," *Journal of Human
Resources,* Supplement, Vol. 3 (1968), p. 106.

[35] Michael K. Taussig, "An Economic Analysis of Vocational Education in the New

tional track in keeping people in school by allowing them to proceed at a slower but far more costly pace."[36]

Expanded vocational training opportunities may also be an effective policy to encourage industry to locate on the reservations by furnishing a pool of skilled or semiskilled labor instead of the present surplus of unskilled workers.[37]

The present policy of limiting vocational training is perhaps most questionable because it apparently runs counter to the desires of the Indian people. Many Indian leaders on the reservations visited during 1968 expressed a preference for an expansion of vocational training in the schools. The Senate Subcommittee on Indian Education under the chairmanship of Robert F. Kennedy (and, after his death, of Wayne Morse) heard a large number of Indian witnesses who favored vocational training in the BIA high schools.[38]

Because research on vocational education has been so limited, many of the statements made here must be regarded as tentative. However, it does appear that some expansion of the vocational offerings in bureau schools may be advisable, particularly if there is student demand for them. Recent research indicates that job mobility may make it more realistic to teach clusters of skills rather than the specific skills necessary for a given occupation.

To determine the validity of these recommendations, the Bureau of Indian Affairs should undertake a benefit-cost analysis of its existing vocational training program. Isolating the relevant costs and relating them to the earnings differentials (if any) between graduates of vocational courses and other high school graduates not attending college should permit an assessment of the benefit–cost ratio of the program.[39] A ratio considerably greater than one would argue forcefully for an expansion of vocational training in terms of students enrolled, equipment utilized, and courses offered.

York City High Schools," *Journal of Human Resources*, Supplement, Vol. 3 (1968), p. 82.

[36] "Decision to Invest in Vocational Education," pp. 112–13.

[37] It is true that some of those who receive vocational training will leave the reservation, and the pool of skilled or semiskilled labor on the reservation will be smaller than if there were no migration.

[38] *Indian Education,* Hearings, Pts. 1–5.

[39] Unfortunately, at present not enough data has been collected for a study of this kind.

Adult Education

One of the greatest needs of reservation Indians is an effective program of adult education, both to increase the human capital available on the reservation for employers or potential employers and to afford adult Indians greater job opportunities if they leave the reservation.

The need for such a program is indicated by the following table, which shows the educational level at various ages of male reservation Indians:[40]

Age group	Median years of school completed
20–24	9.2
25–35	8.2
35–44	7.9
45–64	6.6
65 and over	3.5

All age groups, except the bracket from twenty to twenty-four, are below the high school level. Since most tribal chiefs and members of the tribal councils are over forty, it is evident that many Indian leaders lack the educational attainment that would help them to understand the modern world.

The scant information available on the bureau's adult education program indicates its limited scope (Table 2-3). Only about half of the Indian communities had an adult education program in 1968, although the percentage more than doubled in the 1962–68 period. Virtually no communities in Alaska had a program in spite of the fact that 12 percent of the total population under BIA jurisdiction lives there.[41] Also, while the number of adult students nearly tripled from 1967 to 1968, fewer than one in seven nongraduates from high school was enrolled in the latter year.[42]

[40] Based on data in *1960 Census, Nonwhite Population by Race*, Table 20, p. 43.

[41] Interview with Jerry Hargis, adult education specialist, Bureau of Indian Affairs, October 1968.

[42] This ratio is a maximum figure, based on no double counting. Since there was double counting, substantially fewer than 33,883 adults participated in formal classes. This is a poor way for the Bureau of Indian Affairs to keep statistics, mainly because it is impossible to determine over time whether more adults are participating or more courses are being offered.

TABLE 2-3

Coverage and Enrollment of Indian Adult Education Program, 1962–68

Fiscal year	Percentage of communities served	Number of adults in		Total number of adults served[a]	Number enrolled in GED[b]	Number obtaining GED[b]	Total expenditures
		Formal classes	Informal classes				
1962	23.1	n.a.	n.a.	n.a.	n.a.	n.a.	n.a.
1963	25.5	n.a.	n.a.	n.a.	n.a.	n.a.	n.a.
1964	33.3	n.a.	n.a.	30,868	n.a.	n.a.	n.a.
1965	34.9	n.a.	n.a.	n.a.	n.a.	n.a.	n.a.
1966	37.9	n.a.	n.a.	28,900	n.a.	n.a.	n.a.
1967	47.5	12,400	13,500	25,900	416	n.a.	n.a.
1968	51.0	33,883	27,510	61,393	1,353	333	$1,007,000

Sources: 1962–67, Bureau of Indian Affairs, "Statistics Concerning Indian Education" (1962, 1963, 1964, 1965, 1966), and *Indian Affairs* (1964, 1966, 1967). 1968, interview with Jerry Hargis, adult education specialist, Bureau of Indian Affairs, October 1968.

n.a. Not available.

a. This column heading is somewhat misleading. Many adults sign up for both formal and informal classes, so there is an unknown amount of double counting in the statistics; moreover, if one adult is enrolled in three classes, for example, he is counted three times.

b. GED: general educational development program. Enrollees who complete the course satisfactorily receive a high school equivalency certificate.

The entire education budget of the Bureau of Indian Affairs in 1969 was $100 million. Some $1 million was programmed for adult education—only 1 percent of the budget. This seems an incredibly low figure, when the median schooling for adult Indians is only eight years and only half of today's Indian high school students are graduating.[43] Furthermore, expenditures per student seem far below effective levels. If every individual is assumed to have been counted twice (that is, the figure of 61,393 adults served in 1968 in fact represents only one-half that number), total expenditures would be only about $33 per student. If there were no double counting, total expenditures would be a painfully low $16 per student.

Budgetary considerations have forced the bureau to limit the effectiveness of its basic education courses. These courses, in which most of the adults who sign up for formal classes are enrolled, bring educational achievement only up to eighth grade level. Be-

[43] One could argue that, with limited funds available for education, it is more sensible to devote the bulk of the resources to educating the young in order to bring their performance up to satisfactory levels. However, even if one accepts this argument, the portion of the education budget devoted to adult education seems too small.

rapid technological change and industry's need for highly
 manpower, many educators believe that adult programs
 k to raise achievement in the basic skills to a minimum of
 rade level.[44]

In addition, the BIA has only forty professional adult educators
(or one for every four reservations) to establish courses, recruit
teachers, and coordinate their efforts with other reservation educational programs. They are spread too thin to do a really effective
job.

An expansion of the adult education program, both in numbers
served and in effectiveness, seems highly desirable. Many adults
over forty-five who have never attended high school should be given
an opportunity now. Younger adults who may have dropped out of
school need a second chance at an effective education. This program could be integrated with on-the-job training to enable the
participants to learn the skills necessary to advance in their organizations.

Pupil Personnel Services

Another critical need of the federal Indian schools is for skilled
professional nonteaching personnel. School psychologists, social
workers, guidance counselors, and workers in the area of special
education are all in critically short supply.[45]

PSYCHOLOGISTS

According to fairly persuasive evidence, Indian children have
psychological problems in adjusting to a formal school situation in
which the teachers and administrative staff are non-Indian. One
study suggests:

Rapid change from the Indian way of life may leave the Indian with
the problem of being confused as to which set of rules to live by. The
difficulty of making decisions in this situation may result in emotional
problems. The Indian may withdraw from situations where he has to

---

[44] Interview with Jerry Hargis.

[45] The Bureau of Indian Affairs is not unaware of its manpower requirements for
pupil personnel services. Budget limitations are at least partially responsible for the
failure to obtain the necessary staff.

make such decisions or he may even go back to tribal ways altogether
. . . much work needs to be done to relate type and symptoms of mental
illness to the various acculturation situations.[46]

Harry Saslow, who has studied the mental health of students at
the Albuquerque Indian School, an off-reservation boarding
school, points out that a significant number of the students have
serious emotional or social problems before they ever come to
school. From 1963 to 1967, he indicates, 25 percent of the students
at the school were sent there because of behavioral problems.[47]

An investigator evaluating the effectiveness of the Elementary
and Secondary Education Act of 1965 made the following comment:

Over 90% of the children attending the Wahpeton Indian School
come from family milieus in which there is severe economic depriva-
tion and social maladjustment. Parental backgrounds reveal cases of
assault, illicit cohabitation, illegitimacy, rape , theft, larceny, and
chronic alcoholism. Some of the children have been in corrective institutions. Some were dimissed or rejected from other schools for such
stated reasons as "maladjusted, recalcitrant, stubborn, truant, pugna-
cious, uncooperative, incorrigible, depraved and delinquent." Many
of the social histories disclose traumas, which have doubtless contributed to problems in emotional organization and socialization.
Among the emergency situations that led to the enrollment of some
of the children are removal of parental custody, the hospitalization of
parents with serious illnesses, the incarceration of parents in penal institutions, and the violent death of parents or their surrogates.[48]

As indicated earlier, one criterion for acceptance of pupils at
nonreservation boarding schools is a broken home, and another is
emotional or mental problems that cannot be corrected in an ordi-
nary school situation. In spite of a well-established need for psychologists in the BIA schools, especially the off-reservation boarding schools, only one was employed in the entire system in 1968.[49]
In addition, virtually no mental health workers are employed by
the Division of Indian Health in the hospitals. Without psycholo-

[46] Tom Sasaki, "Sources of Mental Stress in Indian Acculturation," in J. Cobb (ed.),
"Emotional Problems of Indian Students in Boarding Schools and Related Public
Schools," Bureau of Indian Affairs (1960; processed), p. 5.

[47] *Indian Education*, Hearings, Pt. 1, pp. 195–99.

[48] ENKI Corporation, "Evaluation Report," Vol. 2, "Detailed Project Evaluation,"
p. 30.

[49] Unpublished tabulation from Bureau of Indian Affairs, Branch of Pupil Personnel Services.

gists or psychiatrists, the off-reservation boarding schools are no better able to meet the needs of the students than are the institutions that referred them.

Since relatively few public schools have psychologists,[50] it is difficult to ascertain how many are needed. At a minimum, there should be one in each of the nineteen off-reservation boarding schools and perhaps one for each 1,000 pupils in the other BIA schools. This would mean a total of sixty-five.

SCHOOL SOCIAL WORKERS

In recent years, with the realization that children with problems reflect communities with problems, urban school systems have begun to hire personnel with master's degrees in social work. Social workers could be most useful in federal Indian schools in such areas as dropout prevention, help for underachievers, and assistance to the psychologist.

Social workers could visit the homes of potential dropouts and discuss with the entire family the importance of completing school. Since fewer than one-fifth of reservation parents have completed high school, the social worker's best arguments may be needed to convince the older members of the family of the importance of a high school education. For students attending boarding schools long distances from home, working directly with the students would appear to be more practical.

Most studies indicate that the achievement of many Indian children of above average or average intelligence is far below their capabilities.[51] School social workers, in conjunction with the teaching staff, could seek ways of increasing student motivation and general interest in school. Perhaps trained workers could remove some of the impediments to learning that seem to exist for many Indian children.

The social worker could also supplement the work of the psy-

[50] According to a survey by the U.S. Office of Education, the number of public school psychologists increased between 1950 and 1960 from 520 to 2,724. Reported in Bureau of Indian Affairs, Branch of Pupil Personnel Services, "School Psychological Services" (1968; unpublished).

[51] For example, see ENKI Corporation, "Evaluation Report," Vol. 3, "Detailed Test Data."

chologist with children identified as emotionally disturbed or with varying degrees of mental illness. The social worker could work with parents when home conditions are a cause of the child's problems.

No study of casework standards for school social work appears to have been made, but schools in Baltimore, for example, try to maintain a standard of 75 cases per worker.[52] In 1968 the Bureau of Indian Affairs had only two social workers in its entire school system.[53] In several off-reservation boarding schools 80 percent of the children enrolled had problems.[54] Since 11,000 students attend off-reservation boarding schools, this implies a need for 120 social workers for those schools alone.

SPECIAL EDUCATION

With so many Indian children severely retarded in educational achievement, there is great need for teachers trained in special education. The pupil–teacher ratios that special educators believe are optimal for children with a variety of functional disabilities are shown in the following table:[55]

Type of disability	Number of pupils per teacher
Hard of hearing	15
Partially sighted	12
Mentally retarded	12
Social emotional disorders	9
Psychoneurological learning disorders	12

If only one-tenth of the pupils in federal Indian schools require the services of a special educator (a very conservative estimate, considering that the achievement level of a reservation Indian twelfth grade student is three to four years below the national average), approximately 460 would be required (assuming a ratio

[52] V. P. Shook, "Professional-Pupil Ratios in School Social Work," Bureau of Indian Affairs, School Social Work Section (1968; unpublished).

[53] Unpublished tabulation from Bureau of Indian Affairs, Branch of Pupil Personnel Services.

[54] Shook, "Professional-Pupil Ratios."

[55] Bureau of Indian Affairs, "Teacher-Pupil Ratios in Areas of Special Education" (1968; unpublished).

of twelve students per educator). The Bureau of Indian Affairs in 1968 had only seven special educators for a school system of 250 schools and 57,000 students.[56] Obviously these seven can meet only a tiny fraction of the need for their services.

GUIDANCE COUNSELORS

The problem in using guidance counselors in BIA schools is as much one of manpower effectiveness as of manpower shortage. Counselors in Indian schools, like those in public schools, should be counseling on after-graduation job opportunities, helping the student select an appropriate college, and assisting in various school testing programs. They should also be responsible for easing the adjustment of students entering public schools with a minority of Indian pupils[57] and for interpreting to Indian pupils tests that were originally designed and standardized for students with quite different cultural and social development.

It is generally recognized that guidance personnel have been used ineffectively in BIA schools. According to a bureau memorandum:

As we closely observe the general practices that are presently followed in Bureau of Indian Affairs schools, it is readily apparent that the area of guidance has assumed the major responsibility for looking after the general welfare of the students, e.g., developing health habits, conducting recreational activities, developing eating practices, providing clothing, meting out punishment, and putting children to bed. To place the discipline of guidance in such an untenable position leads to the castration of the possible effectiveness that professional guidance personnel could perform.[58]

Guidance personnel are being used ineffectively partly because they are pressed into service to relieve a shortage of dormitory aides in virtually every Indian school. Furthermore, many of the counselors have the title but lack the standard qualification for the

[56] Unpublished tabulation from Bureau of Indian Affairs, Branch of Pupil Personnel Services.

[57] A large number of Indian children attend all-Indian schools operated by the Bureau of Indian Affairs up to grade eight or nine and then enter a public high school where a majority of the students are non-Indian.

[58] Bureau of Indian Affairs, Branch of Pupil Personnel Services, "Professional Services to Pupils Through Guidance and Counseling" (1968; unpublished).

TABLE 2-4

Manpower Requirements, Pupil Personnel Services,
Bureau of Indian Affairs Schools, 1968

Profession	Actual staff	Manpower needs	Manpower deficit
Psychologist	1	71[a]	70
School social worker	2	120[b]	118
Special education worker	7	430[c]	423
Guidance counselor	173	259[d]	86
Total	183	880	697

Sources: Actual, unpublished tabulation from Bureau of Indian Affairs, Branch of Pupil Personnel Services; needs, author's estimates.

a. Assumes one psychologist for every nineteen off-reservation boarding schools and one psychologist for every 1,000 pupils.

b. Off-reservation boarding schools only. Assumes 80 percent of pupils with problems and 75 cases per worker.

c. Assumes ratio of one teacher per 12 pupils and 10 percent of children in need of services of special educator.

d. Assumes ratio of one guidance counselor per 200 pupils.

work, a master's degree in guidance. In far too many cases they have not had enough formal training to undertake an effective guidance program.

It appears also that there is a shortage of guidance counselors (there are now 173), although it is not so severe as in other skilled nonteaching professions. On the basis of discussions with educators and guidance workers on thirteen reservations during 1968, it would seem that an increase of 50 percent (86 counselors) would be enough to eliminate the shortage, assuming that all guidance counselors were qualified and used effectively.[59]

The manpower needs in the various pupil personnel services that have been discussed are summarized in Table 2-4. The estimates are based on quite conservative assumptions, and actual staffing needs are probably higher than indicated. If one accepts

[59] Since this is not the case, the 50 percent increase is an underestimate of actual staffing needs. A 50 percent increase would produce a ratio of one counselor to 1,200 students, twice the number generally found in public schools. However, a high proportion of Indian students live in boarding schools and thus require more counseling than in the usual school situation. Moreover, since Indian parents generally have limited schooling and off-reservation experience, counseling is vital to acquaint the child with the training and education prerequisite for successful living in an off-reservation setting.

the argument that government schools should be model institutions for the education of disadvantaged children, it is clear that bureau schools are seriously deficient in skilled nonteaching personnel. At least four times as many are needed as are currently employed.

Teacher Turnover in BIA Schools

There is an excessive rate of teacher turnover in BIA schools, which is bound to adversely affect the quality of education. Some students do not have the same teacher all year (about 40 percent of the teachers who leave the schools each year do so during the school year). Recruitment costs are high, leaving less money for other educational purposes. Moreover, teacher turnover is, to some extent, an indication of dissatisfaction with the schools and the students, and a dissatisfied teacher cannot function at maximum effectiveness.[60] The rate of turnover in BIA schools is almost double that in the public schools of the country as a whole or that of the New York State system (Appendix Table A-5) and almost two and one-half times as high as the rate in Connecticut or Tennessee. It is roughly comparable to the turnover in public school systems located in the sparsely settled state of Montana, or of the West and Southwest as a whole. It could be argued that, since most BIA schools are located in sparsely settled western and southwestern states and have turnover rates not much greater than public schools in those areas, the problem is not especially important. On the other hand, it seems reasonable that the federal Indian schools should be at least equal in all aspects of educational quality, including teacher turnover, to the public schools of the nation as a whole, especially when one goal of the bureau should be to operate a model school system for disadvantaged children. This calls for a much lower turnover rate than now prevails. The federal government has far better recruiting and orientation facilities to attain this lower rate than do local school districts in western and southwestern states.

[60] Total teacher turnover is defined as the total number of vacancies to be filled in a local school system; it does not include vacancies in newly created positions.

TABLE 2-5

*Reasons for Leaving after One Year, Bureau of
Indian Affairs Teachers, 1964–67*

Principal reason for leaving	Percent of those leaving
Isolation	38.6
Return to school	20.1
Economic	13.2
Marriage and homemaking	13.2
Maternity	5.8
Community difficulty	4.0
Military service	1.7
Retired	1.7
Deceased	1.7
Total	100.0

Source: Bureau of Indian Affairs, Division of Education, "Teacher Turnover Survey for 1964–67" (1968; processed), p. 58.

The greatest turnover by administrative area (Appendix Table A-6) occurs in isolated parts of the country, such as Alaska, Montana, and Wyoming, and the lowest in the more populous states of Oklahoma, Washington, and Oregon. The turnover rate in small day schools in sparsely settled portions of the reservation is about double the rate for non-reservation boarding schools, which are generally in, or close to, more populated areas.[61]

More than one-half of all turnover occurs among teachers with two years or less of experience, and less than 15 percent among those with more than five years' experience (Appendix Table A-7). It is thus important to examine the reasons for leaving given by teachers with only one year's experience in the system, as presented in Table 2-5. More than 50 percent of these teachers left because of isolation or for economic reasons.

Much of the turnover problem plaguing the bureau school system appears traceable to the rigidity of the civil service system. Virtually all new teachers begin at the same starting salary (GS-7, $8,098 for twelve months in 1970), whether the teaching location is isolated or near a heavily populated area. It would seem reason-

[61] Three of the largest non-reservation boarding schools are Albuquerque Indian in New Mexico, Phoenix Indian in Arizona, and Sherman Institute in California.

able to adjust starting salaries and increments to reflect the disutility of a particular situation. A single salary structure, unresponsive to the location assigned, is unrealistic and results not only in a higher turnover rate in the more isolated areas but also in great difficulty in finding qualified individuals to fill positions, even on a temporary basis.[62]

Another hardship under the civil service system is the two to three weeks' vacation given new teachers, as against two to three months for public school teachers. This increases the feeling of isolation and consequently BIA problems of recruitment and retention. Bureau teachers may take up to thirty days of educational leave, but since most summer school courses last from six to ten weeks, teachers are forced to use annual leave if they wish to take them for credit. Otherwise leave is sufficient only to attend educational workshops.

Considering the amount of time teachers must spend in the classroom, bureau salaries (per hour) are not competitive with those of the public schools. The starting salaries are about 2 percent higher than the U.S. average, but bureau teachers spend 25 percent more time in their classrooms.[63]

Finally, new teachers receive little or no orientation to living and working conditions on an isolated Indian reservation. Recruited from the eastern parts of the United States, many have had no experience with either Indian culture or the sparsely settled regions of the country where the reservations are located. Perhaps an orientation would frighten off many applicants, but at least those who accepted employment would have a reasonable idea of the conditions.

Moreover, monetary incentives might encourage teachers with reservation experience to take positions in very isolated areas and eliminate the assignment of new teachers in such areas.

[62] Henry M. Levin has shown that a single salary structure in schools in metropolitan areas results in shortages of teachers in those subjects where nonteaching alternatives offer relatively high salaries. "Recruiting Teachers for Large-City Schools" (unpublished). Moreover, the ENKI Corporation "Evaluation Report" indicated that it had been virtually impossible to obtain qualified teachers to operate the Title I program in bureau schools located in isolated areas.

[63] As mentioned above, in most cases they are not teaching during the summer but are required to be there nevertheless.

Proposed Transfer of Education to HEW

A proposal has recently been advanced by congressmen and officials of Indian organizations to transfer responsibility for Indian education to the Office of Education in the Department of Health, Education, and Welfare. Three reasons are offered by the proponents.

First, the Department of the Interior is a resource-oriented agency whose primary concern is the development of natural resources, while the Office of Education is directly concerned with developing human resources and could concentrate solely on this task. This argument is strengthened by the fact that the Bureau of Indian Affairs has much more adequate statistics on uses of Indian lands, forests, and minerals than on the quality of human resources.

Second, the Office of Education could use its research capability (especially through the regional education laboratories) to study methods of improving Indian education. The BIA does almost no research and is consequently handicapped in solving such fundamental problems as high dropout rates, poor achievement levels, or decisions on types of secondary school education to be offered.[64]

Finally, it is argued that it would be easier for the Department of Health, Education, and Welfare to obtain the appropriations necessary for an effective school system. The Bureau of Indian Affairs has not had especially good relations with Congress over the years, and this has limited its appropriations. Supporting this view is the fact that since 1955, when the Public Health Service took over Indian health programs from the BIA, appropriations have increased substantially and levels of Indian health have improved markedly.

However, many problems in Indian education would not be solved by a transfer of responsibility. Without reforms in pay scales and vacation policy, the problem of obtaining qualified

[64] As an example of BIA lack of interest in educational research, it was not until 1968 that the bureau initiated a survey of the Indian dropout problem, and then the study was made by the Northwest Regional Educational Laboratory under contract with the BIA.

teachers for isolated reservations will continue. Also, at least part of the low-achievement and dropout problem is due to poverty and lack of opportunity on the reservations; a shift of responsibility for education would not change these conditions. Finally, that BIA schools are inadequate despite above-average expenditures per pupil suggests that the more ample funds that might be available for Indian education under the HEW aegis would produce only limited improvement unless they were used effectively.

Thus it would appear that the expected benefits to be derived from shifting the responsibility for Indian education from BIA to HEW are insufficient to justify the transfer. Rather, an emphasis on making several of the reforms discussed above (while retaining Indian education within BIA) should have a significant effect on the quality of Indian education.

CHAPTER III

Health

Congress first appropriated funds for Indian health in 1832, a modest $12,000.[1] In 1836 the federal government began providing limited health services, including physicians, to the Ottawa and Chippewa Indians under the provisions of a treaty establishing their reservations.

By 1880, the Bureau of Indian Affairs was operating four hospitals and had a staff of seventy-seven physicians.[2] During the next seventy-five years the number of health facilities and personnel employed by the BIA gradually expanded, but because of limited appropriations the level of services was not adequate.

Responsibility for the health care of Indians and Alaskan natives was transferred on July 1, 1955, from the Bureau of Indian Affairs to a special Division of Indian Health in the Public Health Service (PHS) of the U.S. Department of Health, Education, and Welfare. It was thought that the Public Health Service would have greater success in recruiting physicians to work on reservations, partly because of higher salaries and better fringe benefits. Furthermore, Congress was not as hostile to HEW appropriations as to those of the BIA. Indian health has improved substantially in the decade and a half since that time, largely because of increased appropriations, which tripled on a per-Indian basis between 1955 and 1966. With few exceptions, reservation Indians are entitled to comprehensive medical care free of charge if they are of one-fourth or more Indian blood.

[1] 4 Stat. 514.
[2] See William A. Brophy and Sophie D. Aberle (comps.), *The Indian: America's Unfinished Business* (University of Oklahoma Press, 1966), p. 160.

Before the Public Health Service was given the responsibility for Indian health, conditions were deplorable. Death rates from infectious diseases such as tuberculosis and influenza were comparable to those for all races twenty years earlier. There was a severe shortage of health manpower, and facilities such as hospitals were outmoded and understaffed. Provision for Indian health was niggardly, as shown in the following table of appropriations before and after the transfer:[3]

	Appropriation
Fiscal year	*(thousands of dollars)*
Before transfer	
1940	5,088
1945	5,734
1950	10,017
1952	13,345
1955	24,555
After transfer	
1957	47,537
1959	48,337
1961	59,985
1963	66,171
1965	71,775

Death and Disease Rates

A marked reduction in infant mortality and in deaths from infectious diseases is one of the more important accomplishments since 1955. Table 3-1 shows a greater percentage decline in infant and tuberculosis death rates for Indians than for all races for the years 1955–67. In 1955 the Indian infant mortality rate was the same as that for all races in 1931—a difference of twenty-four years. By 1967 the rate was that for all races in 1950—the difference had decreased to seventeen years. A similar comparison for 1955–65 for tuberculosis shows a decrease from seventeen years' to fourteen years' difference: the 1955 Indian death rate was equal to that of

[3] Data for 1940–52 from U.S. Public Health Service, *Health Services for American Indians* (1957), p. 249; data for 1955–65 from Public Health Service, *Indian Health Highlights* (June 1966), p. 43.

all races in 1938; the 1965 rate was equal to that of all races in 1951.[4]

In 1955 some 2,500 Indian tuberculosis patients for whom beds were not available were awaiting hospitalization.[5] The backlog was soon eliminated, and since 1956, the peak year of hospitalization, the tuberculosis census has declined steadily, chiefly because

TABLE 3-1

Infant and Tuberculosis Death Rates, Indians and All Races,
Selected Years, 1955–67

Year	Infant death rates[a] (per 1,000 live births)		Tuberculosis death rates[b] (per 100,000 population)		
	Indian	All races	Indian	Alaskan natives[c]	All races
1955	61	26.4	47	158	9.1
1957	57	26.3	34	83	7.8
1959	50	26.4	28	42	6.5
1961	44	25.3	25	35	5.4
1963	40	25.2	25	28	4.9
1965	37	24.7	19	16	4.1
1967	30	22.4	16	17	3.5
Percentage change, 1955–67	*−51*	*−15*	*−66*	*−89*	*−62*

Source: U.S. Public Health Service, "Indian Health Trends and Services," 1969 ed. (processed), pp. 8, 32. Figures for Indians are for those in twenty-four reservation states.

a. Indian rates are three-year moving averages, 1957–65; other rates are based on single-year data.

b. Indian and Alaskan native rates are three-year moving averages, 1955–65; other rates are based on single-year data.

c. Includes Indians, Aleuts, and Eskimos.

of the use of new drugs. The chemotherapy program, for ambulatory patients, not only reduced the need for hospitalization but the length of stay in the hospital. As a result, by 1963 two sanitariums with a total of 500 beds had been closed and two tuberculosis units in Indian general hospitals had been converted to general medical and surgical use. Tuberculosis bed utilization in contract hospitals (those not operated by the PHS but given specified fees for

[4] Mortality data for all races (before 1955) from U.S. Bureau of the Census, *Historical Statistics of the United States, Colonial Times to 1957* (1960), pp. 25, 26.

[5] *A Review of the Indian Health Program*, Hearing before the Subcommittee on Indian Affairs of the House Committee on Interior and Insular Affairs, 88 Cong. 1 sess. (1963), p. 7.

TABLE 3-2

Gastritis & Enteritis and Influenza & Pneumonia Death Rates,
Indians and All Races, 1954–64[a]

(Per 100,000 population)

Year	Gastritis & enteritis[b]		Influenza & pneumonia[c]	
	Indians	All races	Indians	All races
1954	56	4.9	n.a.	n.a.
1955	41	4.7	88	n.a.
1956	36	4.5	93	n.a.
1957	35	4.7	94	n.a.
1958	34	4.5	89	n.a.
1959	30	4.4	83	31.2
1960	27	4.4	77	37.3
1961	28	4.3	n.a.	30.2
1962	26	4.4	n.a.	n.a.
1963	22	4.4	n.a.	n.a.
1964	19	4.3	n.a.	n.a.
Percentage change, 1954–64	−66	−12		

Source: Public Health Service, *Indian Health Highlights* (June 1966), pp. 31, 32. Figures for Indians are for those in twenty-four reservation states.
n.a. Not available.
a. Indian rates are three-year moving averages; other rates are based on single-year data.
b. Includes duodenitis; does not include deaths from diarrhea of newborn.
c. Does not include deaths from pneumonia of newborn.

each Indian patient) was reduced from more than 900 in 1955 to about 200 in 1963.[6]

Besides the drop in tuberculosis, there has been a marked reduction in the death rate of reservation Indians from other infectious diseases, particularly from gastritis and enteritis, which declined during the 1954–64 period more than five times as rapidly as the rate for all races (Table 3-2). However, the Indian mortality rate from these diseases was similar in 1954 to that for all races in 1919 (a difference of thirty-five years), and in 1964 to that for all races in 1931, still more than thirty years behind.

The death rate from influenza and pneumonia among Indians declined moderately between 1955 and 1960. The 1955 rate corresponded to that of all races in the middle 1930s (a difference of some twenty years). The 1960 rate was similar to the rate for all races in 1939—a difference of twenty-one years.

[6] *Ibid.*, p. 49.

TABLE 3-3

*Incidence Rates for Various Infectious Diseases, Reservation Indians
and All Races, Selected Years, 1952–65*

(*Annual rate per 100,000 population*)

Disease	Indians			All races		
	1952–54	1965	Percentage change	1955	1965	Percentage change
Tuberculosis	643.3	175.9	−72.7	60.1	25.3	−57.9
Syphilis	385.3	113.4	−70.6	74.9	58.2	−22.3
Dysentery	857.2ª	365.9	−57.3	10.5	5.7	−45.7
Strep throat	n.a.	2,189.1	n.a.	89.8	203.9	127.1
Whooping cough	128.2	17.8	−86.1	38.2	3.5	−90.8
Measles	842.5	761.3	− 9.6	337.9	135.1	−60.0
Chickenpox	248.7	553.7	122.6	198.9	127.6	−35.8
Mumps	213.3	291.6	36.7	159.5	108.7	−31.8
Hepatitis	125.5	139.1	10.8	19.5	17.5	−10.3
Trachoma	279.2	1,478.4	429.5	n.a.	n.a.	n.a.
Influenza	1,600.5	1,103.1	−31.1	n.a.	n.a.	n.a.
Pneumonia	1,306.5	4,023.1	207.9	n.a.	n.a.	n.a.
Gastroenteritis	860.0	6,078.8	n.a.	n.a.	n.a.	n.a.

Sources: Public Health Service, *Health Services for American Indians* (1957), pp. 57, 248; "Illness Among Indians, 1966" (processed), p. 14; *Indian Health Highlights* (1959), p. 44.

n.a. Not available.

a. Includes all forms of dysentery.

While reductions in mortality rates from infectious diseases have been significant, the incidence of infectious diseases has not declined notably (Table 3-3). Although the incidence of tuberculosis, syphilis, and dysentery has declined rapidly (more rapidly than for the non-Indian population), there have been large increases among reservation Indians in the incidence of trachoma, pneumonia, gastroenteritis, and chickenpox. These statistics probably exaggerate the actual increase, especially of trachoma. Improved techniques of case finding and the development of better medical records in recent years mean that fewer cases go undetected and unrecorded.

Table 3-3 shows that a reservation Indian is seven times as likely as a non-Indian to contract tuberculosis, sixty-four times as likely to be stricken with dysentery, and eight times as likely to contract hepatitis.

The principal causes of the high incidence of infectious disease

are the low socioeconomic status of reservation Indians and deplorable housing. According to a 1966 survey, 75 percent of all reservation homes are substandard, with 50 percent so dilapidated as
to be beyond repair.[7] On the Navajo Reservation, where nearly
one-third of the nation's reservation Indians live, only 20 percent
of the homes have running water and adequate means of waste disposal and only 17 percent have electricity. One-half of all the families use a potentially contaminated water source.[8]

To improve the situation, Congress in 1959 passed the Indian
Sanitation Facilities Construction Act (Public Law 86-121),
which authorized federal funds for the construction and improvement of sanitation facilities in reservation homes and community
buildings. Safe water and waste disposal improvements have since
been authorized for nearly 44,000 families, at a total cost of some
$50 million.[9]

Personnel

Increased appropriations by Congress resulted in an increase between 1955 and 1966 of 50 percent in total personnel in the Indian
Health Division, while the number of physicians and dentists increased 152 percent and 162 percent, respectively. The increase for
many other categories was even higher (Appendix Table A-8).
Nevertheless, there are still proportionately far fewer personnel
for Indians than for the population as a whole, as shown in Table
3-4. There are twice as many dentists for the general population as
for reservation Indians, and more than three times as many pharmacists. The lack of physicians and public health nurses is not as
great: in 1962 there was one full-time practicing physician for each
840 of the general population compared with one for 1,460 res-

[7] Task Force on Indian Housing, "Indian Housing: Need, Alternatives, Priorities
and Program Recommendations," Bureau of Indian Affairs (December 1966; processed).

[8] *Federal Facilities for Indians: Tribal Relations with the Federal Government,*
Report by Mamie L. Mizen, Staff Member, Senate Committee on Appropriations
(1966), p. 455.

[9] See U.S. Department of Health, Education, and Welfare, "To the First Americans:
A Report on the Indian Health Program of the U.S. Public Health Service" (1967;
processed), p. 2.

TABLE 3-4

Number of Persons Served by Each Physician, Dentist
Public Health Nurse, and Pharmacist, 1955, 1962, 19

Profession	Indian health program			General population, 1962
	1955	1962	1966	
Physician	2,200	1,460	1,220	840[a]
Dentist	7,000	4,600	3,670	1,800
Public health nurse	4,000	3,500	3,300	2,500
Pharmacist	51,400	6,460	5,000	1,500

Sources: Data for 1955 and 1962 (except physicians, 1962, and pharmacists) are from *A Review of the Indian Health Program*, Hearing before the Subcommittee on Indian Affairs of the House Committee on Interior and Insular Affairs, 88 Cong. 1 sess. (1963), pp. 27, 51; ratios for 1966 (except nurses) computed from data in Appendix Table A-8, using population reported in Public Health Service, "Illness Among Indians, 1966," p. 3. Other data are author's estimates.

a. Does not include physicians in full-time teaching or research.

ervation Indians, and one public health nurse for every 2,500 of the general population compared with one for every 3,500 reservation Indians.

Physicians applying for positions with the Division of Indian Health must have served a one-year internship in an accredited hospital. Nearly 70 percent of the physicians and dentists in the Indian service are there in lieu of military service, and few remain more than the required two years (the time draftees are required to serve in the armed services). There is thus a great turnover in staff, which affects program continuity. The principal reason is the higher pecuniary rewards offered elsewhere. A doctor or dentist entering the Indian Health Division in 1970 received a base salary of $13,400 a year,[10] which could reach a maximum (with major administrative responsibility and twenty-six years' service) of $24,000. The average income in private practice in 1968 was $36,000 for physicians[11] and an estimated $24,500 for dentists.

Since most of the physicians employed by the Division of Indian Health are not specialists (nor is it likely that at present pay scales many specialists could be attracted), patients requiring a specialist are usually referred to private physicians under contract in urban

[10] Unpublished tabulation, Public Health Service (salaries effective Jan. 1, 1970).
[11] Arthur Owens, "The New Surge in Physicians' Earnings and Expenses," *Medical Economics*, Vol. 46 (Dec. 8, 1969), p. 85.

areas near the reservations. Funds for contract care are generally adequate, so that the lack of specialists for Indians is minimal.

Nurses who have graduated from a two-year college program are hired by the Indian Health Division at $7,000 a year. Those who have completed three- or four-year programs enter at $7,400.[12] These salaries are reasonably competitive with non-Indian service alternatives in major metropolitan areas, where nurses generally receive starting salaries ranging from $6,000 to $7,000 per year. However, to attract good nurses to some of the isolated locations will require higher salaries than they would receive elsewhere. Many Indian hospitals suffer from high turnover of nurses and from unfilled vacancies. For example, at the PHS hospital on the Papago Reservation the position of head nurse had been vacant six months as of June 1968; the thirty-six-bed hospital on the Zuñi Reservation had five vacant registered nurse (RN) positions; at the hospital on the Blackfeet Reservation three of the ten RN positions were vacant; the hospital on the Pine Ridge Reservation had twenty-five RN positions with twelve vacancies.[13] Because of the nursing shortage, the surgery suite at Pine Ridge could not be used.

Although salary levels higher than those outside the Indian service would probably reduce unfilled vacancies and turnover, there would still be a nursing shortage in the Indian hospitals. The isolation of the reservations, with the concomitant lack of social life and recreation, affects staff turnover and morale. A high rate of turnover among nurses will probably continue until more Indian RNs are brought into the service, since more of them would be familiar with this type of area and thus less likely to object to such a location. At present, only a small percentage of service RNs are Indian, but the percentage has been rising in recent years.

One factor in the high turnover among the professional health personnel has been inadequate housing, but this situation has improved in recent years. For example, between 1955 and 1958 three

[12] Information from Division of Indian Health.

[13] Interviews with PHS hospital personnel: Dr. Steimohl, medical officer in charge, Sells, Ariz., June 29, 1968; Dr. Zebrack, Zuñi Reservation, June 20, 1968; Dr. Brown, Browning, Mont., July 6, 1968; Dr. Woldridge, Pine Ridge, S.Dak., July 15, 1968.

hundred temporary housing units for health personnel were built,[14] and between 1955 and 1960, seventy one permanent units were built. Although precise data on the number of new housing units built since 1960 are not available, most of the facilities for doctors, dentists, or nurses on the reservations visited were quite new and generally superior to those provided for professional employees of the Bureau of Indian Affairs.

Most Indian service physicians reported some competition from indigenous practitioners of medicine (better known as medicine men). It was estimated that nearly 50 percent of the Indians on the Zuñi and Choctaw Reservations see medicine men before seeking treatment at the PHS hospital, but at most of the other reservations visited the estimate was much lower. At the hospital at Shiprock, New Mexico, on the eastern edge of the Navajo Reservation, it is common practice to allow the medicine men to visit hospitalized patients as long as they do not interfere with the patients' medical treatment.[15] Apparently the practice of medicine by medicine men is declining. Not only is there a growing confidence in modern medicine among reservation Indians, but as the older medicine men die there are no younger ones to take their place.

TRAINING PROGRAMS

It is the policy of the Division of Indian Health to train and employ as many Indians and Alaskan natives in its programs as possible. From 50 to 60 percent of the health personnel employed by the division are Indians, although the number of Indian physicians and dentists employed is less than 1 percent of all professional Indian personnel. Between 1955 and 1965 more than a thousand Indians and Alaskan natives were trained for auxiliary positions, including practical nurses, dental and nursing assistants, sanitarian aides, community health aides, medical records technicians, and clerks. The division operates a school at Albuquerque, New Mexico, where some sixty girls of Indian descent are trained as practical nurses each year. Three centers are operated to train

[14] *Indian Sanitation Facilities,* Hearings before a Subcommittee of the House Committee on Interstate and Foreign Commerce, 86 Cong. 1 sess. (1959), p. 52.

[15] Interviews with PHS hospital personnel: Dr. Zebrack; Dr. Gibson, Philadelphia, Miss., April 1968; Dr. Read, Shiprock, N.Mex., June 24, 1968.

Indian and Alaskan native high school graduates as dental assistants in Brigham City, Utah, Lawrence, Kansas, and Mount Edgecumbe, Alaska. About thirty graduate each year and are then employed at various Indian health facilities.

The division has recently started three residency training programs, in general practice, pediatrics, and public health.[16] On-the-job training is provided for service personnel, housekeepers, and ambulance drivers.

INCREASES IN PRODUCTIVITY

A crude but tolerable measure of the productivity of health personnel can be obtained by dividing the number of units of service performed per year by the number of employees, thus obtaining the number of service units per year for each professional.[17] This measure ignores any change in productivity if the quality of service increases or decreases.

The productivity of physicians remained constant between 1958 and 1967 (approximately 4,400 outpatient visits per physician per year). Although there is some question whether each physician could have handled more, the time per patient is usually only five to seven minutes (about one-third to one-half the time allotted to outpatients by physicians in private practice).[18] Thus an increase in the number of patients seen per hour could result in reduced quality of care. However, most Indian service physicians believe that a modest increase in productivity could be realized if there were more auxiliary personnel. Between 1955 and 1966 the number of physicians grew more rapidly than the number of nurses and other auxiliary personnel. Had the reverse been the case, probably each physician could have assumed a slightly higher patient load. Some physicians felt that a greater number of examining rooms would allow them to see more patients per hour and thus increase productivity.

While there was no gain in the productivity of physicians, there was a moderate growth in the productivity of dentists. During the

---

[16] Public Health Service, *The Indian Health Program of the U.S. Public Health Service* (PHS Publication 1026, rev. 1969), pp. 12–13.

[17] See Appendix Tables A-8, A-9, and A-10 for the underlying data. Definitions of units of service for various kinds of personnel are given in the notes to Table A-10.

[18] "Doctors' Earnings Dissected: The Productivity Factor," *Medical Economics*, Vol. 45 (Dec. 9, 1968), p. 76.

years 1956–58 each dentist averaged 3,100 units of service per year, compared with 4,100 in the period 1962–65, an increase of 32 percent. Two factors appear to account for this. First, the number of auxiliary personnel rose from 0.80 dental assistant and technician per dentist in 1955 to 1.14 in 1966, or 43 percent. Second, two-chair clinics were used instead of the traditional single-chair clinics, and high-speed equipment, such as air turbine handpieces and high-efficiency suction devices, was widely employed.[19]

The most dramatic gain in productivity occurred among pharmacists. In the years 1955–57, each man's output was 10,200 workload units a year, but by 1964–66 it was 19,980 units a year—an increase of nearly 100 percent. The important factor appears to have been the gradual shift from one pharmacist per hospital to two or more. This freed one or more of them from time-consuming administrative duties.[20] Probably the productivity of pharmacists will grow more slowly in the future, because they are now encouraged to explain privately to each patient the purpose of the medicine and drugs prescribed and the importance of following directions regarding their use.[21] While this will leave less time for the pharmacist to spend on the traditional activities by which his productivity is measured, it will probably increase his effectiveness and thus his real productivity.

Health Facilities and Services

When the Public Health Service took over the Indian health program in 1955, the obsolescence of the hospitals was critical. Twelve of the forty-four general hospitals in operation had been built before 1925 and only one after 1945; nine were of frame construction and thus potential fire hazards. Few of the operating rooms were adequately safeguarded against explosion and special fire hazards; many lacked conductive flooring, shockproof and

[19] Public Health Service, *Dental Services for American Indians and Alaska Natives* (PHS Publication 1406, 1965), pp. 11–12.

[20] Interview with Allen J. Brands, chief, Pharmacy Branch, Division of Indian Health, Public Health Service, Feb. 7, 1969.

[21] A study by H. Gilbert, PHS Hospital, Sacaton, Ariz., "Drug Utilization on the Pima Indian Reservation" (1966, unpublished), indicated that many patients did not use, or used incorrectly, the medicine or drugs prescribed.

sparkproof lights and outlets, and reliable auxiliary electrical systems.[22] Only eleven of the hospitals were accredited by the Joint Commission on Accreditation of Hospitals. Less than half had blood banks, a medical records department, or metabolism apparatus.

Since 1955 twelve hospitals have been constructed and others have had extensive modernization. Seven obsolete ones have been closed. Although staff shortages have been somewhat reduced, they are still acute by community hospital standards. For example, in 1955 there were 121 employees for each 100 patients in an Indian hospital. By 1962 this ratio had increased to 147 employees per 100 patients, but was still far behind the community hospital ratio of 227 employees per 100 patients.[23] In spite of the improvement in facilities, only twenty of the forty-nine hospitals maintained by the Indian Health Division were accredited in late 1968,[24] because of lack of blood banks, inadequate separation of patients with various infectious diseases, and small size (hospitals with fewer than twenty-five beds were not eligible for accreditation).

The Division of Indian Health also maintains health centers and stations. The centers are outpatient facilities staffed by full-time personnel and providing medical care and teaching preventive health measures. The stations, which are intermittently staffed, hold scheduled clinics and supply medical care and other health services. Between 1955 and 1967, eleven centers and forty-six stations were built.

Since 1955 there has been a rapid growth in the services provided under the Indian health program. (See Appendix Tables A-9 and A-10 for data on selected hospital-oriented health services, 1955–65.) Admissions to hospitals have increased more than 50 percent, and hospital visits have more than doubled. Hospital births have increased by over 40 percent. By 1963, 97 percent of all Indian babies were born in hospitals, compared with 85 percent in 1952. Also, total outpatient visits to health centers and health stations increased more than fivefold between 1951 and 1965. Physician visits more than trebled, and the level of dental services pro-

[22] Public Health Service, *Health Services for American Indians*, pp. 111–12, 249–50.

[23] *A Review of the Indian Health Program*, Hearing, pp. 11, 56.

[24] Interview with personnel in Program Analysis and Statistics Branch, Office of Program Planning and Evaluation, Division of Indian Health, Silver Spring, Md., December 1968.

vided increased two and a half times. The most rapid expansion took place in pharmaceutical services, which were virtually nonexistent when the PHS took over the program.

Some physicians at Indian hospitals maintain that a small charge for outpatient visits (particularly after-hours visits) and drugs would reduce the number of nuisance visits (for example, for mosquito bites or for diet pills) and thus allow more time for patients with more urgent health needs. However, there are reservations where the median family income is less than $1,000 a year,[25] and many families could not afford even a nominal fee. In the long run, better health education will permit the patient to determine more realistically when he needs to see a physician. (This also applies to the non-Indian population.)[26]

A related question is whether reservation Indians with sufficient means to obtain private medical care should be given comprehensive medical care free of charge. In the past, Oklahoma Indians with incomes above a minimum level were required to pay for medical care: for example, a family of five with an income of $4,500 or more annually.[27] However, because of bookkeeping problems and because of political pressure, the requirement was dropped.

From the standpoint of equity, Indians with incomes above some specified level should be required to pay for medical care. However, on the lowest-income reservations the number seeking treatment who could afford to pay more than a nominal fee would be so small that the revenue would not compensate for the increased administrative costs.

Family Planning

Because of the poverty and unemployment that too often prevail on Indian reservations and among Alaskan natives and birthrates

[25] Bureau of Indian Affairs, "Selected Data on Indian Reservations Eligible for Designation under Public Works and Economic Development Act" (December 1966; processed).

[26] Moreover, better screening by auxiliaries would eliminate the need for the doctor to treat these patients, and he could spend a larger part of his time with the seriously ill.

[27] Interview with Dr. Abend, PHS hospital, Claremore, Okla., June 15, 1968.

two to two and a half times the national average,[28] population pressure is acute. As a result, Indian health personnel have begun disseminating birth control information and devices. By the end of 1969, an estimated 32.5 percent of Indian women between fifteen and forty-four years of age were receiving family planning services, compared with 5.6 percent in 1965 and 20.6 percent in 1967.[29] There is some indication that birth rates are dropping in response to these increased services. On the Zuñi Reservation the total number of births declined from 190 in 1967 to 150 in 1968; on the Blackfeet Reservation they declined from 225 in 1964 to 170 in 1967 and 150 in 1968.[30]

Some Continuing Problems

Considerable progress has been made in Indian health improvement. Between 1940 and 1964 the life expectancy of a reservation Indian increased from fifty-one to sixty-three and a half years, largely as a result of improved health measures. However, much more must be done in some areas. One of the greatest needs is a mental health program. There is a high incidence of suicide on some reservations, and Indian adolescents, especially those living in boarding schools, have emotional problems; the need for trained psychiatrists and psychologists is obvious.[31]

In the past, only limited psychiatric services have been available to Indians and Alaskan natives through contract arrangements made by the Division of Indian Health, and patients placed in state mental hospitals have often received only custodial care.

[28] Public Health Service, *Indian Health Highlights* (June 1966), p. 8.

[29] Public Health Service, "Charts on Health Trends and Services" (April 1968; processed), p. 2.

[30] Interviews with Dr. Zebrack and Dr. Brown.

[31] See for example, Larry Dizmang, "Suicide Among the Cheyenne Indians," and Sol Goldstein and Philip R. Trautmann, "Report on the Quinault Indian Consultation," in *Indian Education*, Hearings before the Special Subcommittee on Indian Education of the Senate Committee on Labor and Public Welfare, 90 Cong. 1 and 2 sess. (1969), Pt. 5, pp. 2177–81, 2343–50. On the problems of adolescents, see Harry L. Saslow and May J. Harrover, "Research on Psychosocial Adjustment of Indian Youth," *American Journal of Psychiatry*, Vol. 125 (August 1968), pp. 224–31; Robert L. Leon, "Mental Health Considerations in the Indian Boarding School Program," in *Indian Education*, Hearings, Pt. 5, pp. 2203–08.

However, in recent years the division has begun to develop a mental health program. In 1965 a pilot project was set up for the Pine Ridge Reservation in South Dakota. The staff includes a psychiatrist, an anthropologist, a psychologist, three social workers, and two aides.[32] In 1966 a psychiatrist, a psychologist, and a mental health social worker were added to the Anchorage area staff; this team provides services to all PHS hospitals and BIA schools throughout the state. Psychiatrists have been added to area offices at Phoenix, Albuquerque, and Window Rock. But compared with some of the other services, the mental health program is still in its infancy.

Closely related to mental health is alcoholism, which is a serious problem on the reservations.[33] On some reservations over 90 percent of the arrests are alcohol-related. Most Indian hospitals have no special treatment facilities for alcoholism, which is generally treated as a crime, not an illness. (Interestingly, on reservations where the Public Health Service hospitals have inadequate facilities for blood storage, blood is sometimes obtained from the inmates of the tribal jail, most of whom were arrested for alcohol-related violations.) Research into the causes of the high rate of alcoholism among Indians is badly needed. There appears to be a wide range of opinion about its causes, but little in the way of hard information.

A third problem is that of dental services to adults. Because of lack of funding and personnel, most Indian service dentists devote the major part of their time to children. Generally, service for adults is limited to extractions. In 1967 only about 20 percent of the Indian population over the age of eighteen received dental treatment, while almost 50 percent of those under eighteen were cared for.[34]

Finally, to meet immediate needs, the Indian Health Division has concentrated almost exclusively on curative health services and very little on preventive services. An increase in the personnel engaged in preventive work would permit the division to establish a truly comprehensive health care system.

[32] Calvin A. Kent and Jerry W. Johnson, *Indian Poverty in South Dakota* (University of South Dakota, 1969), p. 111.

[33] See Maurice L. Sievers, "Cigarette and Alcohol Usage by Southwestern American Indians," *American Journal of Public Health and the Nation's Health*, Vol. 58 (January 1968), pp. 71–81.

[34] Public Health Service, "Charts on Health Trends and Services."

CHAPTER IV

Agricultural Development

In 1968 gross agricultural production from Indian lands was valued at nearly $300 million.[1] However, only $114 million, or slightly more than one-third, was accounted for by Indians; the remainder was produced by non-Indians. This imbalance occurred principally because the Indians leased the bulk of their lands (often the most productive tracts) to non-Indians or permitted some of the lands to lie idle, as is shown in the following table:[2]

| | Number of acres in use | | Number of acres idle |
Land use class	Indians	Non-Indians	
Open grazing	27,809,358	5,530,941	644,986
Dry farming	415,335	1,296,703	60,666
Irrigated	139,887	232,917	113,936

In 1968 Indians were using less than 30 percent of their irrigated lands, about 25 percent of their dry farming lands, and 80 percent of their open grazing lands.

One reason for leasing a large part of the land to whites is that the return from agriculture for Indians is extremely low. In 1960 reservation families engaged in agriculture earned about $1,000, while rural nonfarm families earned about $1,800.[3] Under these

[1] U.S. Bureau of Indian Affairs, "Land Use Inventory and Production Record, Calendar Year 1968," Report 50-1 (1969; processed). No statistics on Indian agricultural income have been collected by the BIA since 1944.

[2] Ibid.

[3] U.S. Bureau of the Census, U.S. Census of Population: 1960, Subject Reports, Nonwhite Population by Race, Final Report PC(2)-1C (1963), p. 26.

circumstances many Indians find they can raise their incomes if they lease their land to whites and take nonagricultural jobs.

Factors in Low Productivity

One of the salient elements hindering Indian agricultural development is the low productivity of Indian farm operators. For example, in 1954 Indian production per acre on the Blackfeet Irrigation Project was much lower than non-Indian: 56 percent less wheat, 25 percent less barley, and 61 percent less alfalfa hay.[4] From 1948 to 1956 on the White Swan Irrigation Project there were great disparities in average values per crop—Indian operators averaged $89, white operators on Indian land $126, and white operators on non-Indian land, $222. Gross income per acre on Indian rangelands was about one-third that on non-Indian land.[5] While the quality of reservation lands was undoubtedly poorer than that of non-Indian rangelands, this probably was not of major importance.

MANAGEMENT

The key factor in the low productivity of Indian farm operators is poor management. As agricultural operations have become more complex and more competitive, efficient management has become increasingly necessary to ensure adequate returns. Indian adults are willing to attend dances and ceremonials that last several days, leaving only the children to make crucial judgments in case of such calamities as an irrigation failure.

The land operations officers on the Blackfeet Reservation cited several typical examples of poor management. Many Indian farmers grow hay. When hay is ready for mowing, it must be cut within a short time or it loses much of its nutrient value and, consequently, of its market value. However, Indian operators will delay,

[4] William A. Brophy and Sophie D. Aberle (comps.), *The Indian: America's Unfinished Business* (University of Oklahoma Press, 1966), p. 79.

[5] Peter P. Dorner, "The Economic Position of the American Indians: Their Resources and Potential for Development" (Ph.D. dissertation, Harvard University, 1959), p. 33.

ceremonials or through carelessness, until the crop has lost
ıch of its commercial value. Again, the calf crops of Crow cattle
ᴐerators average 70 to 72 percent of the maximum potential,
while 85 percent is considered the minimum for building up a
herd of economic size. According to one observer, "Small grain
operators produce 80 to 85 percent of what they could (with proper
management); on irrigated farms about 50 percent."[6]

Several bureau land operations officers declared that Indian cattlemen could earn a higher income per dollar invested if they
switched from cattle- to sheep-raising. Because sheep require more
intensive care and better management, inexperienced Indian operators prefer to raise cattle.[7]

Why is Indian management ability significantly below that of
non-Indians? First, with the exception of the Pueblo Indians, most
tribes have traditionally not been agricultural but have secured
food by hunting and gathering, often covering hundreds of miles
in their search. During the last half of the nineteenth century they
were forcibly placed on reservations and kept alive with free government rations. Cattle donated by the government for the development of ranching were frequently butchered for food. The
Dawes Act of 1887, which allotted much of the reservation land to
individual Indians in 80- or 160-acre tracts, was based on the assumption that Indians could become family farmers, even though
they had virtually no experience in agriculture. Unlike white
farmers, who learned how to farm from their fathers, Indian operators had to learn for themselves. (Since they had virtually no
experience in farm operations, it is little wonder that the majority
of them soon lost their land.)

Second, given the Indian's lack of experience in agriculture, the
technical assistance provided has been inadequate. Indian agricultural extension programs were first undertaken in the 1930s, but
funds were not sufficient to make them effective. Because of a shortage of personnel, the BIA extension agents were also responsible
for administering credit programs and often spent more than half

[6] Interview with Billy E. Butts, land operations officer, Blackfeet Reservation,
Mont., July 7, 1968.

[7] There are undoubtedly other reasons why Indians (with the exception of the
Navajo) are reluctant to raise sheep. Competent sheepherders are in short supply.
Also, according to those familiar with reservation agriculture, Indian operators like
to raise cattle partly for status reasons.

their time on them. A former assistant commissioner of the BIA said in 1947:

Agricultural extension work as now carried on by the Indian Service is inadequate in coverage, due principally to lack of funds to provide even the same ratio of workers to farm operators as exists on the non-Indian areas. Because of the greater need for training and extension work that exists at most reservations, due to the lesser experience and training of Indians, the ratio should be higher in Indian work. Were the extension work of the Indian Service transferred to the Extension Division of the Department of Agriculture as now proposed in a recent Senate bill, it is possible that more funds than are now available could be obtained for this greatly needed work among Indians.[8]

Agricultural extension work was finally transferred to the Department of Agriculture (USDA) in the late 1950s, but funds for the program are still provided by the Bureau of Indian Affairs on a contract basis; in 1969 the amount was approximately $1 million.[9] The professional personnel (numbering about 200 full- and part-time) are hired by and under the administration of the Extension Service of the USDA and of the state colleges of agriculture. Since there are about 160 sizable Indian reservations, there is only 1 agent per reservation. While it is difficult to specify the number of agents needed on an average reservation (it obviously depends on the agricultural potential of the reservation), a study cited by Dorner indicates that 3 were needed for the rather small Nez Percé Reservation in Idaho.[10] If the needs of this reservation are an indication, 400 to 600 agents would be needed overall.

Third, the poor management ability of Indian farmers is often a result of their limited formal education. Rural adult Indians in 1960 averaged about 6.5 years of schooling, as compared with about 8.5 years for all males, and 14 percent of rural Indians in 1960 had no education at all, compared with 2 percent of the total rural population.[11] With the increasing complexity of agriculture, farmers

[8] Quoted from a paper by Assistant Commissioner John H. Province, BIA, presented at the National Conference of Social Work, San Francisco, Calif. (April 15, 1947), as cited in Dorner, "Economic Position of American Indians," p. 83.

[9] Interview with Will J. Pitner, chief, Branch of Land Operations, Bureau of Indian Affairs, October 1969.

[10] Bureau of Indian Affairs, "Development Plan, Nez Percé Reservation" (1958; processed).

[11] Helen W. Johnson, "Rural Indian Americans in Poverty," U.S. Department of Agriculture, Economic Research Service (1969; unpublished), p. 5.

with limited education are poorly equipped to understand modern agricultural techniques.

CAPITAL

Another factor limiting productivity growth is a lack of capital equipment. Because of their poverty, it is virtually impossible for most reservation Indians to buy the necessary machinery, fertilizer, or seed for efficient operation. The Bureau of Indian Affairs administers a revolving loan fund, which is available to tribal Indians or to those of one-fourth or more Indian blood, and to Indian organizations, but the total amount appropriated under this authorization between 1934 and 1961 was only $18 million. From 1934 through fiscal year 1952, 77.3 percent of all loans from this fund were for less than $1,000 and were largely for emergency subsistence.[12]

The inadequacy of the revolving fund has led Indian operators in recent years to obtain an increasing share of their financing from the U.S. Farmers Home Administration (FmHA). That agency can make loans for a variety of purposes, including farm operations and supplies, family living needs, purchases of land, or farm improvements and homes. Under a provision of the Economic Opportunity Act, the FmHA makes loans to poor farmers and other rural people for small enterprises that will help them raise their incomes. In 1966 the FmHA made 659 loans valued at $4.5 million to Indians. By December 31, 1966, outstanding loans to Indians numbered 1,855 and were valued at $11.1 million.[13]

RESOURCES

A third factor in the low productivity and income of Indian operators is the small size of holdings. On the Zuñi Reservation in New Mexico only five families out of several hundred have an economically viable operation.[14] The Navajos have traditionally supported themselves by raising sheep, but it takes 600 sheep to pro-

[12] Brophy and Aberle, *The Indian*, p. 109.

[13] Henry W. Hough, *Development of Indian Resources* (World Press, 1967), pp. 100–07.

[14] Interview with Quentin C. Sulgie, chief, land operations, Zuñi Reservation, June 20, 1968.

duce a net income of $3,000, and over half of the Navajo families have fewer than 50. On the San Carlos Reservation in Arizona a similar situation exists. The great majority of cattle owners have from 10 to 40 head. Only a few have more than 100 head, with the largest probably running to 200.[15] In 1968, of the 28,500 reservation Indian families engaged in agricultural enterprises, only 5,080 (less than one-fifth) had an operation large enough to be considered a "full-time operational enterprise."[16]

DIVIDED OWNERSHIP

Still another major factor working against the Indian farmer is the immensely complicated and difficult problem of "fractionated" or "fragmented" heirship land. The General Allotment Act of 1887 providing for the division of tribal land made it possible for a large number of persons to hold interests in a tract of land too small to be economically viable. This act and similar laws required the federal government to retain title until the Indian "owner" had assimilated the white man's desire for individual private ownership. The laws failed to anticipate the difficulty of dividing an Indian's land holdings after his death. The holdings are often scattered, and an heir must secure approval of all other owners of a tract in order to work it himself. Finally, the procedure for disposing of allotted lands in heirship status is determined on the basis of state laws, not tribal laws.[17]

At present, more than 6 million acres (about 11 percent of all Indian land) are in heirship status. About 25 percent of this land is used by non-Indians, 65 percent is used by Indians (half of these tracts are owned by five or more heirs), and 10 percent lies idle, largely because of the difficulty of making leases or subdividing the property among the owners.[18] It will be impossible to solve the problem of land use on many reservations until the heirship prob-

[15] Dorner, "Economic Position of American Indians," p. 30.

[16] Bureau of Indian Affairs, "Land Use Inventory, Calendar Year 1968."

[17] Brophy and Aberle, *The Indian*, p. 74. The amount of time that BIA clerical personnel must devote to keeping records on heirship land is enormous. Where heirship land is leased (which is possible only under certain circumstances), the BIA may, for example, divide $1,000 among seventy-five heirs, with some receiving a check for less than $1.

[18] *Ibid.*

lem is solved. A bill introduced in Congress in 1966 (which did not pass) offered a two-pronged attack on the difficulties. It specified that when the fractional share in a tract was below a specified figure or when the income from the property was less than a certain level, the land should be given to the closest relative of the original owner. The bill also provided for the establishment of a "fractional interests acquisition fund," to be used by the secretary of the interior to consolidate land by buying tracts or shares of tracts from owners who wished to sell.

If such a bill is again introduced, several modifications are needed to make an effective attack on the heirship problem. First, it would be more realistic to establish a fund to be used by the tribes for land consolidation purposes than to give sole authority to the secretary of the interior. The individual tribes know which tracts offer the most potential, and they could, with adequate safeguards, carry out a competent land consolidation program. On the basis of Dorner's 1959 figures, tribal purchase of all heirship lands in the 1970s would cost $75 million to $100 million. Moreover, such a bill would be at best only a holding action. It would prohibit the fractionation of land among more than a specified number of claimants, but many tracts with only slightly fewer claimants would remain divided into inefficiently small units. Unless the legislation provides for consolidating many of these uneconomic units, the heirship problem will continue.

Tribal Enterprises

Tribally owned lands have none of the heirship problems of allotted lands, and tribes enjoy superior financial resources and access to credit. Not suprisingly, most of the successful agricultural operations are carried out by the tribes or by producers' cooperatives.

Papago Indians on the Maricopa Reservation in southern Arizona have formed a corporation which operates an 8,000-acre cotton and ranching operation that yielded a profit of $240,000 in 1967. In order to increase efficiency, the tribal corporation in 1963 hired as manager a successful farmer with considerable experience from outside the tribe. The operation is increasing in size as the tribe takes back land as leases expire. In 1967 the corporation provided fifty Indians and five non-Indians with full-time employment. Some of the profits are used to develop a tribal housing program.[19]

The Hualapai tribe, located in northern Arizona, has only about 700 members, and the livestock industry provides its major income. Its herd has more than a thousand cows and produces a small annual profit. In 1963 the reservation became the first USDA "certified brucellosis-free area" in Arizona. Tribal ranchers generally employ modern production techniques such as supplemental feedings, effective pest control, and efficient breeding practices to yield high quality stock. In 1961 the Hualapai purchased a carload scale, enabling them to save $1 per head by weighing cattle at the time of sale. Between 1961 and 1966, 6,000 head of cattle were shipped to market. An important share of the credit for the success of the operation belongs to the BIA land operations branch, which invested more than $1 million for a variety of ranching improvements such as reseeding, new fencing, and construction of dams.[20]

On June 22, 1938, the San Carlos tribe in eastern Arizona established ten cattle associations (later reorganized into eleven).[21] A man who wanted to begin ranching applied to one of the associations. If he was approved for membership, he received a loan of twenty head of breeding stock from the association's herds. The loan had to be repaid in eight years with twenty-two head of cattle. Each owner was expected to help in the roundups preceding the yearly sales, send a substitute, or pay $5 to the association for each calf branded on his behalf. However, the fine was too low to provide sufficient incentive to work and there was frequently a shortage of qualified workers at roundup time.

In 1956 the tribal council reorganized the San Carlos cattle industry. The eleven associations were combined into five, resulting in more efficient and economically viable range units. A manager was hired to increase the effectiveness of the livestock operations by promoting the use of more productive ranching techniques. Under his supervision the cattlemen prepare for the annual cattle sales by, for example, dividing the sale stock into classes, and handle the sale activities themselves. Since the reorganization, owners

[19] Hough, *Indian Resources,* p. 79.
[20] *Ibid.,* p. 83.
[21] Harry T. Getty, "San Carlos Apache Cattle Industry," *Human Organization,* Vol. 20 (Winter 1961–62), p. 182.

are prohibited from working on the range with their own cattle. The association pays all the men required for the various range tasks, including roundup chores, and in consequence the efficiency of the operations has increased. Gradually the cattle owners and their associations are employing the principles of controlled breeding and earlier weaning of calves, leading to an increase in the calf crop. During 1960 the gross income derived by the five associations was $1.6 million.[22]

Need for Training

Two measures might promote greatly improved use of Indian agricultural resources. First would be the reintroduction of vocational agriculture in BIA schools and in public schools attended by Indians. Bureau land operations officers and tribal officials believe that vocational agriculture was instrumental in teaching basic agricultural skills and the rudimentary methods of farm management. One officer asserted: "One can just tell the difference between livestock and farming practices of those who went and did not go to vocational agriculture school. I think they made a big mistake to eliminate it."[23] While few believe that a high school course in vocational agriculture could produce a successful farmer, this high school experience followed by additional study at an agricultural college would probably develop a fairly successful commercial operator (if he were able to finance the endeavor).

A vocational agriculture program would require the redevelopment of bureau-owned farms formerly used for teaching purposes, a fairly expensive undertaking. Furthermore, on some reservations agriculture may not be a satisfactory economic alternative to other types of employment. It should be possible to determine by a questionnaire (perhaps distributed in the junior high schools) how many students would be interested in a high school program of vocational agriculture. On reservations where interest is high and agricultural development seems promising, the reintroduction should prove feasible.

[22] *Ibid.*, pp. 183–84.

[23] Interview with Albert L. Keller, land operations officer, Shiprock, N.Mex., June 25, 1968.

A second way to improve the skills of farmers and potential farmers would be to make agriculture and ranch management part of the curriculum of a managerial training center. Since the most successful Indian farm operations appear to be the large-scale tribal or cooperative ventures, the training center could provide courses in the management of large agricultural enterprises.[24] To provide practical experience, a farm would have to be established as part of the center. A large number of competent graduates from this program would eliminate the need for tribes to hire non-Indian managers for their enterprises.

Agricultural Development Projects

In response to a request from the Bureau of the Budget, the Bureau of Indian Affairs in 1967 made a benefit-cost study of various resource development programs,[25] including irrigation, open range, and dry farming lands. According to bureau specialists, there were nearly 400,000 acres of irrigation land, 100,000 acres of dry farming land, and 26 million acres of grazing land remaining to be developed under BIA programs. In determining the ratio of benefits to costs, the BIA generally assumed that the projects would last 100 years.[26] The direct or primary benefit of the irrigation and other projects was calculated as "the value of goods or services directly resulting from the project, less associated costs incurred in realization of the benefits and any induced costs not included in project costs," the guidelines set forth five years earlier by the President's Water Resources Council in response to President John F. Kennedy's request for a review of existing standards.[27]

With these guidelines, normal yields were estimated for princi-

[24] This program should not be limited solely to those employed by tribes or producers' cooperatives. Individual producers with holdings of at least minimal operational size should be permitted to enroll.

[25] See Bureau of Indian Affairs, "Indian Irrigation Projects" (July 1967; processed).

[26] *Ibid.*, pp. 2, 5, 20, 23.

[27] *Policies, Standards, and Procedures in the Formulation, Evaluation, and Review of Plans for Use and Development of Water and Related Land Resources*, S. Doc. 97, 87 Cong. 2 sess. (1962), p. 9.

TABLE 4-1

Benefit–Cost Ratios and Total Costs for Irrigation, Grazing,
and Dry Farming Projects Proposed for 1968 and
Later Years, Selected Reservations

Reservation	Irrigation		Grazing		Dry farming	
	Benefit–cost ratio	Total cost (millions of dollars)	Benefit–cost ratio	Total cost (millions of dollars)	Benefit–cost ratio	Total cost (millions of dollars)
Blackfeet	2.9	2.3	9.1	1.0	20.9	0.2
Colorado River	8.9	13.8	n.f.	n.f.	n.f.	n.f.
Crow	3.3	1.5	9.3	1.5	53.8	0.2
Duck Valley	1.7	5.7	2.4	1.0	n.f.	n.f.
Flathead	1.8	1.9	7.8	0.2	18.3	0.1
Fort Apache	1.9	2.5	5.7	2.9	n.f.	n.f.
Fort Belknap	3.1	0.3	5.9	0.8	n.f.	n.f.
Fort Hall	4.2	2.6	4.2	0.8	18.2	0.1
Fort Peck	4.0	0.5	10.3	0.5	43.9	0.3
Gila River	6.4	2.4	n.f.	n.f.	n.f.	n.f.
Navajo	3.0	186.9	3.0	56.8	n.f.	n.f.
Papago	2.5	1.3	9.1	1.0	n.f.	n.f.
Wind River	2.7	3.4	14.7	0.6	n.f.	n.f.
Yakima	6.7	0.5	3.4	1.0	n.f.	n.f.
Total		225.6		68.1		0.9

Source: Bureau of Indian Affairs, "Indian Irrigation Projects" (July 1967; processed), Tables F, 1, 4, 6.
n.f. Not feasible (usually because of soil or climatic conditions).

pal crops under the projected pattern of land use, and an average level of management competence was assumed in projecting land use and crop yields. Agricultural prices and costs were taken from a series developed by the Department of Agriculture.[28] The BIA added to the primary benefit a secondary one: wage income from employment directly created by the benefit.[29] The rate of discount used was 3.125 percent. While most economists consider this too low, it is the rate used by the Bureau of Reclamation and by the Army Corps of Engineers. The benefit–cost ratios and total costs of the three types of development projects are presented in Table

[28] Bureau of Indian Affairs, "Indian Irrigation Projects," p. 6.
[29] This procedure is followed by the Bureau of Reclamation; the inclusion of a secondary benefit is generally considered acceptable.

4-1. The total cost would be nearly $300 million if all of the projects were undertaken.

It is probable that the benefit–cost ratios calculated by the BIA are overoptimistic. First, the productivity of the land is assumed to be the same as that of any agricultural development, but (as shown earlier) Indian productivity on irrigated and grazing land is far below that of non-Indians.[30] Second, it is assumed that Indian operators would be as competent managers as non-Indians. On the basis of examples given earlier, this is doubtful.

A more fundamental objection is the assumption that the opportunities made available for agricultural development of reservations will be fully used.[31] There is some evidence, although it is not conclusive, that the interest of Indians in agricultural pursuits is waning. Under the Navajo-Hopi Rehabilitation Act of 1950, $3.3 million was spent on capital improvements for 40,000 acres of undeveloped and uninhabited land near the Colorado River. Funds were also provided to assist colonization by making farm loans of $3,500 to $6,000 per family for the purchase of machinery and equipment, for housing, and for other purposes, when the settlers received their land assignments.[32] During the period 1945–60, 244 loans with an aggregate value of $700,000 were advanced to colonists.[33] Of the 148 families who were resettled between 1945 and 1951, only 63 remained by 1960. The main reasons given for withdrawal were domestic and health problems; lack of aptitude for irrigation farming; failure to master the managerial requirements of successful farm operation; inadequately small farm assignments at the beginning of the program; and inability to adjust to the climate. In a congressionally sponsored survey of unemployment on Indian reservations made in 1963, one question concerned occupa-

[30] There have been no published studies of Indian as compared with non-Indian productivity on dry-farmed land, but it is assumed that the results would be similar to those for irrigated and grazing lands.

[31] Will Pitner, chief of land operations, Bureau of Indian Affairs, estimated that with complete development of Indian agricultural resources, 60,000 reservation families could be accommodated in full-time agricultural pursuits on economic-sized units.

[32] Robert W. Young (comp.), *The Navajo Yearbook* (Window Rock, Ariz.: Navajo Agency, 1961), pp. 205–07.

[33] Loans before the 1950 act became effective were made from tribal funds. By 1960, one-half of all loans had been repaid.

TABLE 4-2

Number of Indian Families Engaged in Agriculture,
by Profitability of Operation, 1965 and 1968

Profitability of operation	Number of families		Percentage change
	1965	1968	
Operational[a]	9,253	5,080	−45
Part-time operational[b]	12,641	12,843	+ 2
Nonoperational[c]	8,252	10,620	+29
Total	30,146	28,543	−5

Sources: Data for 1965 from Henry W. Hough, *Development of Indian Resources* (World Press, 1967), p. 77; data for 1968 from Bureau of Indian Affairs, "Land Use Inventory and Production Record, Calendar Year 1968," Report 50-1 (1969; processed).

a. Any unit regardless of size that (a) provides a fair margin of profit in sufficient quantity to support the operator and his family at an acceptable standard of living in view of present requirements and conditions, and (b) yields a total income that exceeds the nonfarm income of the operator and dependent members of his family.

b. Any unit regardless of size that (a) provides a fair margin of profit, and (b) yields a total income that does not exceed the nonfarm income of the operator and dependent members of his family.

c. Any unit regardless of size that does not provide a fair margin of profit.

tional preference. On the reservations where the survey was taken, only 5 to 10 percent of the population wished to become full-time independent farm operators.[34]

Furthermore, a more recent survey of Indian high school graduates indicates little interest in agriculture. Of the males who received no additional training, only 8 percent were employed in agriculture, compared with 17 percent of their fathers; of those graduates who received further training, only 4 percent were in agriculture, compared with 14 percent of their fathers. Agriculture was part of the curriculum of only 4 percent of graduates entering a federal vocational-technical school, 2 percent of those attending a four-year college, but 18 percent of those in junior colleges.[35]

Finally, the number of Indians engaged in agriculture on a full-time basis has declined sharply in recent years, as is indicated in Table 4-2.

While there might be more interest in agriculture if more technical assistance and greater capital and material resources were

[34] See *Indian Unemployment Survey*, Pt. 1, *Questionnaire Returns*, A Memorandum and Accompanying Information from the Chairman, House Committee on Interior and Insular Affairs, 88 Cong. 1 sess. (1963).

[35] Alphonse D. Selinger, "The American Indian Graduate: After High School, What?" (Northwest Regional Educational Laboratory, 1968; processed), pp. 14, 41, 23.

made available, it is also possible that the present Indian exodus would continue in spite of increased federal assistance. The data on occupational status in Chapter 1 (Table 1-11) indicate that Indians have been moving away from agricultural pursuits since the 1940s (as have non-Indians), presumably because of the higher income prospects elsewhere. There is no guarantee that even with expanded agricultural development the differential between farm and nonfarm earnings would decline enough to greatly reduce the exodus and to allow full and sustained use of the resources created by the projects proposed in Table 4-1.

Agricultural development, perhaps more than any other type, must be planned on a reservation-by-reservation basis. Projects should not be started unless there is clear evidence that enough Indian families are seriously interested in making a living in agriculture to produce an acceptable benefit–cost ratio. Little would be gained by the federal government's spending large sums of money on development only to discover that, for lack of interest in farming or ranching, Indians had leased the land to whites who did not need aid.[36] On reservations where there is enough interest, the projects that are most promising should be undertaken.

Farming is unprofitable for most individual Indians because of poor management, lack of capital, and the inefficiently small farm sizes. They often lease their land to whites because they cannot earn sufficient income from their own work. Tribal enterprises have proved more successful, since they are not subject to these disadvantages. Steps such as the reintroduction of vocational agriculture and resource development projects need to be studied carefully; but they will not be successful unless the Indian people are interested in becoming full-time, independent farmers.

[36] This could be applied also to additional agricultural assistance of other types. There would be little point, for example, in trebling the number of extension agents working with Indians if their services were not used.

CHAPTER V

Industrial Development

Industrial development of the Indian reservations is comparatively recent. Before 1960 there were only four factories on reservations. The record-breaking expansion in business activity during the sixties, plus the efforts of the Area Redevelopment Administration, the Bureau of Indian Affairs, and the Economic Development Administration, succeeded in attracting a steadily increasing number of small factories.

Table 5-1 shows the number of factories in operation on Indian reservations and the size of their labor force from 1957 to 1968. After 1963 there was an acceleration in reservation industrial development, which generally paralleled the rapid economic growth of the nation. Defense spending, bolstered by the needs of the Vietnam war, stimulated the establishment of approximately a dozen electronics plants making circuits and transistors partly for military purposes. Because some of these new plants were marginal enterprises, with inexperienced managers and little capital, one in five has gone out of business. The mean period during which the twenty-seven unsuccessful plants remained in operation was twenty months.[1] The BIA industrial development analysts tried to find out why each of the plants closed down. They concluded that 50 percent of them had inexperienced management, 20 percent were undercapitalized, and 30 percent were unable to find adequate markets for their product.[2]

[1] Estimated from data in sources for Table 5-1.

[2] Obviously these factors are often interrelated. A firm with effective management is likely to be more successful in obtaining financing and developing markets than one with ineffective management.

TABLE 5-1

*Summary of Plants Established on Indian Reservations,
and Labor Force, 1957–68*

Fiscal year	Number of plants			Labor force	
	Established	Closed down	Operating at end of year	Indian	Non-Indian
1957–59	4	1	3	391	171
1960	3	0	6	525	256
1961	4	0	10	702	505
1962	5	1	14	887	600
1963	6	2	18	1,395	1,719
1964	14	7	25	1,668	2,286
1965	21	6	40	2,011	2,479
1966	21	4	57	3,044	3,224
1967	23	3	77	3,730	3,666
1968	36	3	110	4,112	4,375
Total	137	27			

Sources: Data on plants established from U.S. Bureau of Indian Affairs, "Summary Record of Plants Established as Result of Indian Industrial Development Program" (August 1968; unpublished). Data on plant closings from Bureau of Indian Affairs, "Summary of Plant Closings" (July 1968; unpublished). Data on Indian and non-Indian labor force from unpublished graph provided by Gordon Evans, Division of Industrial and Tourism Development, Bureau of Indian Affairs, September 1968.

The average plant operating on an Indian reservation is fairly small. In 1968 the typical plant had seventy-five employees, of whom 48 percent were Indians.[3] During the 1957–62 period, a majority of the employees were Indians, but in the later period the proportion fell to somewhat less than half. In recent years many of the industrial plants have been located just inside the reservation boundary and draw their labor from Indians living on the reservation and non-Indians living off it.[4] Also, a few plants have found it necessary, for reasons of efficiency, to reduce the number of Indian

[3] The larger plants tend to employ a higher percentage of Indian employees. In 1967, the percentages of Indian workers were the following: in plants with 100 or more workers, 74.7; 50–99 workers, 50.2; 25–49 workers, 70.7 percent; 10–24 workers, 36.4 percent; 1–9 workers, 8.1 percent. See *Indian Resources Development Act of 1967*, Hearings before the Subcommittee on Indian Affairs of the House Committee on Interior and Insular Affairs, 90 Cong. 1 sess. (1967), p. 65.

[4] In Oklahoma, where there is only one Indian reservation, Indians and non-Indians often live side by side.

employees owing to their high rate of turnover and absenteeism. For example, on the Pine Ridge Reservation in South Dakota, a moccasin manufacturing plant cut back its percentage of Indian employees from 95 to 65 because of a 200 percent turnover in personnel during 1967–68. A garment factory on the Yakima Reservation in Washington State, 95 percent of whose employees were Indians, closed in December 1967 because of absenteeism. In April 1968 a new garment factory opened in the same quarters, but only 50 percent of its employees were Indians.[5]

Although there were eight times as many Indian employees in industrial plants in 1968 as in 1960, the total number was small. Of a reservation labor force of about 130,000, only 4,112, or about 3.2 percent, were employed in factories located on reservations or Indian land areas.

Barriers to Development

Although there has been progress on the reservations, several barriers have retarded industrialization in the past and continue to have a depressing effect on development.

TRANSPORT

The first obstacle confronting a businessman interested in locating on an Indian reservation is the totally inadequate transportation system. Since for many manufactured products transportation costs are a significant fraction of total costs, this factor is important.

The Bureau of Indian Affairs is maintaining and improving roads on 165 Indian reservations in twenty-three states, because county road service is not furnished. Generally, there is no local subdivision of state government that can furnish this service. There are only 1,400 miles of bituminous paved roads and 1,800 miles of gravel-surfaced roads on reservations. On most of the larger reservations, the miles of paved or graveled roads per 1,000

[5] Interviews with Thomas Allen, manager, Oglala Sioux Moccasin Company, July 16, 1968; Roger Coonrod, reservation programs officer, Yakima Indian Agency, July 1, 1968.

square miles are far below the level for rural roads in surrounding states, as shown in the following table:[6]

Reservation	Surrounding state	Miles of roads per 1,000 square miles	
		Reservation	Surrounding state
Navajo-Hopi	Arizona-New Mexico	37.3	152
Papago	Arizona	55.4	162
San Carlos	Arizona	37.2	162
Crow	Montana	96.4	230
Wind River	Wyoming	91.1	143

In fact, the condition of reservation roads is comparable to that found in underdeveloped regions of the world—in 1961, Africa had 20 miles of paved or graveled roads per 1,000 square miles, Latin America 20 miles, Asia 159 miles, and Oceania 77 miles.[7]

One reason for the inadequacy of the reservation roads is the relatively low level of expenditure for their maintenance and improvement. During the period 1946–49 the BIA spent about $90 a mile on maintenance for an average of 15,000 miles of road systems, while rural counties spent some $175 a mile. In 1964 the figures were $206 for reservations and $415 for all rural county road systems.[8]

There are no data on the number of miles of railroads on, or adjacent to, Indian reservations. However, the rail service is totally inadequate on the following major reservations, which contain more than half of the total reservation population: Navajo, Hopi, Papago, Zuñi, Pyramid Lake, Pine Ridge, Rosebud, Standing Rock, Cheyenne River, and the United Pueblos (with the exception of Laguna). On some reservations that do have railroad service, newly located firms have persuaded the railroad to build spurs at factory expense from the main line to the factory in order to facilitate shipment of merchandise.

The Bureau of Indian Affairs maintains air strips in seventy-five Indian and Eskimo communities, since most reservations are far from population centers. During the winter the airlines are the

[6] U.S. Bureau of Indian Affairs, Branch of Roads, "Indian Reservation Roads" (1967; processed), p. 1.

[7] Reported in *ibid.*, p. 2.

[8] *Ibid.*, pp. 5–6.

only transportation facilities available to many of the communities. The bureau admits that most of the air strips are inadequate "to serve the communities within aviation safety standards."[9]

LOCATION OF MARKETS

A reservation location is not advantageous for industries that can minimize transportation costs by locating at the market[10] or for service industries that must locate near the source of their demand. The poverty of Indians means that the effective demand for all goods is lower there. Moreover, the population on most reservations is so scattered and the road system so poor that concentration of sufficient demand in any given market to ensure profitable operation is impossible. Many reservations are located far from non-Indian settlements, especially in sparsely settled states. For example, South Dakota, which has the third largest population of reservation Indians among the states, had a total population of only 656,000 in 1968; the few population centers, such as Pierre or Rapid City, are 75 to 150 miles from the fringes of the principal Indian reservations. A similar situation prevails in Montana; of its seven reservations, only the Crow Reservation near Billings is close to a potential market. On the other hand, industry located at the Pueblos would have the advantage of being close to the expanding population centers of Albuquerque and Santa Fe.

Because of high transportation costs and lack of effective demand near the industrial site, production on the reservation is often confined to lightweight, high-value items, which can be produced profitably for either a regional or a national market.

QUALITY OF HUMAN RESOURCES

The reservation Indians and Alaskan natives are the most poorly educated minority groups in the United States. As indicated in

[9] *Ibid.*, p. 7. The BIA has requested funds to improve twenty-five air strips a year over a period of three years, with principal funding provided under the Federal Airport Act.

[10] For example, it takes one-fourth of a ton of syrup to make one ton of Coca-Cola. To minimize transport costs, one would locate a Coca-Cola plant at the market and not at the source of the raw material or somewhere in between the market and the raw material. For further discussion of this point, see Alfred Weber, *Theory of the Location of Industries* (University of Chicago Press, 1957).

Chapter 2, the median number of years of schooling for reservation Indian males in 1960 was 7.9. Although school attendance has increased greatly since the Second World War, only about 40 to 50 percent of Indian youths complete high school. Thus, industries requiring employees with at least a high school diploma would not find it feasible to choose a reservation location.

Also, the limited data available indicate a lack of both semi-skilled and skilled manpower on the reservations.[11] Out of 600 adults living on the Nez Percé Reservation in Idaho, only 47 could be so classified. A survey of the Standing Rock Reservation in North and South Dakota found that of 793 employed individuals 78 percent were in unskilled occupations and 22 percent in semi-skilled or skilled occupations.[12]

Since the Second World War there has been considerable migration from the reservations. Like the migration of Negroes from the South to the North, it has been selective: the better educated have tended to migrate and the less educated to remain.[13] The median amount of schooling of a representative sample of migrants leaving the reservation in 1963 was 10.6 years, or about one year more than that of nonmigrants of comparable age. Moreover, the median for those in the adult vocational training program (see page 128) was 12.0 years, about 2.5 years higher than the median for nonparticipants.[14] In view of this tendency, a rapid improvement

[11] Since the mid-fifties the Bureau of Indian Affairs has offered few vocational courses in reservation schools, as was reported in Chapter 2. Public schools with predominantly Indian enrollment offer few vocational courses, and lack of industrialization has prevented reservation Indians from taking advantage of industry training programs.

[12] Bureau of Indian Affairs, "Nez Percé Human Resources Survey" (May 1963; processed), Tables 3, 18 (this does not include those with arts and crafts skills such as beadwork, leatherwork, and basketry); Employment Security Bureau, "Manpower Resource Survey, Standing Rock Indian Reservation" (Bismarck, N.Dak.: 1967; processed), p. 11 (the survey was conducted by the community action program of the Office of Economic Opportunity).

[13] See C. Horace Hamilton, "The Negro Leaves the South," *Demography*, Vol. 1 (1964), and Rashi Fein, "Educational Patterns in Southern Migration," *Southern Economic Journal*, Supplement, Vol. 32 (July 1965), pp. 106–24 (Brookings Reprint 104).

[14] Estimated from data in Bureau of Indian Affairs, "A Followup Study of 1963 Recipients of the Services of the Employment Assistance Program" (1966; processed), pp. 16, 39; U.S. Bureau of the Census, *U.S. Census of Population: 1960, Subject Reports, Nonwhite Population by Race*, Final Report PC(2)-1C (1963), pp. 42–43.

in the quality of the reservation labor force is difficult to foresee.

LACK OF INFORMATION

Another barrier to the movement of industry to Indian reservations is a dearth of facts on which to base a decision. Data regarding the skills and abilities of the Indians are extremely limited: of 118 technical assistance or feasibility studies sponsored by the Bureau of Indian Affairs between 1962 and 1968, only two were concerned with the quality of human resources.[15] In most cases there is little published information on the cost and availability of power, quality of communications facilities, prevailing wage rates, or plant site availability. Because in the past the BIA has not made such material available (primarily because much of it had never been collected), Indian reservations have been at a disadvantage in competing for industry with various state industrial development commissions, which can more readily provide all the necessary facts.

In recent years the bureau has published brochures on a limited number of Indian reservations. The quality of information provided varies enormously. The brochure concerning the industrial potential of the Zuñi Reservation contains some material that is false and misleading, and other data, while accurate, are irrelevant. For example, it states that a high percentage of the labor force are high school graduates; in fact, the percentage is only 19.[16] It further states that there is quick access to rail service,[17] but in fact, the nearest railroad is at Gallup, New Mexico, forty miles away. The brochure contains information on the history, dress, and recreation of the Zuñi Indians, most of which is of little importance in choosing a plant site.

In contrast, the Pine Ridge Reservation brochure provides data on prevailing wage rates; level of unemployment; transportation facilities; cost and availability of electric power; cost of telephone

[15] Bureau of Indian Affairs, Branch of Credit and Financing, "List of Indian Related Technical Assistance Studies" (April 1968; processed).

[16] Bureau of Indian Affairs, *Zuni* (Zuni, N.Mex.: Zuñi Agency, n.d., 1968), p. 10; Bureau of the Census, *1960 Census, Nonwhite Population by Race*, p. 211.

[17] Bureau of Indian Affairs, *Zuni*, pp. 9, 19.

service; cost, availability, and chemical content of water sup~~~
and information on the health and education facilities of the c~~~
munity.[18]

In the spring of 1968 the bureau, in its effort to increase knowledge of the industrial potential of reservations, sponsored an industrial development conference in New York City, attended by
government officials, Indian leaders, and industrial executives. In-
dustrialists who had located on reservations discussed their experi-
ences and provided potential entrepreneurs with considerable information.

Aids to Development

While many factors have retarded reservation development, there
are some that favor a reservation location. Among the advantages
are the natural resources on the reservation and low labor costs.

LOW LABOR COSTS

Because of the high level of unemployment on the reservations,
prevailing wage rates for the few jobs available are low. Table 5-2
compares the prevailing wages on the Pine Ridge Reservation
with those in the U.S. north central region (a region neither the
highest nor the lowest in the nation).

One reason why many electronics firms have located on the reservations is that the starting wage is $1.60 an hour (the minimum
wage), while on the West Coast starting salaries range from $2.00
to $2.25 an hour.[19] Virtually all nonsupervisory employees in reser-
vation factories begin at the minimum wage. In fifteen plants
visited on reservations, the average wage ranged from $1.60 to $2.00

[18] Consumers Power District, Industrial Development Department, "Industrial
Facts, Pine Ridge, South Dakota" (Pine Ridge, S.Dak.: February 1968; processed).

[19] Philco-Ford Corporation, "Quarterly Report, Madera Employment Training
Center" (April 1968; processed), Chap. 3. Because most electronics firms located on
the reservations are engaged in the assembly of lightweight transistors and circuits,
transportation cost is not an important criterion in plant location. Thus, Fairchild
Semiconductor (a division of Fairchild Camera and Instrument Corporation), the
largest nongovernmental employer of Indians in the United States, located at Shiprock on the eastern portion of the Navajo Reservation, receives raw materials and
ships out its final product by air freight from Farmington, N.Mex., forty miles dis-
tant.

TABLE 5-2

*Wage Levels, Various Occupations, Pine Ridge Reservation
and U.S. North Central Region, 1966–67*

(*In dollars*)

Occupation	Pine Ridge Indian Reservation[a]	U.S. north central region[b]
Laborer (material handling)	1.60	2.34–3.00
Truck driver	1.60	2.52–3.37
Carpenter	2.80	2.99–3.74
Electrician	3.25	3.09–3.96
Painter	2.55	2.93–3.74
Bricklayer	3.30	3.55–3.95
Plumber	3.25	3.59
Crane operator	2.00	2.80–3.20
Cook (female)	1.60	n.a.
Secretary	200.00[c]	390.00–556.00[c]
Typist	175.00[c]	254.00–452.00[c]

Sources: Consumers Power District, Industrial Development Department, "Industrial Facts, Pine Ridge, South Dakota" (Pine Ridge, S.Dak.: February 1968; processed), p. 6; U.S. Bureau of Labor Statistics, *Wages and Related Benefits, 1966–67*, Bulletin 1530-87, Pt. 1 (1967), pp. 18–19, 34–35. Bricklayers' and crane operators' wages are author's estimates.
n.a. Not available.
a. Average wage. Rate is per hour unless otherwise indicated.
b. Wage range for metropolitan areas that reported to the Bureau of Labor Statistics—generally twenty to twenty-five areas (only one area reported plumber's wage rate). Rate is per hour unless otherwise indicated.
c. Per month.

an hour, although it was $2.60 for similar manufacturing industries off the reservation.[20] It is likely that the recent increases in the minimum wage have slowed down the reservation industrialization process, since the "equilibrium" wage of unskilled workers in a labor market with 30 to 60 percent unemployment is probably lower than $1.60 an hour. A lower wage than now prevails on the reservation would probably encourage the location of additional industries there.[21]

LIMITED FRINGE BENEFITS

Labor costs in reservation plants are lower than in comparable plants located off the reservation not only because of the hourly

[20] A 1968 unpublished survey by the Bureau of Indian Affairs of seventeen reservation plants in the Southwest found the average wage to be $2.25 an hour.
[21] This would certainly be true for industries in which labor costs are a large fraction of total costs and the elasticity of demand for the final product is high.

wage differential, but also because most reservation factories have fewer fringe benefits than plants elsewhere. For instance, none of the fifteen firms visited had medical insurance plans, and only one had a life insurance plan for its employees.[22] The amount of paid vacation ranged from three to seven days a year. Employees were required to work from six months to one year before paid vacations were given.

LITTLE UNIONIZATION

Only one of the fifteen plants visited was unionized, and none of the large reservation plants (100 or more workers) were unionized. Since increased unionization would work to eliminate wage differentials and differences in fringe benefits between reservation and non-reservation plants, a manager of one of the reservation plants expressed the opinion that "unionization would deter industrialization on the reservation."[23]

The next several years will probably bring an acceleration in union activity on Indian reservations, particularly if union leaders believe that plants off the reservation are relocating to gain an advantage by employing nonunion labor.[24] Moreover, the rising educational level of the reservation work force and the increasing sophistication of its members as industrial employees may lead to internal pressures for unionization.

Because reservation labor costs are relatively low, most of the industries that have located there are labor-intensive, highly competitive ones, manufacturing products such as furniture, garments, fishhooks and fishnets, wooden items, costume jewelry, baskets, Indian artifacts, and electrical components.

[22] In contrast, 89 percent of plant workers in manufacturing plants were covered under medical insurance plans, 99 percent under surgical plans, 98 percent by life insurance, and 76 percent by noncontributory pension plans. U.S. Bureau of Labor Statistics, *Wages and Related Benefits, 1966–67,* Bulletin 1530-87, Pt. 1 (1967), pp. 61–85.

[23] Interview, Shiprock, N.Mex., June 25, 1968.

[24] Some brochures stress the fact that existing reservation factories are not unionized. Since many of these plants receive subsidies for operating on-the-job training programs, the government appears to be in the unusual position of encouraging the growth of nonunionized plants.

ABUNDANT NATURAL RESOURCES

Several reservations have an abundance of natural resources, so that resource-oriented industries may find a reservation location advantageous. For example, many of the reservations in the Northwest have large timber supplies. If there are markets nearby, a reservation location may prove profitable for a furniture factory. White Swan Industries on the Yakima Reservation in Washington State obtains its raw material from tribal forests and sells its product to firms located in the upper northwest region. The logs are cut to specifications in a sawmill on the reservation.

The Navajo Reservation is thought to be a feasible location for a factory manufacturing construction materials. Raw materials for three products—concrete block, concrete products (pipe and beams), and ready-mix—are especially abundant in the Leupp, Arizona, and Gallup, New Mexico, areas. Between 1964 and 1967 there was an estimated $9 million market potential for the sale of these three products in the New Mexico counties adjacent to the reservation alone.[25]

One of the great oil and gas areas of the Far North is in northern Alaska. Commercial gas production was established near Point Barrow several years ago. The Tyonek band of the Tlingit and Haida tribes have received more than $10 million from oil leases and bonus bids. Exploitation of the oil and gas reserves will doubtless accelerate once the land claims filed by several bands of Alaskan natives are settled.[26] The settlement of these claims has become more urgent with the discovery of new oil fields in northern Alaska with a potential value of several hundred million dollars. In addition, the future value of all of Alaska's mineral resources is estimated to be many billions of dollars.[27] In early 1971, how-

[25] IIT Research Institute, "The Technical and Economic Feasibility of Manufacturing Selected Construction Materials on the Navajo Reservation" (Bureau of Indian Affairs, September 1964; processed), pp. 7–8.

[26] For further information on the magnitude of natural resources on Indian reservations, see Henry W. Hough, *Development of Indian Resources* (World Press, 1967), pp. 115–16. Because Alaskan natives have laid claim to most of the state, the federal government is reluctant to grant new oil leases or renew old ones.

[27] Arlon R. Tussing and Douglas N. Jones, "Economic Development and Alaskan Natives," in *Toward Economic Development for Native American Communities*, A

ever, there was no indication that the federal courts wo\
sider the native land claims in the near future.

Area Redevelopment Administration

During the comparatively short life of ARA (1961–65) various federal aids to chronically depressed areas, including Indian reservations, were provided.

After a community was classified by the agency as an area of chronic unemployment, local leaders submitted an overall economic development plan. If the plan was approved, the community became eligible for several aids to industrial development: long-term, low-interest (4 percent) loans covering up to 65 percent of total costs, to augment public and private investment in new industries or expanding existing ones (to encourage participation by private financial institutions, ARA could subordinate its loans to a loan from a bank); loans and grants for developing public facilities that were directly associated with new or expanded industry; financing of training programs that were operated and staffed by local vocational educators; financing of industrial feasibility studies and surveys of mineral and other natural resources.

Through fiscal 1964 the ARA made eight loans for Indian industrial development purposes; by 1965 two were in default. However, the principal ARA effort to promote development on reservations consisted of financing a large number of industrial feasibility studies by private management consulting firms, since a major obstacle to development was a lack of knowledge of reservation economic potential. Many of the studies were of limited value for these reasons:

1. They concentrated on the feasibility of locating a specific industry on a specific reservation, instead of on the broader industrialization possibilities on a reservation. The titles of two of these reports illustrate the point: "The Possibility for Charcoal Production on the Fort Apache Indian Reservation" in Arizona[28] and "A

Compendium of Papers Submitted to the Subcommittee on Economy in Government of the Joint Economic Committee, 91 Cong. 1 sess. (1969), Vol. 1, p. 325.

[28] Prepared by Hammon, Jensen, and Wallen (Oakland, Calif.: 1963; processed).

Study to Determine Feasibility of Establishing a Wool Processing Plant on or near the Navajo Reservation."[29] Nowhere in any of them is information presented on why the industry under study is more feasible than some other industry.

2. They often examined industries that would provide employment for only a very few Indians. For example, a major investigation for the BIA by a research team from the University of Alaska on establishing a sawmill at Minto, Alaska, concluded that the operation was feasible and nine part-time jobs would be created.[30] The study concerning charcoal production on the Fort Apache Reservation concluded that employment for twenty workers would be furnished.

3. The results were not publicized. Fewer than 100 copies of most of these reports were made. For some studies no copies were sent to Washington for coordination with the BIA industrial development program.

A permanent staff of economic analysts in a federal or regional agency could provide better technical studies of this sort. Not only are management consultants usually unfamiliar with the conditions on reservations, but the quality of the reports varies enormously from firm to firm. Research on Indian problems, especially in the area of economic development, is too important to be left to those with only a transitory interest in the subject.

The Area Redevelopment Administration did not devote a large amount of its resources to reservation development. Through fiscal 1964 the agency spent only $4.8 million on Indian reservations. Of this amount, $2.8 million was lent to businessmen for industrial development, $1.0 million was spent for thirty technical assistance projects, and $1.0 million was allocated for some forty-six training projects that enrolled 1,581 previously unemployed persons.[31]

[29] Ernst and Ernst (1964; processed).

[30] Frank W. Kearns, "Report of the Technical and Economic Feasibility of Establishing a Sawmill Operation at the Native Village of Minto, Alaska," Phase 1 of *Resource Analysis of Minto Flats Area, Alaska* (University of Alaska, Institute of Business, Economic and Government Research, 1965; processed).

[31] U.S. Department of Commerce, *More Jobs Where Most Needed, Annual Report of the Area Redevelopment Administration, Fiscal Year Ended June 30, 1964*, p. 29.

Economic Development Administration

The Economic Development Administration was created in 1965 as a successor to ARA. The agency recognized that one of the main barriers to industrial development is a lack of social overhead capital. This is as true of Indian reservations as it is elsewhere. A trip through the major reservations indicates the lack of sewer, water, and communications facilities. This is most evident in the desert Southwest—for example, on the Navajo, Hopi, Papago, San Carlos, and Fort Apache Indian Reservations.[32] Thus, an important feature of the EDA program is grants of up to 50 percent of the costs for water, sewerage, and community building projects. Supplementary grants of up to 80 percent of project costs are permitted for distressed communities that have difficulty raising local matching funds. Public works loans for up to forty years are also available from EDA, with an interest rate in 1966 of 3¾ percent.[33]

Like ARA, EDA makes loans of up to 65 percent of the cost of land, buildings, machinery, and equipment. The borrower has up to twenty-five years to repay; in 1966 the interest rate was 4¼ percent. In addition to direct loans, EDA's business assistance program provides working capital guarantees of up to 90 percent. These are guarantees on the unpaid balance of private working capital loans made in connection with projects receiving direct EDA loans. The Economic Development Administration provides, in addition, the same type of technical assistance as was given under ARA. From 1966 to 1968 EDA spent $36 million to assist industrial development on Indian reservations, with over half allocated to public works grants (Appendix Table A-11).

Many of these grants are being used to create industrial parks. One such grant of $350,000 was made to the Blackfeet tribe in Montana and another of $150,000 went to the Yakima Indians in Washington State.

[32] For further information, see *Federal Facilities for Indians: Tribal Relations with the Federal Government*, Report by Mamie L. Mizen, Staff Member, Senate Committee on Appropriations (1966).

[33] U.S. Department of Commerce, Economic Development Administration and Office of Regional Economic Development, *First Annual Report, Fiscal Year 1966*, p. 11.

Other Aspects

Indian tribes offer several kinds of assistance to potential manufacturers. Tribal land is provided for industrial sites, and in many cases plants are built to employer specifications by the tribe at no cost to the firms. In such cases, the building and grounds are leased to the company by the tribe, since Indian trust property cannot be sold to a non-Indian. Many tribes have provided capital by investing in the firm, and some factories are exclusively tribal enterprises, such as a sawmill on the Navajo Reservation, or an arts and crafts cooperative on the Zuñi Reservation.

The Bureau of Indian Affairs recognizes that one of the principal reasons why businessmen are reluctant to locate plants on the reservations is that the potential labor force lacks the requisite education, training, and industrial discipline. To minimize this obstacle, the bureau operates an on-the-job training program, which is described in Chapter 6. Employers are reimbursed one-half the minimum wage for each employee in training. This inducement is important because most employers interviewed indicated that the productivity of Indian employees is below the break-even point during the first months of training; without the rebate the entire operation would be jeopardized. The trainees are recruited and screened by local BIA employment assistance officers in cooperation with the local office of the state employment service, thus minimizing firm recruiting costs.

Because most reservation Indians are not familiar with the discipline of industrial employment, there is a rapid turnover in personnel for six months to one year after an operation begins. Most firms reported turnover of 200 to 400 percent during the first year. Rapid turnover and absenteeism play havoc with assembly line production. Some companies reported that workers were often trained to do several tasks in order to avoid bottlenecks in the production process. This initial period of turnover and absenteeism is hardest on small firms, which may not have the necessary financial resources to withstand a period of heavy losses from lagging production. As was pointed out above, some firms in this situation have increased the proportion of non-Indian labor in order to reduce turnover and absenteeism.

Firms that survive this period generally report that after the first year of operation the labor force tends to stabilize. For example, the Fairchild plant on the Navajo Reservation reported that turnover averaged about 6 percent annually. A similar rate was reported for Rosebud Electronics on the Rosebud Reservation.[34]

Anthropologists argue that Indians generally have an orientation to the present and not to the future.[35] This cultural predisposition has created problems for industrial plants on reservations that have a seasonal upsurge in other economic activity. For instance, White Swan Industries on the Yakima Reservation pays untrained workers $1.60 an hour. They are paid once every two weeks. Agricultural laborers receive $1.75 an hour and are paid each day. During harvest time, which lasts about six weeks, some employees leave the furniture plant and obtain employment as agricultural laborers. After the harvest season they are not rehired by the plant and face the prospect of long-term unemployment. Similarly, an electronics plant on the Papago Reservation found that during the firefighting season, which lasts about two months, electronics trainees quit to fight fires. A firefighter earns $2.50 an hour (compared with $1.60 an hour as an electronics trainee), but only some $600 a year. Needless to say, this behavior is very frustrating to employers who are trying to build up a permanent labor force.

A major national effort is being made to promote qualified members of minority groups into managerial and supervisory positions, but employers on Indian reservations indicate that Indians are reluctant to accept promotion.[36] Several firms cited instances of

[34] Interviews with George Higgins, Fairchild Semiconductor Plant, Shiprock, N.Mex., June 25, 1968; Wilson Emory, Rosebud Electronics, Rosebud, S.Dak., July 17, 1968.

[35] See, for example, John F. Bryde, *The Sioux Indian Student: A Study of Scholastic Failure and Personality Conflict* (n.p., 1966); "The Mental Health of the American Indian," *American Journal of Psychiatry*, Supplement, Vol. 125 (August 1968); Clyde Kluckhohn and Dorothea Leighton, *The Navajo* (Harvard University Press, 1946); and Ralph Linton, *Acculturation in Seven American Indian Tribes* (Appleton-Century, 1940).

[36] Even BIA literature promoting the industrial development of the reservations, which often glosses over the problems an employer may face if he locates on a reservation, admits that one of the disadvantages of employing Indian workers is their

employees leaving when given supervisory or additional responsibility. This appears at least in part to be due to the cultural values of certain tribes. Many Indians tend to be noncompetitive in an industrial or school situation.[37] Since a promotion would make an employee superior in status to those he regards as his peers, and in some cases would subject him to ridicule, he is understandably reluctant to accept the position.

Not all tribes are interested in industrial development. For example, the Papago tribe in Arizona refused to lease land for the expansion of an electronics plant, claiming none was available, although it has tens of thousands of acres of desert wasteland that certainly could have been used. The tribe had accepted the firm reluctantly at the urging of the Bureau of Indian Affairs, and by refusing land for expansion so discouraged the plant that it relocated in Tucson.[38]

Some tribes desire industrialization but do not wish to invest tribal resources or develop tribal enterprises. Robert Jim, chairman of the Yakima Tribal Council, said: "Some of us are smart enough not to do all this."[39] He was expressing the reluctance of some tribes to engage in business or commercial activity because of their fear that Bureau of Indian Affairs services would be terminated.[40]

---

reluctance to accept promotion even though they may be fully qualified. For further information, see Bureau of Indian Affairs, "Some Facts About Indian Workers" (n.d.; processed).

[37] For example, Sioux Indian children will not raise their hands or participate in class unless called on by the teacher. See Murray L. Wax, Rosalie H. Wax, and Robert V. Dumont, Jr., *Formal Education in an American Indian Community*, Supplement to *Social Problems*, Vol. 11 (Spring 1964).

[38] Interview with John Artichoker, superintendent, Papago Indian Agency, Sells, Ariz., June 29, 1968.

[39] Interview at Toppenish, Wash., July 2, 1968.

[40] This fear is not without foundation. In 1953 the House of Representatives passed a resolution favoring the termination of government services at the earliest possible time. After two major tribes, the Klamath of Oregon and the Menominee of Wisconsin, who had been pressured to request that their relations with the federal government be terminated, were unfavorably affected, services to other tribes were not terminated. However, the resolution has never been rescinded. The situation is discussed at length in Chap. 7.

Some Policy Proposals and Implications

A bill to increase the self-sufficiency and economic development of the Indian tribes was submitted to Congress in 1967 as the Indian Resources Development Act. Although it was not enacted, some of its provisions and the objections offered by Indian leaders are worth examining. The main provisions were:

1. The authorization of $500 million of new appropriations—but no more than $100 million for the first five years—for a loan guarantee and insurance fund. The secretary of the interior was authorized to insure loans for losses up to 15 percent of the aggregate of loans, but not more than 90 percent of the loss on any one loan.[41] No loan over $60,000 could be insured unless it had been approved by the secretary.

2. Authority for the issuance of federal charters to Indian tribes and groups to form corporations for business or quasi-municipal enterprises.

3. Authority for Indian corporations to issue tax-exempt bonds for municipal purposes such as improving recreational or civic facilities, transportation, and utilities.

4. Authority for tribes to invest, mortgage, sell, or otherwise hypothecate trust property if authorized by the tribe's constitution or by a referendum, the investment of the proceeds to be approved by the secretary of the interior.

Passage of this bill would have expanded the supply of funds for industrial and other kinds of economic development. How much demand there would have been by tribes or individuals to borrow from the fund is not clear. Indian tribes have about $300 million in trust funds, which could be used for industrial and economic development projects,[42] also with the approval of the secretary of the interior. Presumably, if Indian leaders wished to, they could use their trust funds for industrial development, but in 1966 only $12 million of tribal money was so invested. However, some tribes with very small incomes or trust funds do not have enough capital

[41] *Indian Resources Development Act of 1967*, Hearings, pp. 22, 27.
[42] The sources, growth, and use of trust funds are discussed in Chap. 7.

resources to promote economic development and have been forced to rely on the inadequate revolving loan fund of the BIA (see Chapter 4). Some of these tribes undoubtedly would have borrowed extensively under the proposed new loan fund.

One barrier to the industrial development of the reservations, as mentioned earlier, is a lack of social overhead capital. It is not clear whether the bill would have permitted loans for such purposes, since those loans are usually not self-liquidating. (Most of the social overhead capital projects approved under EDA have been financed by grants.) Without massive increases in social overhead capital, most reservations will not be able to attract industry, nor will tribal leaders be likely to show much interest in financing their own industry through a loan fund or other means.

Indian leaders expressed opposition to several provisions of the bill. Although one of the principal goals of the legislation was to increase the self-sufficiency of reservation Indians, the secretary of the interior would have retained authority to approve or disapprove loans over $60,000 as well as the investment of the proceeds of trust property disposed of. Second, the bill would have allowed tribal land to be mortgaged to obtain project financing; some Indian leaders fear that mortgaging their land would open the way to a further loss of land to whites. Finally, many Indians, especially in the Northwest, believed that the bill was a prelude to termination of federal responsibility toward the Indians.

The first two criticisms are generally unfounded. While the statutory authority to approve loans of more than $60,000 and the use of proceeds from trust property would have rested with the secretary of the interior, it is unlikely that this power would have been used restrictively. As Chapter 7 indicates, the secretary has been quite flexible toward the investment and disposal of Indian trust funds and tribal income totaling several hundred million dollars. Moreover, since some Indian leaders are unsophisticated in financial enterprises, safeguards appear in order.

Similarly, it would appear that the advantages of being able to mortgage Indian lands would have outweighed the disadvantages. Not only would the ability of the tribes to borrow funds have been enhanced, but some tribes whose sole asset is land would have been able to participate in the lendable funds market. Approval of all projects by the secretary of the interior would have assured the adoption of sound projects in order to minimize the risk of foreclosure and resulting loss of lands.

While these objections appear unfounded, it may be true, as some opponents charged, that the bill would have been a prelude to termination. At the House hearings Secretary of the Interior Stewart L. Udall commented: "I think this type of legislation, which would encourage initiative, would encourage decisionmaking, would develop the capacity of Indian groups and leaders to make decisions, and would move us down the road toward the right kind of ultimate independence is what the Indian people want." When asked if by "ultimate independence" he meant doing away with the reservations, he answered, "I think this is undoubtedly the ultimate end result; yes."[43]

The fear of termination of federal responsibility for Indians (discussed in Chapter 7) is a powerful barrier to industrial development. Indian tribes are quite reluctant to finance by borrowing or otherwise initiate industrial or economic development projects if this would lead to termination. The Indian people generally do not think they are ready for termination and will do nothing to hasten its coming. Thus, the secretary's remarks tended both to reduce the chances that Indian tribes would wish to borrow if funds were available and to weaken further the Indians' desire for industrial development. Several leaders of major tribes in the Northwest and the northern plains stated in interviews that they planned to use tribal income for land acquisition and not for industrial development. Although this results partly from an emotional desire to expand the size of the reservation by reclaiming ancient Indian lands, it would also be a "safe" investment: unlike industrial development, land acquisition per se does not increase self-sufficiency and hasten termination. Of course, idle land, unlike industry, generates no income or employment, nor does it promote the improvement of human resources.

A firm statement by the federal government indicating that forced termination is not federal policy would eliminate uncertainty and generate in some tribal leaders more enthusiasm about economic development.

[43] *Indian Resources Development Act of 1967*, Hearings, p. 48.

The primary objective of the Indian Resources Development Act was to increase the self-sufficiency of the tribes through development of their own enterprises. A different approach was proposed by Herbert Striner, director of program development for the W. E. Upjohn Institute for Employment Research, in a paper prepared for the Joint Economic Committee.[44] Striner would use subsidies to induce more non-Indians to locate plants on the reservations. He would offer a tax credit to companies establishing new plants on or near reservations and employing a minimum of 10 Indians or 10 percent of a labor force of more than 100. The tax credit would be limited to ten years and would be on a sliding scale based on the expected difficulty of attracting industry. Some reservations would be ineligible for credit; others would be eligible for a credit of $300, $800, or a maximum of $1,200 per twelve man-months of Indian employment. Striner further proposed a rapid depreciation schedule in order to attract capital-intensive industry with relatively high skill requirements, so that Indians might have the opportunity to develop better paying skills, rather than labor-intensive industry with low skill requirements.

While the subsidy advocated by Striner doubtless would increase the number of firms locating on reservations, it is not clear that this would be the most efficient way to do so. Presumably the subsidy would be granted to offset the higher production and distribution costs resulting from the lack of social overhead capital and nearby markets.[45] In the long run it might be more economical for the federal government to undertake the necessary expenditures for social overhead capital so that the additional subsidies advocated by Striner would not be necessary. Most economists believe that subsidies, like tariffs, are most defensible when granted to "infant" industries. The subsidy provided under the bureau's on-the-job training program meets this criterion: that is, when

---

[44] Herbert E. Striner, "Toward a Fundamental Program for the Training, Employment and Economic Equality of the American Indian," in *Federal Programs for the Development of Human Resources,* A Compendium of Papers Submitted to the Subcommittee on Economic Progress of the Joint Economic Committee, 90 Cong. 2 sess. (1968), Vol. 1, pp. 309–11.

[45] The BIA on-the-job training program already provides a subsidy to workers in training.

training is completed, the subsidy ends. However, the subsidy proposed by Striner would last for ten years.

Even if increased subsidies were an efficient way of raising the level of industrialization of the reservations, further problems would arise. Could such a program justifiably be limited to Indians? Other minorities are conceivably entitled to such aid[46] and, in the interest of equity, subsidization of industry would have to be extended to virtually all depressed areas.[47]

Moreover, a heavy subsidy for plants locating on reservations might encourage the relocation of plants from other sections of the country. Striner minimizes this possibility by pointing out that non-Indian labor is mobile and would adjust to plant displacement. However, the immobility of labor is one of the problems of the chronically depressed areas of Appalachia and some sections of New England.

While Striner's sliding subsidy would in theory equalize industrialization opportunities among reservations (thus penalizing the reservations that would not need this aid to attract industry), in practice the plan is not feasible. Not only are there not enough data to make a rational decision about the potential ease of attracting industry (nor are there likely to be in the near future), but the various tribes through their respective congressmen would probably put great pressure on the federal government to get the maximum subsidy for plants that would locate on their reservations.

Finally, the proposal to encourage capital-intensive industry through rapid depreciation schedules seems inappropriate. The

[46] In fact, several legislators have discussed the possibilities of subsidizing industry to locate in urban ghettos. Former Secretary of Defense Clark Clifford in September 1968 proposed locating defense plants in ghettos in order to relieve the unemployment problem. There is no compelling reason why some of these plants could not also be located on Indian reservations. Not only would this ensure that the plants would be dispersed, but the recognized hand and finger dexterity of Indians would be an asset in the manufacture of delicate machinery or instruments. As of 1968, only one defense plant was located on an Indian reservation, the Turtle Mountain Reservation in North Dakota.

[47] The BIA on-the-job training program should not be regarded as providing special treatment for Indians in the same sense as would the Striner recommendations. Many federal manpower programs, whose participants are generally non-Indian, are similar to the Indian on-the-job training program (for example, under the Manpower Development and Training Act). However, there are no federal programs offering permanent subsidies for industry to locate in a particular area.

most serious economic problem on the reservations is unemployment. Labor-intensive industries put more people to work per dollar invested than capital-intensive ones. While the latter pay
higher wages, it would seem that maximum employment should
be the primary objective.

Two measures, which were not incorporated in either the Resources Development Act or the Striner proposals, would assist Indian industrial development. First, to encourage Indian leaders to
plan their own economic development projects, they should be
helped to get the training necessary to make effective decisions on
project formulation and management. Because most Indian leaders are elderly and have a limited formal education, they are currently forced to seek advice from non-Indians on the financing and
operation of major enterprises. Residential training centers, located on or near the reservations, could provide today's leaders
with the expertise to operate tomorrow's reservation development
projects.

Second, to deal effectively with the lack of social overhead capital, large federal expenditures should be made. They would not
only be a direct aid to subsequent industrial development, but
would create new jobs, thus raising reservation incomes, and would
provide job skills that could be an inducement for employers to
locate factories on the reservations. A recent investigation found
that many Indians looked quite favorably on the WPA (Works
Progress Administration) program of the 1930s, because it put large
numbers of Indians to work building roads and irrigation systems.[48]
Federal expenditures on social overhead capital would be most
effective if they were integrated into an overall reservation development plan in which the technical and economic feasibility of selected industries was considered as well as the infrastructure required to support them.

A lack of funding and personnel has caused the Bureau of Indian Affairs to neglect the industrial development program. The
Branch of Industrial Development has only twenty-seven professional employees and a total budget of $800,000. Because most of

[48] Human Sciences Research, Inc., "A Comprehensive Evaluation of OEO Community Action Programs on Six Selected American Indian Reservations" (McLean,
Va.: HSR, September 1966; processed), p. 202.

the personnel are in Washington, the reservations have few employees whose primary responsibility is to attract industry. The Washington staff is too small to tabulate and analyze the kinds of information that prospective employers would need before deciding whether to locate on a reservation. Nor is it possible to publicize the program adequately or to follow up initial contacts. More funds and staff are needed for an effective development program.

CHAPTER VI

Manpower Development

To improve economic conditions on the reservations and to reduce unemployment, the Bureau of Indian Affairs during the 1950s developed a variety of employment assistance programs for persons who are members of a recognized tribe, band, or group of Indians, and of at least one-fourth Indian blood. One program is the direct relocation of unemployed or underemployed Indians and their families to major urban centers, where employment is found for the breadwinners. Another provides advanced vocational training in an off-reservation institution, with job placement in the city where training is obtained. There is also an on-the-job training program for Indians who wish to stay on the reservation. This chapter describes these three programs and attempts to evaluate them. Still another program, undertaken in the late 1960s, combines vocational education with basic education for those who cannot qualify for advanced training; contracts with three corporations to operate such training were in effect in 1968. Since the program is too recent for appraisal of results, it is described in Appendix B.

The first mass migration of Indians from the reservations took place during the Second World War. Some 23,000 men served in the armed forces; this was 32 percent of all able-bodied male Indians between eighteen and fifty years of age. (Some 800 women also served.) An undetermined number did not return to the reservations after the war, but remained in urban centers.

In addition, 46,000 Indians left the reservations in 1943 to obtain wartime employment. About half of them went into industry, where manpower shortages were severe, and the other half into agricultural occupations. Another 44,000 left in 1944.[1] After the war most of those in defense-related industries were laid off, and a large proportion returned to the reservations. In 1948 the Bureau of Indian Affairs established a program of job placement services for Navajos, many of whom were engaged in seasonal farm and railroad track work.[2] The BIA worked closely with the Arizona and New Mexico State Employment Services and the Railroad Retirement Board in expanding employment opportunities for Navajos in Arizona, New Mexico, and the cities of Los Angeles, Denver, and Salt Lake City, where sizable groups of Indians were living.

Direct Relocation

In the fall of 1950 the bureau launched a full-scale relocation program for Indians who desired permanent employment away from the reservations. Field or placement offices were established in several cities and are still operating in Chicago, Cleveland, Dallas, Denver, Los Angeles, Oakland, San Francisco, and San Jose (California). In 1968 two smaller centers were opened in Oklahoma at Tulsa and Oklahoma City.

The first applicants were placed in February 1952, and by mid-1967 the program had relocated more than 60,000 persons, including dependents. The program grew rapidly from 1952 to 1957, but thereafter the annual number relocated fluctuated and has not exceeded the number placed in 1957, principally because an increasing number of Indians are engaged in other manpower programs (see Table 6-1).

To participate in the direct relocation program, an Indian files an application with an employment assistance officer on or near the reservation. The officer ascertains the Indian's work preferences, then refers him to the state employment service for aptitude testing (usually the General Aptitude Test battery). The employ-

[1] *International Labour Review*, Vol. 51 (June 1945), pp. 781–82. Also it was estimated in 1944 that 14,059 Indians could have been recruited and placed in off-reservation employment if more intensive recruitment and placement services had been instituted and if transportation had been made more readily available.

[2] U.S. Bureau of Indian Affairs, "The Bureau of Indian Affairs Voluntary Employment Assistance Services Program" (n.d.; processed), p. 2.

TABLE 6-1

Number of Participants and Costs, Bureau of Indian Affairs
Manpower Programs, Selected Years, 1952-67

Fiscal year	Direct relocation		On-the-job training		Adult vocational training	
	Partic- ipants[a]	Cost (dollars)	Partic- ipants	Cost (dollars)	Partic- ipants[a]	Cost (dollars)
1952	868	567,480	—	—	—	—
1954	2,553	577,763	—	—	—	—
1956	5,119	991,617	—	—	—	—
1958	5,728	3,163,671	207	31,495	873	515,515
1960	3,674	2,732,663	276	73,759	1,809	2,999,592
1962	3,494	3,100,000	736	187,400	2,500	3,312,600
1964	4,097	2,747,000	552	292,517	3,054	6,380,483
1966	3,747	3,007,000	1,302	520,075	5,502	10,868,925
1967	5,599	3,912,000	1,344	820,277	5,545	12,515,723
Total[b]	61,641		6,223		31,556	

Sources: Program participants from U.S. Bureau of Indian Affairs, Branch of Employment Assistance, "Statistical Summary of Activities from Inception of Individual Program through June 30, 1967" and "Annual Statistical Summary, 1969" (unpublished tabulations); data on costs from unpublished tabulation provided by Branch of Employment Assistance.

a. Includes dependents.

b. For all years from beginning of program through fiscal year 1967.

ment officer discusses the results of the examination with the applicant and counsels him on the conditions he will encounter after relocation.

Because the Indians who apply for direct relocation are usually unable to defray the cost of relocating, the Bureau of Indian Affairs has established various kinds of assistance to ease the financial burden of moving for the Indian and his family:[3] a medical examination for the whole family (if serious illness is discovered, relocation is delayed until the health problems are eliminated); transportation for the family to the place of employment, and additional travel expenses; low-cost temporary housing, clothing if necessary, additional counseling, and advice in job seeking; health insurance (generally necessary only until the applicant obtains his first job); assistance in moving into permanent housing; household furniture and basic housewares to meet minimum requirements for urban living (tables, chairs, sofas, refrigerators, washing

[3] Bureau of Indian Affairs, "Policies and Programs of the Bureau of Indian Affairs" (n.d.; unpublished).

machines, linens, dishes, and eating utensils); and assistance for emergencies such as death in the family or illness that results in unemployment.

The field office staff follows up the applicant for one year after placement, providing counseling and additional job placement services if he leaves his first position. Eligibility for grants is limited to three years after the initial relocation.

This program is altogether voluntary. According to Indian leaders as well as BIA personnel, the bureau does not pressure Indians in any way to apply for relocation.

On-the-Job Training

Many Indians prefer to remain on the reservation, regardless of the economic consequences. The Indian Vocational Training Act of 1956 authorizes the secretary of the interior to contract with private industry to provide subsidized on-the-job training (OJT) for reservation Indians eighteen to thirty-five years of age:

> . . . in order to help adult Indians who reside on or near Indian reservations to obtain reasonable and satisfactory employment, the Secretary of the Interior is authorized to undertake a program of . . . apprenticeship, and on the job training, for periods that do not exceed twenty-four months. . . . For the purposes of this program the Secretary is authorized to enter into contracts or agreements with any . . . corporation or association which has an existing apprenticeship or on-the-job training program which is recognized by industry and labor as leading to skilled employment.[4]

Each BIA area office currently employs an industrial development specialist, whose job is to contact employers who might qualify to participate in the program. The commissioner of Indian Affairs, or anyone to whom he delegates the authority, is responsible for negotiating the contract and ensuring compliance with it. The amount of the wage rate to be paid by BIA and the length of the training period for each skill are negotiable. The subsidized portion of the wage rate must not exceed one-half of the established minimum wage under the prevailing standards of the Fair Labor Standards Act. For example, with a legal minimum wage of $1.60

[4] 70 Stat. 986.

an hour, the BIA may pay $0.80 if the trainee's beginning wage rate is $2.50 an hour. If the trainee begins at $1.50, the BIA could pay $0.75. If the trainee were to work fifty-four hours a week, the BIA could subsidize only forty of those hours.[5]

After contract details are settled, prospective trainees are screened, evaluated, and referred to the participating firm by the area employment assistance officer. The final selection of Indians to be trained is made by the participating employer, and he is not required to hire every person referred to him by the BIA.

In addition to reimbursing the firm for a portion of the trainee's wages, the Bureau of Indian Affairs pays for the Indian's transportation to the training facility and his subsistence en route. The training period ranges from three months to two years, depending on the occupation.[6] The employer providing the training agrees to retain the Indians as permanent employees if they complete the program satisfactorily.

A BIA study indicates that about 97 percent of on-the-job training has been conducted within the reservation area.[7] Although the number of participants in the program grew rapidly from 1964 through 1967 (see Table 6-1), the total number is small compared with the total reservation labor force of 130,000, and the proportion of women trainees is quite high. The small total is generally not due to any weakness in the program, but to the difficulty of inducing businessmen to locate plants on the reservation, as discussed in Chapter 5. In recent years Congress has allocated about twice as much money for on-the-job training as has actually been disbursed.[8]

[5] Loren C. Scott and David W. Stevens, "An Economic Evaluation of On-the-Job Training Conducted Under the Auspices of the Bureau of Indian Affairs: Concepts and Preliminary Findings," in *Toward Economic Development for Native American Communities*, A Compendium of Papers Submitted to the Subcommittee on Economy in Government of the Joint Economic Committee, Vol. 1, 91 Cong. 1 sess. (1969), p. 180.

[6] The length of training for the various positions is determined by the U.S. Department of Labor.

[7] Bureau of Indian Affairs, "A Followup Study of 1963 Recipients of the Services of the Employment Assistance Program" (October 1966; processed), p. 23.

[8] Based on unpublished data provided by the BIA Branch of Employment Assistance. Other reasons for the discrepancy between allocation and disbursal, aside from lack of business interest, are the cancellation of contracts due to bankruptcy of the firm or failure to operate a suitable training program.

Adult Vocational Training

Partly because so few Indians were employed in positions above the unskilled category, the Indian Vocational Training Act of 1956 provides for a wide variety of courses for reservation Indians. By 1966, vocational training courses in 125 occupations had been approved at accredited schools in twenty-six states. These schools are located both in urban centers and near reservations. However, most graduates eventually move to urban areas, regardless of where they have taken their training. The lack of economic opportunity on the reservation makes it likely that, even if the trainees were able to find jobs, they would not be commensurate with their levels of skill.

Applicants for adult vocational training (AVT) must be between eighteen and thirty-five, although older applicants may be selected if they appear able to take full advantage of the training and have a reasonable prospect of being employed in the jobs for which they are trained.[9] Preference is given to unemployed or underemployed applicants who need training to obtain satisfactory jobs. The applicants' employment and school records are scrutinized to select those who are most likely to benefit from the training.

As in the direct employment program, potential trainees are given the General Aptitude Test battery to determine the occupations for which they show the greatest potential. Eligibility for the various courses depends, however, on the educational requirements for entry, which are related to the educational requirements of the occupation and vary from eight to twelve years of schooling. Because the program uses existing training facilities, there is no minimum enrollment for courses.

Persons accepted for training are eligible for the same grants as those participating in the direct relocation program.[10] In addition, vocational trainees are provided with the necessary tuition, books, supplies, and tools essential to their courses of study, and financial

[9] Bureau of Indian Affairs, Branch of Employment Assistance, "Adult Vocational Training Services: Questions and Answers" (n.d.; processed), p. 1.
[10] *Ibid.*, p. 3.

assistance is adjusted to provide funds to maintain the trainee's family at the center.

The field employment assistance offices or the reservation employment assistance officers help the Indian to secure employment after training is completed. Transportation, moving expenses, housing assistance, and health and welfare benefits are provided (on the same basis as in the direct relocation program) to help him get to the job location.

Since 1960 the number of participants and the total cost of the program have steadily increased (Table 6-1). However, as many Indians are still being relocated without training as are receiving training.

The total cost per participant in each of the Indian manpower programs has risen dramatically since their inception. In the adult vocational training and direct relocation programs, greater costs are attributed to increased staffing of field offices and rising subsistence allowances for trainees. Costs for on-the-job trainees have risen primarily because of increases in the minimum wage.

Criteria for Evaluation

In evaluating these three programs, the following criteria might be used: the internal rate of return and benefit–cost ratios, compared with similar programs for non-Indians; the proportion of Indians removed from poverty; reduction in unemployment, compared with programs for non-Indians; the proportion of Indians obtaining jobs related to their training; the proportion returning to the reservation after relocation; the dropout rate, compared with that of non-Indians; incentives to participants for undertaking additional investment in human capital; reduction in antisocial behavior; and the effect on the overall economic progress of the Indian people.

Much of the information for assessing the programs is based on a BIA survey of 327 of the 5,108 persons who took part in these programs during 1963. The sample is proportionately stratified to reflect the categories of persons participating in each program: 33 percent were relocated without training; 11 percent received on-the-job training; and 56 percent were given adult vocational training before employment. Data were collected on the participants' economic status for three years before training and/or relocation and for three and five years afterward.[11]

Studies that focus on the increment of income attributable to a manpower program often use a control group to indicate what income would have been if the individual had not participated in the program. No control group was used in the BIA study; however, age-earnings profiles of reservation Indians plus information on secular changes in reservation income (derived from Census Bureau data) provide a tolerably good estimate of what the individual's earnings would have been if he had not participated. Moreover, control groups cannot effectively "control" for such intangible characteristics as personality, motivation, or temperament. Since the sample data used in this study refer to the economic status of individuals at different points in time, there is at least partial control for variations in these characteristics.

Benefit-Cost Analysis

Each of the Indian programs represents an investment in human capital[12] that involves costs and renders returns. From data on costs and returns, the ratio of present value to cost and the internal rate of return can be calculated.[13] It is assumed that the returns

[11] Bureau of Indian Affairs, "A Followup Study of 1963 Recipients of the Services of the Employment Assistance Program" (October 1966; July 1968, rev.; processed).

[12] Three studies of similar programs as an investment in human capital are the following: of relocation, Larry A. Sjaastad, "The Costs and Returns of Human Migration," *Journal of Political Economy*, Supplement, Vol. 70 (October 1962), pp. 80–93; of on-the-job training, Jacob Mincer, "On-the-Job Training: Costs, Returns, and Some Implications," *ibid.*, pp. 50–79; of vocational or technical schooling, Adger B. Carroll and Loren A. Ihnen, "Costs and Returns for Two Years of Postsecondary Technical Schooling: A Pilot Study," *ibid.*, Vol. 75 (December 1967), pp. 862–73.

[13] The ratios and internal rates of return presented are biased in an unknown direction by two factors that cannot be quantified. First, because Indian reservations contain closely knit communities, where English is often the second language, the psychic costs of relocation (with or without training) are very high. Second, there is a nonmonetary return arising from locational preferences, representing consumption with a zero cost of production; for many Indians this return may be large. For

will accrue over the entire working life of the participant. Since the average age of the participants in the programs was twenty-five, returns are computed for forty years, assuming retirement at age sixty-five.[14] Discount rates of 5 and 10 percent are calculated for illustrative purposes (there is little agreement among economists about the appropriate rate). It can be argued that the discount rate for low-income individuals is much greater than 5 to 10 percent, but since these are publicly supported programs, this point does not seem to be particularly relevant.

The benefit-cost estimates for the various Indian programs are given in Table 6-2.[15] For the direct relocation program, the internal rate of return of 93 percent is comparable with estimates in a study by Osburn of 106 percent for whites and 132 percent for nonwhites. However, it is considerably lower than the estimate of 409 percent obtained by Robbins in a similar analysis of low-income migrants relocated with public funds from the eastern to the Piedmont section of North Carolina.[16]

The rate of return for on-the-job training is much higher than that found by Mincer for metal, printing, and building apprentices. He found that, depending on alternative assumptions concerning income streams, the rate of return varied from 9.0 to 18.3 percent.[17] The rate of return for the Indian OJT program is much higher because the training period is much shorter than that in the Mincer study and, as a result, training costs are lower. Moreover, a larger relative increment to income resulted from partici-

---

example, many of them prefer to settle in California, presumably because the climate is not very different from that on the Indian reservations where they previously lived.

[14] This may overestimate the number of years over which returns will accrue, since the returns are adjusted on the basis of non-Indian mortality tables. The present life expectancy for reservation Indians is sixty-three and a half years. While the improvement in housing and income that follows program participation will undoubtedly increase the life span, it is unclear how much longer than nonparticipants an Indian participating in these programs can expect to live.

[15] See Appendix C for the data and the methodology used in deriving the estimates.

[16] D. D. Osburn, "Returns to Investment in Human Migration" (Ph.D. dissertation, North Carolina State University, 1966), cited in Richard D. Robbins, "An Evaluation of Publicly Supported Mobility of Low Income Rural Residents" (Master's thesis, North Carolina State University, 1967), p. 41. This latter program yielded a higher rate of return than the one for Indians because costs per migrant were lower and the increment to income was higher.

[17] Mincer, "On-the-Job Training," p. 64.

TABLE 6-2

Internal Rates of Return and Benefit–Cost Ratios for 1963 Participants
in Direct Relocation, On-the-Job Training, and
Adult Vocational Training Programs

Description	Direct relocation	On-the-job training	Adult vocational training
Internal rate of return (percent)			
Total	*93*	*132*	*57*
Men	*88*	—	*63*
Women	*127*	—	*45*
Benefit–cost ratio at 5 percent discount rate			
Total	15.8	22.6	9.8
Men	15.0	—	10.7
Women	21.8	—	7.6
On reservation (men and women)	7.4	—	6.2
Near reservation (men and women)	6.5	—	11.9
Field office areas (men and women)	25.0	—	12.2
Benefit–cost ratio at 10 percent discount rate			
Total	9.3	12.9	5.5
Men	8.9	—	6.1
Women	12.4	—	4.4
On reservation (men and women)	4.1	—	3.6
Near reservation (men and women)	3.7	—	6.8
Field office areas (men and women)	14.2	—	6.8

Sources: Derived from data in Bureau of Indian Affairs, "A Followup Study of 1963 Recipients of the Services of the Employment Assistance Program" (October 1966; July 1968, rev.; processed). See Appendix Tables C-1 and C-3 for the cost and benefit figures (rounded) used in calculating the ratios.

pation in the Indian training program than in the apprenticeship programs examined by Mincer.

Carroll and Ihnen in their study of institutional vocational training found that, depending on assumptions made about alternative income streams, the rate of return to technical training varied from 11.7 to 16.5 percent.[18] These results are below those for the Indian program, partly because the increments to income after training are not as great in the institution they examined as those in the Indian program.

The benefit–cost ratios for the Indian adult vocational training program are similar to the findings of Ribich, who examined the benefits and costs of three retraining programs undertaken by Connecticut, West Virginia, and Massachusetts. (Connecticut and

[18] "Costs and Returns," p. 868.

West Virginia collaborated with the Area Redevelopment Administration.) The workers in Connecticut were trained primarily in
machine shop operations, pipe fitting, and ship fitting. More than
half of the group in Massachusetts were enrolled in schools for
barbers and technicians, and the remaining trainees were spread
over a variety of fields from drafting to auto repair. The West Virginia program trained men as auto repairmen, construction workers, electricians, riveters, machine tool operators, and welders; and
women as nurse's aides, typist-stenographers, and waitresses.[19] Ribich, assuming a 5 percent rate of discount and benefit streams continuing to age sixty-five (adjusted for mortality), obtained a benefit–cost ratio of 10.1 for the Connecticut retraining program, 4.2 for
Massachusetts, and 15.0 for West Virginia.[20]

The benefit–cost ratio for the Indian AVT program may also
be compared with that for the Job Corps. Both programs provide
vocational training in an institutional setting; however, the Job
Corps also provides basic education. In a survey of the Job Corps,
Cain concluded that the realistic ratio of benefits to costs ranged
from 1.02 to 1.70, although varying assumptions led to ratios between 0.60 and 1.89.[21]

While incomes after participation in direct relocation are
slightly higher than after OJT (see Appendix Table C-2), the cost
per trainee and forgone earnings in the OJT program are only
slightly less than half the cost per migrant in the direct relocation
program.

Moreover, although earnings after participation in AVT are
higher than after the other two Indian manpower programs, the
benefit–cost ratio is lower because forgone earnings and training
costs under AVT are double the cost per migrant (without training) and four times the cost per trainee under OJT.[22]

[19] Thomas I. Ribich, *Education and Poverty* (Brookings Institution, 1968), p. 39.

[20] *Ibid.*, p. 49. Ribich's investigation involves retraining, which implies that the
participant is being taught a skill different from one he originally had. Vocational
training for Indians involves teaching a skill to previously unskilled individuals.

[21] Glen G. Cain, "Benefit/Cost Estimates for Job Corps" (University of Wisconsin,
Institute for Research on Poverty, 1967; processed).

[22] One can argue that the data in Table 6-2 are biased upward in regard to the
effectiveness of the AVT program. Since vocational trainees are both trained and
relocated, it can be maintained that much of the earnings increment was not due
to training but to migration. (See Appendix Table C-4 for an internal rate of return and benefit–cost ratios adjusted for this.) Moreover, the average level of school-

In 1966 (three years after program participation), those in the direct relocation program who remained in the urban centers to which they had been sent were earning $1,400 more a year than those who returned to the reservation, and the vocational trainees who remained were earning $920 more a year than those who returned to the reservation. Since the benefit-cost estimates given in Table 6-2 include both those who remained and those who returned, it follows that if more program participants could be induced to remain in the urban centers in which they were originally placed, the benefit–cost ratios of the direct relocation and AVT programs would be even higher.

This analysis suggests that, measured by benefit–cost ratios at current program levels, all three of the employment programs for Indians are relatively efficient compared with similar programs for non-Indians; apparently on-the-job training is somewhat more efficient than the other two. However, because present programs may have skimmed off the most promising trainees, because they are relatively small, and because variables not included in the analysis may have influenced the results, the analysis should not be used to establish priorities for program expansion.

Indians might have relocated or sought training without governmental programs; if so, the government is absorbing a cost that would otherwise have been met by the Indians themselves or by private industry located outside the reservation. However, the Bureau of Indian Affairs estimates that 80 to 90 percent of the participants in the off-reservation employment assistance programs require financial aid, and thus it is likely that very few Indians would have been able to relocate or seek training without the programs.

Employment Programs and Poverty

While the benefit–cost ratios indicate that these programs are highly efficient, it is important to find out how effective they are in

---

ing of the adult vocational trainees was approximately 1.5 years greater than that for the direct migrants or OJT trainees. Thus, part of the increment in income received by the AVT trainees may be ascribed to their education.

removing Indians from poverty. Using poverty levels established by the Social Security Administration for 1963 and 1966 (adjusted for location), the percentage of reservation Indians and of the sample of program participants with incomes above the poverty level in those years is estimated as follows:[23]

	1963	1966
All reservation Indians	21	26
Program participants (1963 sample)		
Direct relocation	25	52
On-the-job training	28	53
Adult vocational training	27	60

Since the income data used in this study refer only to the individual participants and not to their families, poverty calculations are based on the assumption of no dependents. If dependents and their earnings were included in the calculations, the percentages would probably remain about the same.

While the incidence of poverty in 1963 before participation was similar for each of the employment programs, three years after enrollment more participants in AVT than in the other two programs were earning incomes above the poverty level. This is not surprising, since in general the incomes of those in the vocational program were higher in 1966 than the incomes of the others (Appendix Table C-2). Even though the average 1966 income of OJT trainees was $370 less than that of direct relocation participants, the incidence of poverty was the same for both groups.[24] Most of the OJT program recipients lived in rural areas, where the poverty level threshold is considerably lower than in urban areas, where many migrants lived.

Although program participants had a much lower incidence of poverty three years after relocation and/or training than nonparticipants, nearly one-half still had incomes below the poverty threshold.

[23] Estimated using poverty levels as defined in Mollie Orshansky, "Counting the Poor: Another Look at the Poverty Profile," *Social Security Bulletin,* Vol. 28 (January 1965), pp. 3–19; Orshansky, "The Shape of Poverty in 1966," *Social Security Bulletin,* Vol. 31 (March 1968), pp. 3–32; data for all reservation Indians for 1963, author's estimate, and for 1966, Task Force on Indian Housing, "Indian Housing: Need, Alternatives, Priorities and Program Recommendations," Bureau of Indian Affairs (December 1966; processed); data for program participants from Bureau of Indian Affairs, "A Followup Study of 1963 Recipients" (July 1968, rev.).

[24] Thus, an Indian who remained on the reservation and underwent training earned nearly $400 less a year than one who migrated with no training.

Reduction in Unemployment

The employment programs were intended to increase the participants' productivity; hence one would expect lower unemployment rates after training and/or relocation than before. Although the direct migrants received no training, their productivity would also have increased and their likelihood of unemployment decreased, because labor was transferred from an area of oversupply (an Indian reservation) to one of relative shortage. Consequently, the effectiveness of the programs depends on the *difference* in unemployment rates between trainees and other migrants, not on the change in unemployment rates among trainees before and after training.

A direct comparison of the unemployment rates of the Indians in the sample before and after participation in the programs cannot be made because data are available only on rates after they had taken part. However, it is possible to derive a reasonable estimate of the unemployment rate before program participation. The earnings of those in the sample before participation in the programs were similar to those of all reservation Indians of comparable age, and the unemployment rates of OJT trainees on the Pine Ridge Reservation before training were approximately equal to the unemployment rate of the entire reservation.[25] This limited evidence suggests that the labor force status of program participants before training and/or relocation is not significantly different from that of nonparticipants. In 1963 (the year the sample of Indians took part in the employment assistance programs), the unemployment rate for reservation Indians was about 42 percent.[26]

Table 6-3 presents data on the labor force status of beneficiaries before and after program participation. For those enrolled in the direct relocation program, it appears (to the extent that the 1963 estimates are accurate) that unemployment was much lower three to five years after migration than before. Moreover, the labor force participation rate of these migrants increased steadily. How-

[25] Bureau of Indian Affairs, Missouri River Basin Investigations Project, "The Social and Economic Effects of Reservation Industrial Employment on Indian Employees and Their Families" (Billings, Mont., 1968; processed), p. 59.

[26] Estimated from data in *Indian Unemployment Survey*, Pt. 1, *Questionnaire Returns*, A Memorandum and Accompanying Information from the Chairman, House Committee on Interior and Insular Affairs, 88 Cong. 1 sess. (1963).

TABLE 6-3

*Labor Force Status, 1966 and 1968, of a Sample of 1963 Participants
in Bureau of Indian Affairs Manpower Programs*

(*In percent*)

Labor force status	Direct relocation			On-the-job training			Adult vocational training		
	1963	1966	1968	1963	1966	1968	1963	1966	1968
Employed	35–40	69	75	35–40	80	72	35–40	68	71
Unemployed	40–50	20	18	40–50	6	8	40–50	10	6
Not in labor force	20–25	11	7	20–25	14	20	20–25	22	23

Sources: 1963, author's estimate based on U.S. Bureau of the Census, *U.S. Census of Population: 1960, Subject Reports, Nonwhite Population by Race*, Final Report PC(2)-1C (1963), Table 33, p. 104; 1966 and 1968, Bureau of Indian Affairs, "A Followup Study of 1963 Recipients" (1968, rev.).

ever, the unemployment rates are much higher than those for non-Indians of comparable age and education. For example, in 1966 the median age of the sample of migrants was twenty-three, and they averaged about ten and one-half years of schooling. Non-Indians of this age and level of schooling had an unemployment rate of 7.6 percent, but it was 20 percent for the Indians in the sample,[27] indicating a serious unemployment problem among Indian migrants.[28]

For on-the-job trainees the unemployment rate of the sample was lower in 1966 than the rate for participants in the other programs and in 1968 was nearly as low as that of adult vocational trainees. Since the employer was obligated to hire all of the trainees who completed the OJT program, relatively low initial unemployment rates for this group are not unexpected, but it is encouraging to note that substantial benefits lasted for three and five years.

Significant changes occurred in the pattern of labor force participation of OJT trainees. Before training, an estimated 20 to 25 percent were not in the labor market. The high unemployment rate on reservations persuaded some of them to believe that no jobs were available. However, after factories began locating on the reservations and OJT programs were established, a number of them sought and found employment, and by 1966 the labor force

[27] Harvey R. Hamel, "Educational Attainment of Workers, March 1966," U.S. Bureau of Labor Statistics, Special Labor Force Report No. 83 (1967), p. A-15.

[28] Part of their problem is that some of them had returned to the reservation by 1968.

participation rate of those trained in 1963 was relatively high. Between 1966 and 1968 the rate declined as a number of female former trainees left the labor force to become housewives.

Although AVT trainees had much lower unemployment rates after training, these rates were still considerably above those for non-Indians of comparable age and education. In 1966 the unemployment rate for non-Indian high school graduates aged twenty-five (the average age and level of schooling of the vocational trainees) was 4.8 percent, compared with 10 percent for the vocational trainees.[29]

Some of the discrepancy between the unemployment rates for Indians and non-Indians of comparable age and education is probably due to greater adjustment problems for the former. Since about 63 percent of those in the BIA manpower programs were either seven-eighths or full-blooded Indians, it is likely that the cultural shock of leaving the reservation caused problems of adjustment and concomitantly of unemployment.

It appears that the Bureau of Indian Affairs employment programs are about as successful in reducing the unemployment rates of participants as several well-known programs for non-Indians: the Job Corps, the Neighborhood Youth Corps, and the Work Experience and Training Program designed primarily for welfare recipients (Appendix Table A-12). However, the Manpower Development and Training Act (MDTA) program appears to effect a greater absolute decline in the unemployment rates of participants than the Indian manpower programs, although the unemployment rates after participation in MDTA are higher than the unemployment rates of those who have completed the Indian training programs.

Employment Related to Training

Another measure of the effectiveness of a manpower training program might be the proportion of graduates who are in jobs related to their training. In 1966, 67 percent of the sample of OJT trainees were in training-related occupations and by 1968, 52 percent.[30]

[29] Hamel, "Educational Attainment of Workers."
[30] Bureau of Indian Affairs, "A Followup Study of 1963 Recipients" (1966), p. 30, and (1968, rev.), p. 10.

It is difficult to say whether these percentages indicate success. A study in early 1968 of 54,500 trainees in the federal OJT program under the Manpower Development and Training Act who completed their training in 1967 found 90 percent of the group regularly employed and 95 percent of them in training-related jobs.[31] Though this is a far higher percentage than those for the BIA program, the BIA data were gathered two to five years after training, while the MDTA data were obtained only nine to twelve months later. The high rate of job mobility among American workers makes it likely that the number of MDTA graduates in training-related positions will decline substantially over time. Furthermore, participants in the Indian program are faced with a problem that concerns few of the MDTA trainees—closing of the factories in which they are employed. Six of the thirteen reservations visited in 1968 had lost industries. Since industrial development of the Indian reservations is so limited, a plant closing forces the trainee to seek employment outside the area of his specialty.

Of adult vocational trainees, 61 percent were in employment related to training in 1966 and 59 percent in 1968.[32] This is comparable with a figure of 60–65 percent of MDTA graduates (not including OJT trainees).[33]

The chief influence in the lower ratio of training-related employment for Indian AVT participants is that many return to the reservation hoping that there will be a demand for their skills, but they are disappointed. Not only is there scant likelihood that they will find training-related employment, but there is a greater probability of their being unemployed than there is for those who live off the reservation. In 1968, 10 percent of vocational trainees on the reservation were unemployed, as compared with 3.5 percent of those off the reservation. Also, about 20 percent of the trainees leave the program without enough training to enable the BIA to place them in related positions.[34]

[31] U.S. Department of Labor, *Manpower Report of the President, 1968,* p. 206.

[32] Bureau of Indian Affairs, "A Followup Study of 1963 Recipients" (1966), p. 43, and (1968, rev.), p. 26.

[33] Data for MDTA trainees, 65 percent of whom were classified as disadvantaged, estimated by author from information in *Manpower Report of the President, 1968,* p. 205.

[34] This does not include partial completions—dropouts who have had enough training to allow them to accept employment in the field (or a related field) for which they have been trained.

Returnees

A large proportion of participants in the direct relocation program return to their reservations. This does not necessarily indicate a failure to adjust to urban living. The Indian may return because of expanded employment opportunities on the reservation. However, the great earning differential between migrants who remain in urban areas and those who return to the reservation (Appendix Table C-2) reflects the fact that most who return suffer an income loss.

The Bureau of Indian Affairs maintained statistics from 1953 to 1957 which showed that three out of ten who were relocated returned during the same fiscal year in which they migrated (Appendix Table A-13). The data do not indicate how many Indians eventually returned home, a figure that would be much higher.[35]

In 1958 the U.S. comptroller general's annual report criticized the BIA for maintaining inadequate statistics on various activities, including the relocation program. The bureau's response to this criticism was to eliminate, in 1959, its statistical series on the status (returnee or nonreturnee) of Indians; it concluded that statistics on returnees were furnishing ammunition to critics of the program.[36]

Most of the research on Indian migrants who return home has been done by anthropologists. Martin showed that Indians who are younger, higher in level of educational attainment, and of mixed blood are more likely to adjust successfully to an urban environment than older, less educated, full-blooded Indians. Graves and Van Arsdale demonstrated that the principal factor causing migrants to leave Denver and return to the reservation was their lack of economic success. Since older, less educated Indians may have more difficulty in locating and holding a job, Martin's finding is not surprising.[37] Ablon found that when an Indian gets

[35] Probably some 50 percent of the Indians relocated eventually return home. See Joan Ablon, "American Indian Relocation: Problems of Dependency and Management in the City," *Phylon*, Vol. 26 (Winter 1965), pp. 365–66. She suggests that in the early years of relocation the return rate may be about 75 percent.

[36] Interview with employment assistance officer, Branch of Employment Assistance, July 1968.

[37] Harry W. Martin, "Correlates of Adjustment Among American Indians in an

into economic difficulty, he does not take his problem to a community welfare agency (which, in many cases, he probably does not know exists), but instead tends to return home.[38]

In a study of Navajo relocation, Cullum pointed out:

The only sharply positive findings . . . [are] related to attendance at public school and previous occupational experience at skilled trades. Definitely negative findings emerged with regard to families containing five or more children, to heads of families over forty, and in lesser degree to persons completing less than four grades of school. The person using alcoholic beverage "to excess" did poorly.[39]

Two possible influences on the returnee rate that have not been examined directly by anthropologists or others may have a profound effect—the locations to which migrants are sent and the amount of follow-up they receive. From the beginning of the relocation program, the Bureau of Indian Affairs has usually emphasized the movement of Indians to major metropolitan centers, including several of the largest cities in the United States. Adjusting to the highly competitive, fast-paced life of a large city, with its seemingly endless rules and regulations, after living on a tranquil Indian reservation is undoubtedly difficult.[40] Moreover, for many Indians the relocation centers are so far from the reservation that traditional family ties must be severed.

Except in emergencies, the BIA usually limits the follow-up of relocated Indians to a period of one year, on the ground that to continue services after that would prevent the Indian from becoming self-sufficient—a major bureau goal. However, it seems unnecessary to take such a rigid position on the matter. Some persons need more follow-up services than others, and an extension beyond

---

Urban Environment," *Human Organization,* Vol. 24 (Winter 1964), pp. 290–95; Theodore D. Graves and Minor Van Arsdale, "Values, Expectations and Relocation: The Navaho Migrant to Denver," *Human Organization,* Vol. 25 (Winter 1966), pp. 300–07 (in recent years migrants to Chicago and Denver have tended to form Indian residential enclaves or ghettos).

[38] Ablon, "American Indian Relocation," p. 368.

[39] Robert M. Cullum, "Assisted Navajo Relocation, 1952–1956," Bureau of Indian Affairs, Gallup Area Office (1957; processed), p. 8, as cited in Peter P. Dorner, "The Economic Position of the American Indians: Their Resources and Potential for Development" (Ph.D. dissertation, Harvard University, 1959), p. 191.

[40] For example, in the Cullum study of Navajo returnees, 53.1 percent listed adjustment problems as their reason for returning. The largest single cause listed was excessive use of alcohol, which was named by 15 percent.

the one-year limit for those still unadjusted to urban life would not be unreasonable. Moreover, there appears to be great variation in returnee rates by tribe. For example, a recent study of the Salt River Reservation in Arizona (with Pima and Maricopa Indians) showed that, in the years 1960 through 1964, 97 percent of those relocated returned to the reservation.[41] However, only 20 percent of migrants return to the Yakima Reservation in Washington.[42] This may indicate that the cultural patterns of some tribes make it more difficult for their members to adjust to an urban environment. In any event, extending special follow-up services to migrants from the tribes that show persistently high returnee rates may prove feasible.

Dropouts

One of the most discouraging aspects of the BIA on-the-job training program is that a large number of participants leave the program before completing training.[43] Not only is the dropout faced with finding employment in a reservation economy, where unemployment rates of 40 to 60 percent are the rule, but fragmentary data suggest that benefits increase at a rising rate with time spent in training. Thus, a program with a high percentage of graduates would have a greater benefit–cost ratio than a program with fewer graduates, even if the initial costs were the same in both programs and increased at the same rate over time,[44] and if the time stream

[41] Harry W. Martin, Robert L. Leon, and John H. Gladfelter, "The Salt River Reservation: A Proposal for the Development of Its Human and Natural Resources," a consultation report to the BIA (1967; processed), p. 11.

[42] Interview with reservation employment assistance officer, July 2, 1968.

[43] The analysis on dropout rates refers to all Indians who have participated in the OJT program, and not to the sample of trainees.

[44] For example, two-thirds of those who stayed in the Job Corps six months or longer were still working half a year after they left, an increase in their employment status of 12 percent over their pretraining status. The employment rate of those who stayed less than three months was actually lower after training than before. Although both groups had identical wage rates before training, those who left after six months of training earned a median of 32 cents more per hour than before training, but those who left after three months or less earned only 15 cents more per hour than before training. For further information see Sar A. Levitan, *Antipoverty Work and Training Efforts: Goals and Reality* (joint publication of Institute of Labor and Industrial Relations and National Manpower Policy Task Force, 1967), pp. 31–32.

FIGURE 6-1

Comparison of Benefit–Cost Ratios for Persons Dropping Out of Training Programs after Three and Six Months

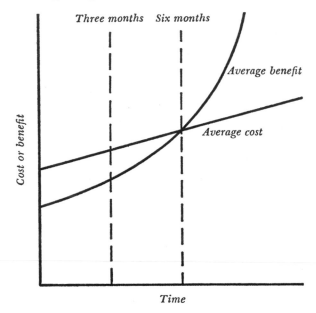

of benefits followed the hypothetical pattern illustrated in **Figure 6-1**. In this example, the benefit–cost ratio is less than unity for a person who drops out after three months and equal to unity for one who leaves after six months.

Statistics on dropouts from the Indian OJT programs for 1958–68 show that almost half of all enrollees terminated without completing training (Appendix Table A-14). This is much higher than the rate of 20 percent in the similar MDTA program.[45]

To determine possible reasons for the high dropout rate from the Indian program, two kinds of analyses were undertaken. The first related the dropout rate to the type of product manufactured (or training given) by the organization providing the training; the second related it to the size of the firm and of the training program.[46]

---

[45] *Manpower Report of the President, 1967*, p. 97.

[46] The data on which these analyses are based refer to the total number of OJT trainees and not to the sample of trainees.

Considerable variation was found in the dropout rate by type of product manufactured or of training (Appendix Table A-14). The rate ranged from 21 percent for trainees in the nurse's aide program to 50 percent for sawmill workers, 54 percent for trainees making Indian artifacts, and 62 percent for furniture workers. Two highly specialized occupations had dropout rates that were even higher.[47]

One might expect that small firms would have higher dropout rates than large ones. Conversations with owners and managers of reservation factories suggested several possible reasons:

1. Firms that enroll few trainees tend to be small, marginal enterprises that are under strong competitive pressure to survive. As a consequence, great stress may be placed on the employees to bring productivity up to maximum levels in a short time. Many of them cannot function in this kind of environment and leave the program.

2. In small firms enrolling few trainees, there is probably more interpersonal communication between the officials and the trainees than in larger firms. These officials criticize the progress of the trainees just as they would if the program were designed primarily for non-Indians. For example, at one firm that manufactured wood and plastic products on a South Dakota reservation the owner made a regular practice of going up and down the assembly line screaming at employees for the slightest mistake.[48] Although generalizations concerning cultural differences can be hazardous, anthropologists say that Indians are much more sensitive to criticism than non-Indians, especially if it is given while fellow employees are present.[49] Thus, the Indian often reacts to public criticism

[47] The two "high dropout" occupations are diamond processing and women's fashion specialty items. Diamond processing is the most highly skilled occupation for which an OJT program has been operated. It is likely that the high dropout rate for this program is due to the difficulty of learning the occupation. The occupation referred to as "women's fashion specialty items" includes the making of wigs by attaching one hair at a time. Apparently most Indians did not have the patience for this intricate process.

[48] The employees reacted by engaging in various acts of industrial sabotage. (Based on an interview with Bureau of Indian Affairs housing officer, July 1968.)

[49] See, for example, Murray L. Wax, Rosalie H. Wax, and Robert V. Dumont, Jr., Formal Education in an American Indian Community, Supplement to Social Problems, Vol. 11 (Spring 1964).

not by improving his productivity but by quitting. Larger firms operating more extensive programs usually arrange for former trainees to teach and train new enrollees. The former trainees, being Indians themselves, use methods of criticism that do not hurt and embarrass the trainee. This probably lowers the separation rate for firms with large training programs.

3. Partly because small firms enrolling few trainees are often marginal enterprises, their training programs are not always conducted effectively and the enrollees may become discouraged and leave. Firms operating large training programs are likely to have more employees in guidance work and more effective personnel managers. These persons not only help the trainee with adjustment problems, but also screen out applicants who might have such problems.[50]

Despite these considerations, a different factor tends to equalize the dropout rate among firms, even though the conditions and type of training vary—the cultural background of the reservation Indian. Before a factory locates on a reservation, most of the Indians living there have never seen a manufacturing plant, let alone worked in one. The lack of sustained employment experience, of industrial discipline, and of personal responsibility must be thoroughly changed if the trainee is to become an effective employee. This demand for adjustment—for making pastoral man into industrial man (at a much faster rate than was ever achieved among non-Indians)—has had a profound influence on the separation rate.

Computation of the dropout rate by the size of the training program yielded the following rates (weighted averages): trainees numbering from 1 to 30, 48.8 percent; 31 to 100 trainees, 52.8 percent; 101 or more trainees, 48.2 percent.[51] The small variation indicates that cultural factors and lack of industrial experience are more important explanations of dropout rates than the size of the firms administering the training programs.

[50] Because of the high rate of unemployment on most Indian reservations, firms operating training programs often have many more applicants than they can accept. Thus highly selective screening is feasible.

[51] Computed from data in Bureau of Indian Affairs, Branch of Employment Assistance, "Annual Statistical Summary, 1968" (processed). These data are not based on the sample of trainees, but include all who have participated in the program from its beginning through June 30, 1968.

Most dropouts from the adult vocational training program are unable to obtain work in the field for which they were trained. This, plus the high investment cost per trainee, makes it vital to keep the number of dropouts to a minimum. About one-third of these trainees in the period 1958–62 failed to complete training. (Appendix Table A-15 gives information for all courses enrolling forty or more students in those years.) While this is higher than the dropout rate for participants in the MDTA program (20 percent in 1965), it is much lower than that for Job Corps enrollees, 71 percent of whom left within the first six months. The AVT dropout rates were analyzed by type and length of course and educational requirements for enrollment.[52] Rates varied considerably among courses. For example, the welding, heavy equipment, and auto diesel mechanic courses had rates of less than 25 percent, while for the practical nurse, cooking, and accounting courses they were more than 45 percent.

To try to explain this variability, the rates were analyzed by length of course and prerequisite formal schooling. Persons without a high school education had somewhat less tendency to leave (32.8 percent dropout rate for nongraduates, as compared with 36.7 percent for graduates). Regardless of the educational requirement for enrollment, those courses continuing for a year or more had higher dropout rates (40.3 for those lasting one year or more, 32.5 for those lasting less than a year).

The variation in dropout rate by length of training, especially for nongraduates from high school, seems reasonable. Enrollees in courses of a year or more may become discouraged when completion still seems far off. Moreover, the longer training period allows more opportunity for such random factors as illness, death in the family, or marital problems to affect a trainee's status. Probably there are other factors, for which data are not available, such as size of classes, sex of trainee, job opportunities for the partially trained, and availability of specialized skills required for certain courses.

---

[52] Based on data from Louis Harris and Associates, as presented in Levitan, *Antipoverty Work*, p. 28.

Further Investment in Human Capital

One result of an investment in human capital is that it often stimulates an additional investment. For example, Jacob Mincer found that the amount of on-the-job training received by individuals was positively correlated with the level of educational attainment.[53]

The educational achievement in later years of those who took

TABLE 6-4

Educational Achievement, 1966 and 1968, of a Sample of 1963 Participants in Bureau of Indian Affairs Manpower Programs

(*In percent*)

Years of school	Direct relocation		On-the-job training		Adult vocational training	
	1966	1968	1966	1968	1966	1968
0–8	31	23	28	22	9	9
9–11	33	36	41	47	23	21
12 or more	36	41	31	31	68	70
Median number of years	10.6	11.1	10.5	11.0	12+	12+

Source: Bureau of Indian Affairs, "A Followup Study of 1963 Recipients" (1968, rev.).

part in the BIA employment and training programs during 1963 is shown in Table 6-4. The median level of schooling of both those who relocated and OJT trainees increased by one-half year. However, the table gives an incomplete picture of the additional investment in human capital made by the sample of program participants. By 1966, 14 percent of those who relocated had attended night school, and by 1968 this figure had risen to 39 percent.[54] By

[53] "On-the-Job Training," p. 59. On a related point, Burton A. Weisbrod, in the same issue of the *Journal of Political Economy* (Vol. 70, Supplement, Pt. 2), points out that one of the "benefits" of achieving a given level of schooling is that one can take advantage of even more schooling: "Education and Investment in Human Capital," pp. 106–23. This point could be applied to other types of human capital.

[54] The latter figure seems high when one considers that incomes are relatively low in comparison with those of non-Indians and that the expenses are borne by the Indians themselves.

1966, only 3 percent of the OJT trainees had attended night school, but by 1968 the figure was 25 percent. Although this is a substantial increase, it is well below the 39 percent of the direct migrants,[55] partly because adult education programs on the reservations where most of the former OJT trainees reside are inadequate compared with the off-reservation programs available to the direct migrants.[56]

By 1966, 16 percent of the sample of AVT trainees had attended or were attending night school, and by 1968 the figure was 36 percent. The proportions of AVT trainees and direct migrants may have been similar because their opportunities were similar.

The sample of Indian manpower program participants showed more tendency to make a subsequent investment in their own education than did participants in other federal manpower programs. Only 6 percent of Job Corps participants, 10.2 percent of Neighborhood Youth Corps, and 4.5 percent of those in the Work Experience and Training Program received additional education or training after leaving the programs.[57] Census information on the educational attainment of reservation Indians indicates that those in the fourteen to twenty-four age group in 1950 showed no increase in schooling by 1960. Since only a small fraction of reservation Indians participated in manpower programs (and those who did usually left the reservations), there is evidence that enrollees furthered their schooling while nonenrollees of comparable age did not.

Changes in Behavior

One of the noneconomic benefits of a manpower program for the disadvantaged is a decline in antisocial behavior, which may be

[55] Bureau of Indian Affairs, "A Followup Study of 1963 Recipients" (1968, rev.).

[56] The annual BIA publication, "Statistics Concerning Indian Education," indicates that in recent years many additional Indian communities have established adult education programs. However, there are still hundreds of communities, particularly in Alaska, that have no such programs.

[57] Data on the Job Corps from Harris and Associates, "Study of Job Corps Terminations," as cited in Levitan, *Antipoverty Work*, p. 31 (the percentage is for the age group twenty to twenty-one only); data for Neighborhood Youth Corps from

measured by examining arrest records. Indians seem prone to arrest. Police records in Denver indicated that about half of the Navajo migrants were arrested at least once during their stay in the city, with about 95 percent of the arrests alcohol-related.[58] If Indians show a decrease in arrests after participating in a manpower program, it seems reasonable to conclude that the program has reduced antisocial behavior. A comparison of the numbers in the 1963 sample arrested before and after taking part in one of the programs showed a substantial decline:[59]

| | Number of arrests | | Decline |
Program	1960–62	1964–66	(percent)
Direct relocation	51	21	59
On-the-job training	9	6	33
Adult vocational training	48	30	38

That the decrease in arrests for vocational trainees is smaller than for those relocated without training[60] is probably not due to economic factors, since the former earn more money and are less subject to unemployment than the latter. Perhaps the pressure placed on the vocational trainees in their skilled and semiskilled positions (untrained migrants in unskilled positions are less subject to pressure) led the trainees to turn to alcohol and resulted in the subsequent arrests.[61] The smaller decline in arrests of OJT trainees probably reflects the fact that the small group included in the survey were law-abiding to begin with.

Levitan, *Antipoverty Work*, p. 62; data for Work Experience and Training from *ibid.*, p. 96. These data must be interpreted cautiously, since it is not clear from the figures how much time had passed since the participants in the programs enrolling primarily non-Indians had left them.

[58] For further information, see Theodore D. Graves, "Alternative Models for the Study of Urban Migration," *Human Organization*, Vol. 25 (Winter 1966), p. 299.

[59] Bureau of Indian Affairs, "A Followup Study of 1963 Recipients" (1966), pp. 21, 34, 47. No distinction was made between misdemeanors and felonies. The data for on-the-job trainees should be accepted cautiously, since the sample was very small.

[60] A chi square test indicates the difference is significant at the 0.05 level.

[61] Nationally, drunkenness alone accounts for 71 percent of all Indian arrests. See Omer Stewart, "Questions Regarding American Indian Criminality," *Human Organization*, Vol. 23 (Spring 1964), p. 61.

Deficiencies of the Programs

The three employment assistance programs appear to be successful, but each has weaknesses.

The greatest shortcoming of the direct relocation program is that half of those relocated eventually return to the reservation. Also, the high unemployment rate of these migrants, shown in Table 6-3, indicates that job placement and follow-up services may be inadequate. Probably the high returnee rate is associated with the difficulty of finding and holding a job. Since this is the oldest of the BIA manpower programs, it is unfortunate that better results have not been achieved. Perhaps it is partly because the bureau has not accumulated useful statistics about the program that would help in understanding the problem and in formulating policies to reduce the return rate.

For the OJT program, the most fundamental criticism is that a high proportion of women are enrolled, while males and nominal heads of households remain unemployed. This problem was stated most eloquently in a letter to the editor of a New Mexico newspaper by a Catholic priest, Father Justus Writh of St. Anthony Indian Mission on the Zuñi Reservation, who wrote:

As you know, many new industries are locating on our Indian reservations. . . . [But] the jobs are not going to our Indian men—to the fathers of families who really need the work. Instead the tendency is to give the jobs to women. . . . For our Indian mothers to be forced to take on outside work because there are almost no jobs available for our men, or because the jobs that are available are given to women—is . . . to fail our Indian people completely. . . . How much of a man would you feel if you wiped the running noses of your children and washed their diapers while the mother of your children went off to work each day so that she might feed you and buy your clothes?[62]

The Bureau of Indian Affairs does not keep statistics on the distribution of trainees by sex, but some information was gathered from some of the larger Indian reservations visited during 1968 (Table 6-5). More than two-thirds of the trainees in the plants visited were women. When questioned about the high percentage of

[62] *Gallup* (N.Mex.) *Independent,* June 19, 1968, p. 2.

TABLE 6-5

*Proportion of Women Trainees, Nine Manufacturing Plants
on Indian Reservations, June–July 1968*

Operating company	Type of industry	Women trainees (percent)	Total number of employees
Burnell	Electronics	80	60
Amizuñi	Electronics	20	50
Fairchild Semiconductor	Electronics	95	550
White Swan	Furniture	40	100
Big Horn Carpet Mills	Carpet, rugs	30	60
Wright & McGill[a]	Fishhooks	50	400
Oglala Sioux Moccasin	Moccasins	95	100
Rosebud Formica Laminated Products	Cabinets, tabletops	5	25
Rosebud Electronics	Electronics	95	50
All plants		70	1,395

Source: Personal visit to plants, June–July 1968.
a. The Wright & McGill fishhook manufacturing operation was permanently shut down on July 30, 1968.

female trainees, most owners or managers gave unsatisfactory responses such as: "If we have men and women, there will be too much fraternization"; "Men won't do the same work as women"; "This work calls for skills men don't have."

The first statement, voiced by several persons, implies that Indians are less able than whites to manage their relations with the opposite sex; there is no evidence to support this prejudiced belief. The second comment also appears to be incorrect. For example, before the shutdown of the Wright & McGill Corporation, 200 men and 200 women worked side by side doing the same work.[63] There was no tendency for the men to feel insecure or to object to the situation. The third comment was made at several of the electronics firms, whose employees make transistors, intricate parts for computers, and other equipment. However, the Amizuñi Corporation, on the Zuñi Reservation, does essentially the same work and finds no difficulty training male workers.

One suspects that the primary motive for hiring a large number of women is strictly economic. It may be possible to pay women

[63] Nevertheless, the turnover rate was higher for men than women.

less than men for the same work, and women may be more difficult to unionize and less insistent on fringe benefits.[64] Since firms usually locate on the reservation because it is a low-wage area, it is not unreasonable to assume that if women are easier to recruit at low wages, women will be hired.

Another problem, which is not a fault of the on-the-job training program per se but is caused by it, is a critical shortage of housing near some of the manufacturing plants. Housing on reservations is usually scattered and of very low density. When an expanding manufacturing plant locates in an area, it creates a great demand for housing nearby. For example, Fairchild Semiconductor placed a major installation at Shiprock, New Mexico, at the eastern end of the Navajo Reservation. In July 1968, the corporation employed 550 workers, most of whom were from other sections of the reservation. The resultant housing shortage was so critical that low-cost public housing built for welfare recipients living in the area was turned over to the Fairchild employees.[65] Fairchild curtailed a planned expansion until the housing shortage could be eased.

A major criticism of the adult vocational training program also concerns the large enrollment of women. Many of those entering the program leave the labor force shortly after completing training; of the women who were enrolled in 1963–64, only 49 percent were in the labor force in 1968.[66] Women in the direct relocation program earned more on the average during the three years after relocation than female vocational trainees, because fewer of the former left the labor force (earnings data include all former trainees or relocatees). It would be desirable to decrease the enrollment of single women in vocational training; undoubtedly the benefit–cost ratio would be greater if this course were followed.

About one-third of the vocational trainees are not high school graduates and many others would probably fall below the high school level on standardized tests. Therefore it might be useful to include some basic or remedial education, as has been done in the

[64] In addition, some personnel managers feel that the monotonous noncreative nature of the work is better suited to the female temperament.

[65] Interview with employment assistance officer, Shiprock Agency, June 25, 1968.

[66] About 35 percent of the trainees were single women.

Job Corps and MDTA programs. One investigator found that MDTA trainees who were given basic education earned $12 more a week after completing the program than those who received technical training only.[67]

Impact on Reservation Economy

Although the level of funding and number of participants in Indian manpower programs have increased in recent years, the question remains whether removing excess labor from the reservation and upgrading part of the labor force through training have had a significant impact on the reservation economy. The change in unemployment rates, shown in Table 1-6, during the period 1958–67 was very much smaller for reservation Indians than for all males (the percentage change for 1958–67 was −14.3 for the former and −54.4 for the latter). Although the programs were a success from the point of view of the individual participants, they operated on too small a scale to have a significant impact on the reservation economy.[68]

As the level of education of reservation Indians continues to increase, more of them will want to be relocated, with or without training. Already most manpower programs operated by the Bureau of Indian Affairs have backlogs of applicants who cannot be accommodated because of a lack of funds. For example, on virtually all the reservations visited in the summer of 1968 budget limitations prevented anyone from being sent to vocational training centers from January until the end of the fiscal year, June 30. As a result, there were six- to nine-month backlogs of potential trainees. A similar situation occurred in 1967. Employment assistance officers reported that many potential trainees lost interest and were no longer available for training when they could be sent. About one-third can never be accommodated. Unless appropriations are increased, these programs, which have been successful in raising

[67] William F. Brazziel, "Effects of General Education in Manpower Programs," *Journal of Human Resources*, Vol. 1 (Summer 1966), pp. 39–44.

[68] The present level of net migration from the Indian reservations is estimated at 10,000 a year, and there are about 3,000 deaths a year among reservation Indians. But the birthrate is double the average for non-Indians—about 16,000 births each year. This means an increase in reservation population of 0.9 percent annually.

the standard of living of the participants, will continue to have only a limited effect on the reservation economy.[69] It is difficult to understand why programs that return $10 to $20 for every dollar spent receive such small appropriations in the face of the urgent need.

[69] However, as mentioned above, funding for the on-the-job training program has been in excess of current needs.

CHAPTER VII

Property and Income Management

While most reservation Indians live in poverty, many tribes have substantial deposits in the federal Treasury or in commercial banks in the form of tribal trust funds. Some Indians have money in individual accounts invested in their behalf by the Bureau of Indian Affairs. The combined total is nearly $350 million. The sources and growth of the funds, bureau investment policy, the role of the secretary of the interior as guardian or trustee, and the part these funds could play in the economic development of the reservations are discussed here. This chapter also examines the pros and cons of the argument for terminating federal responsibility, with special attention to the experiences of several tribes whose relation with the federal government was terminated in the 1950s.

Tribal Trust Funds: Sources and Investment

In the early treaties with the Indian tribes the federal government often made lump sum cash settlements or agreed to provide goods and services as an annuity, occasionally supplementing the annuity with a cash payment at the outset.

The 1819 treaty with the Cherokees was the first in which the government provided a trust fund to be used for the benefit of the tribe.[1] During the remainder of the nineteenth century tribal trust

[1] Laurence F. Schmeckebier, *The Office of Indian Affairs: Its History, Activities and Organization* (Johns Hopkins Press for Institute for Government Research, 1927), p. 190.

funds were established for various reasons. Sometimes the funds were created as a payment to Indians who were forced from their ancestral homelands to reservations farther west, as was done for the Cherokees. In other instances the government simply purchased the lands and deposited the proceeds in the Treasury to the credit of the tribe. Finally, in some cases the government seized the lands, sold them to non-Indians, and deposited the money in the Treasury.

Between 1840 and 1926, Indian trust funds increased from $4.5 million to $23.5 million. After the Second World War they grew more rapidly, from $28.5 million in 1947 to more than $300 million in 1967. The funds are very unequally distributed among tribes: over half of them have less than $100,000 in trust funds, while eight tribes each have more than $5 million. The per capita amount is not impressive, averaging about $750 per reservation Indian. A few tribes have funds amounting to more than $5,000 per member, but for most the figure is less than $300 (Appendix Tables A-16, A-17, A-18).

The recent growth in tribal funds is the result of settlements made by the Indian Claims Commission and earnings received from deposits of oil, gas, and minerals found on reservations. The Claims Commission was created in 1946 to hear claims based on various inequities under the U.S. Constitution, laws, or treaties; errors in treaties or other agreements; or for land taken by the United States without compensation. The first cases were completed in 1949. From then until July 1, 1969, 304 claims were heard; 154 were dismissed, and 150 were decided in favor of the Indian tribes. During that period, almost one-third of a billion dollars was awarded in settlement of claims.[2] In fiscal year 1969, $37 million was awarded. The amounts varied greatly. For example, the Blackfeet and Gros Ventre received $9 million, while the Snoqualmie-Skykomish received $258,000 (Appendix Table A-19).

Only part of the funds received in the settlement of claims is deposited on the tribe's behalf. A large portion is immediately distributed in per capita payments that are usually divided equally among the members of the tribe. Thus, if $1 million is awarded a

[2] Indian Claims Commission, *1969 Annual Report*, p. 2.

tribe with 2,000 members, each member receives $500. Of $106 million awarded by the commission between 1950 and 1966, approximately $42 million was distributed in per capita payments.[3]

Between 1949 and 1966 the earnings from oil and gas deposits on Indian lands amounted to $543 million and other minerals returned $28 million.[4] Precise figures are not available, but it is estimated that more than half of the income from these sources was distributed in per capita payments. The Osage tribe in Oklahoma disbursed approximately $120 million from mineral income in such payments from 1949 to 1966. The Navajos have received more than $80 million from reserves of oil and gas on their lands and have placed it in tribal trust funds. The Tyonek band of the Tlingit and Haida tribes has placed most of its mineral income in trust funds; in 1966 and 1967 the band received $14.4 million in mineral royalties and "bonus bids."[5] (See Appendix Table A-20 for data on tribal income from oil and gas for 1966.)

An act of 1837 ordered the secretary of war to invest the money held in those Indian trust funds that were committed to pay interest to the tribes. After the creation of the Department of the Interior in 1849, responsibility for Indian trust funds was transferred to the head of that department. Because the Treasury lacked sufficient funds, the capital of all trust funds was not invested for some time, although Congress did appropriate funds to pay the interest due. By the late 1850s money was available to invest the principal.[6]

The funds were generally invested in United States or state bonds and railroad securities. An 1876 act transferred custody of the bonds to the treasurer of the United States. He was empowered to make all purchases and sales of the stocks and bonds, but actual control of these securities remained with the secretary of the interior. Beginning in 1880, the trust funds were retained in the Treasury with congressional appropriations providing the funds for interest payments. When the bonds matured, the proceeds were de-

[3] Computed from Robert Pennington, "Summary of Indian Claims Commission Dockets," U.S. Bureau of Indian Affairs, Memorandum (Jan. 12, 1968), Statement No. 5, pp. 1–3. Congressional legislation is necessary to carry out most of the awards of the Claims Commission.

[4] Henry W. Hough, *Development of Indian Resources* (World Press, 1967), p. 118.

[5] See *ibid.*, pp. 120–24, and Bureau of Indian Affairs, Anadarko, Okla., Area Office, Osage Agency, "The Osage People and Their Trust Property" (1953; processed).

[6] Schmeckebier, *Office of Indian Affairs*, p. 191.

posited in the Treasury, and by June 30, 1898, none remained outstanding.[7]

Since 1918 the tribal trust funds deposited in the Treasury have drawn 4 percent simple interest paid from a separate interest account (Appendix Table A-16). In July 1966 the Bureau of Indian Affairs (BIA), in consultation with the tribes, initiated a program for increasing the rate of return by channeling trust funds into approved investments in government securities and commercial bank certificates of deposit, which are secured by bonds or collateral approved by the Treasury Department. The rate of return on these investments has been 5 to 6 percent (Table 7-1), thus increasing by more than $2 million the earnings of participating tribes.

TABLE 7-1

Investment of Indian Trust Funds, Selected Tribes, 1968

Tribe	Type of investment	Amount invested (dollars)	Rate of return[a] (percent)
Tlingit and Haida	Certificates of deposit	5,500,000	6.25
Tlingit and Haida	Treasury bills	1,051,000	5.55
Navajo	Certificates of deposit	39,987,000	5.90
Navajo	Treasury bonds	181,500	4.00
California Indian	Certificates of deposit	27,897,501	5.50
Ute Mountain	Certificates of deposit	10,000,000	6.25
Ute Mountain	Treasury bonds	197,000	4.00
Mescalero Apache	Certificates of deposit	5,933,016	5.75
Creek	Certificates of deposit	4,772,916	5.70
Ute (Utah)	Certificates of deposit	6,925,000	5.65

Source: U.S. Bureau of Indian Affairs, "Investments as of September 30, 1968," unpublished tabulation provided by Assistant Commissioner of Indian Affairs J. Leonard Norwood, November 1968.

a. Weighted average if a tribe held several certificates of deposit, Treasury bills, notes, or bonds with varying interest rates.

In September 1968, Indian tribes had $157 million in tribal funds on deposit in various banks, plus an additional $10 million in Treasury securities. The funds totaled some $300 million; therefore slightly less than one-half of them were still on deposit in the Treasury.

[7] While the trust funds were invested, the government lost several million dollars through embezzlement of bonds and defaults in interest payments. Nearly all of the bonds in default were those of states that seceded from the Union in 1861.

The tribes do not always purchase certificates of deposit in the banks that pay the highest interest rate. For example, one tribe in Montana purchased certificates of deposit paying 5 percent interest at a local bank, although out-of-state banks were paying up to 6¼ percent. The tribal leaders preferred the local bank because they felt that a substantial deposit would make the bank more amenable to extending loans to individual tribal members.

Under the supervision of the BIA and in consultation with private financial analysts, the tribes have begun to invest some of their funds in common stocks and mutual funds. The BIA does not recommend which stocks or mutual funds the tribes should invest in, but it does determine whether the financial advisers used by the tribes are capable. The bureau also holds a veto power over the transfer of moneys from one type of earning asset into common stocks or mutual funds or, if the income has just been realized, its investment in such assets. Not only must all investment projects be approved by the BIA (in practice most tribes leave it to the bureau to invest the money for them), but major expenditures of moneys from the trust funds must be approved by the secretary of the interior.

Although few data are available on the amount of these investments, the Navajo tribe appears to have been the most active. It has established a $10 million educational fund with money invested in common stocks and mutual funds.[8] The proportion of tribal funds invested in such assets will probably increase in the future. Not only is the BIA becoming more amenable to the purchase of stocks and mutual funds by tribes that have the advice of private investment consultants,[9] but the increasing financial sophistication of some tribal leaders is creating a desire that tribal funds earn the highest possible rate of return, which the bureau is making a determined effort to secure.

It seems likely that the funds held in trust for Indians by the BIA will continue to grow but at a slower pace than in the recent past.

[8] Interview with Assistant Commissioner of Indian Affairs J. Leonard Norwood, November 1968.
[9] One could not expect the BIA to buy stocks or mutual funds for the tribes, since this would put the government in the position of selecting some companies as better investment prospects than others.

The docket has closed on the filing of claims with the Indian Claims Commission, and all claims are scheduled to be settled by 1973. Thus, an important source of trust funds will be gone. Income from oil and gas has declined from the peak levels of the late 1950s, but there are still possibilities in this area for some tribes, such as the Standing Rock, Cheyenne River, Rosebud, Brule, Crow Creek, Yankton, and Pine Ridge Sioux and several tribes in the Puget Sound area of Washington State.[10]

Trust fund deposits in the Treasury will probably continue to decline as more moneys are invested in common stocks or certificates of deposit. If the rate of return on these continues to be much higher than the Treasury rate of 4 percent, it is likely that almost no Indian trust funds will be on deposit in the Treasury by the mid-1970s.

Policy Questions

The several hundred million dollars in tribal trust funds under the guardianship of the BIA (via the secretary of the interior) raise questions concerning federal Indian policy. Is the bureau, as legal guardian of these funds (and of most of the land from which a large portion of these funds is derived), following a prudent course in investing tribal money? Should the federal government be in the position of guardian, in effect telling the Indians how to handle their money or other trust property? What use is being made of these funds to assist the economic development of the tribes? Although the BIA is doing a competent job of managing the Indian trust funds, is it serving the long-run interests of the tribes by continuing to do so?

There are several arguments in favor of continuing the BIA's guardianship of Indian trust funds and other property. The low educational level of many tribal officials leaves them without the financial sophistication to make wise investments, and unscrupulous investment consultants could take advantage of them. This argument becomes less valid as the level of education among reservation Indians increases.

[10] Hough, *Indian Resources*, pp. 128–29.

The argument that most tribal leaders prefer guardianship, since it frees them from responsibility for developing an adequate investment program, is essentially valid. It could also be used in favor of a system of voluntary guardianship instead of compulsory guardianship: tribes that wished to have the BIA manage their funds could continue to do so, while those that preferred to manage their own funds could sever the relation.

Not all tribes want the bureau to continue as guardian of the trust funds. Several Indian leaders who were interviewed expressed resentment at the present state of affairs. However, former Commissioner Robert L. Bennett pointed out in an interview that a large number of Indians and tribal leaders (often the most advanced economically) prefer to have outside management of trust property, whether by the BIA or by a bank. Bennett believes that as the tribes continue to progress pressure for continued management of trust funds by outside agencies as an instrument of economic development will increase because they believe the trust is an ideal tool in property management.

Perhaps the most important argument against guardianship is that the money belongs to the tribes and they should be able to control its disposal. Thus, if a tribe (through a special referendum or through elected officials) decided to invest in a project that government officials considered unwise, the responsibility should remain with the Indians. On the other hand, the trust fund is the principal asset of many tribes and dissipation of the funds as a result of bad investments would leave them destitute.[11] Such a financial disaster would be a mistake that many believe the government in good conscience cannot allow the tribes to make.

Nevertheless, the BIA is maintaining a paternalistic role by acting as guardian for the trust funds and other trust property. By continuing to serve as the master banker for the Indian tribes, it is perpetuating a system of dependence. One of the goals of the present commissioner of Indian affairs is to increase the self-sufficiency of the tribes, but this objective cannot be fully accomplished if the bureau functions permanently as guardian of the trust funds. The

[11] Many tribes with little or no current income received settlements from the Indian Claims Commission, which were used to create the tribal trust fund. Other tribes have substantial current income, so possible business losses could be replaced.

BIA might allow tribes to work out their own investment and expenditure plans, under the guidance of private consultants and with little or no interference from the bureau. For tribes that chose to do this the federal government would be guardian in name only.[12]

A final point in assessing federal policy on Indian trust funds is that they must be seriously considered in any discussion of possible termination of the Indian tribes. If a tribe believes it cannot effectively manage its trust funds, the government, for that reason alone, would be committing a serious policy error if it went ahead with termination proceedings without trying to obtain competent nongovernmental investment counseling for the tribe.[13]

Resources and Economic Development

In 1966 the Indian tribes had $58 million of their own funds invested in economic development projects, including $12 million in reservation industry.[14] However, as mentioned earlier, the major portion of Indian financial resources, including current income, is either distributed in per capita payments or deposited in banks or the Treasury. Many tribes have declined to commit a significant portion of their resources to economic and industrial development, for several reasons. The majority of tribal leaders are relatively untrained in business and finance and are understandably reluctant to commit funds to tribal enterprises that would probably have to be managed and operated by non-Indians, very few Indians having had any experience operating a business, especially a large-scale one.[15]

On some reservations the disposition of tribal income or the al-

[12] While it is true that paternalism is minimized if the Bureau of Indian Affairs' authority is used selectively, discretionary limitations of power can often be temporary, particularly if there is frequently a new commissioner of Indian affairs.

[13] The Menominees of Wisconsin and the Klamaths of Oregon, two tribes that were terminated in the 1950s, suffered severe depletion of individual and tribal assets after bureau supervision was ended. This is discussed in greater detail later in this chapter.

[14] Bureau of Indian Affairs, *Indian Affairs* (1967), pp. 12, 13.

[15] Most of the industrial feasibility studies made on Indian reservations in the 1960s recommended that management initially be non-Indian.

location of trust funds is a matter of dispute. One group—for example, older Indians who are not interested in possible long-term gains to be realized from investment in industrial development—may insist on a per capita division of the income among members. If annual incomes are extremely low, pressure for per capita payments will also come from younger members of the tribe. Another group may wish to spend the money on improving human resources through expenditures for higher education and employment-creating and income-earning projects. Often no action is taken, since tribal leaders prefer to postpone a decision until a consensus is reached. The Blackfeet Indians in Montana received a sizable award in 1968 from the Indian Claims Commission, but strife among tribal members about its disposition (many insist on per capita payments) may postpone a decision for years.

Another deterrent to commitment of tribal funds to economic development projects is the rate of return, which may not be any greater than that accruing from investment in Treasury certificates or time deposits. Various industrial feasibility studies undertaken by the Area Redevelopment Administration and the BIA, which indicated low prospective rates of return in many cases, support this point.

However, this position is shortsighted. The biggest problem on an Indian reservation is unemployment; there is a great need to put people to work. For tribes with several million dollars in trust funds or bank deposits, investment in economic development projects with low rates of return would be preferable to the mental and physical degeneration that can result from prolonged unemployment.[16] Long-run human resource development is more important than current short-run interest earnings.

It is not clear whether the BIA should be criticized because only a small portion of tribal trust funds has been used for economic development. If the tribes wish to retain their funds in banks or the Treasury, perhaps the bureau, as guardian, should acquiesce in this decision. However, if the tribes desire to withdraw substantial amounts from the trust funds and are prevented from doing so by

[16] The Navajo tribe has invested millions of dollars in public works projects of doubtful necessity and additional funds in tribal enterprises with low rates of return because, without these expenditures, jobs on some parts of the reservation would be nonexistent.

the BIA's opposition, the bureau might be considered short-sighted. In its goal of obtaining the highest rate of return with a minimum of risk, the bureau appears to have taken a narrow view of its guardianship of tribal funds. Since development projects may deviate from this objective, they are not advocated. There is no evidence that the bureau has ever encouraged the tribes to use their funds for development purposes or, on the other hand, that it has ever prevented one from doing so. In fact, several tribes, such as the Navajo, have used tribal funds in this way.

Tribes with several million dollars in trust funds might be encouraged to use some of them for development in projects planned jointly by the tribe and the BIA. (Thirty-eight tribes have more than $1 million in trust funds, and eight have more than $5 million.) If the tribes failed to show interest, government shortsightedness at least would not have been the stumbling block to development.

PER CAPITA PAYMENTS

The policy of distributing income derived from reservation mineral wealth and awards from the Indian Claims Commission as per capita payments is questionable. Distribution of tribal assets in this way eliminates the opportunity to use the money for long-term reservation development. Since incomes of individual tribal members are frequently very low, personal savings can make little or no contribution to development. Thus the "exogenous" sources of income (minerals or awards by the Indian Claims Commission) are usually the only ones available for this purpose.

Many Indians who are unable to find suitable employment on the reservation are reluctant to leave because they do not wish to miss a per capita payment.[17] From an economic point of view this is irrational. Many tribes give per capita payments to those who have left the reservation, but in any case the economic sacrifice of remaining on the reservation (in terms of income lost) would sel-

[17] Some tribes distribute per capita payments to all persons on the tribal roll as of a specific date in the past, or to their heirs. Others, after the award of the Indian Claims Commission is finally paid, draw up a tribal roll and distribute the money to those who are on the new roll.

dom be made up by a single per capita payment, which rarely exceeds $3,000.

Because reservation Indians are accustomed to poverty and are not well educated, many of them are unable to manage large sums of money effectively. This problem is made worse by the high-pressure salesmanship of non-Indian merchants who flock to the reservation as soon as a large per capita distribution is made. For example, a few Osage Indians in Oklahoma purchased a new car each time there was a per capita distribution (every three months), although others have used their payments for housing and education.

On the other hand, if the majority of tribal members prefer per capita payments, should not this be a guide to policy? Congress has been especially sympathetic to this view and has usually permitted per capita distribution of Indian Claims Commission awards if the majority of tribal members favor them. Similarly, the secretary of the interior has permitted such payments from current mineral income.

While the poverty of the reservation Indian creates in him a strong desire for immediate realization of the benefits of a Claims Commission award or other income, should not the interests of future generations also be considered? In recognition of future needs, it might be a wise policy to distribute in per capita payments only a portion of a Claims Commission award or mineral income.

NAVAJO PROJECTS

The Navajos have used more tribal income (supplemented by government loans and grants) for development purposes than any other tribe. Theirs is an excellent example of government-Indian cooperation without federal domination, which could serve as a model to other tribes with substantial current income. The tribe's principal income—$80 million received from oil and gas—has been used to provide jobs for thousands of Navajos as well as to develop Navajo-owned enterprises. Navajo Forest Products Industries, a tribal enterprise, provided 500 permanent jobs in 1966 and had a payroll of $1.2 million, primarily at a new $6.5 million lumber mill.[18] One of the new facilities at the mill, a cut-stock plant, provides 80 jobs for Indian workers.

[18] Hough, *Indian Resources*, pp. 152–53.

In 1959 the tribal council decided to buy electricity from the town of Farmington, New Mexico, for distribution by a tribal utility system, and appropriated $450,000 to construct the transmission lines needed to serve the area of Shiprock, New Mexico. Service began in late 1960. Plans called for complete electrification of the reservation during the decade 1960–70, at a cost of an additional $6.6 million. Water and sewer systems were constructed and maintained at tribal expense to serve the areas of Window Rock, Tohatchi, and Tuba City, Arizona. In 1961 the tribe appropriated $390,000 to construct natural gas lines to serve the Window Rock–Fort Defiance–Navajo area.[19]

The Navajos have taken the initiative in training their people in modern agricultural techniques. The Navajo Training Farm at Shiprock provides a two-year course in scientific farming. It has been estimated that the total tribal investment in each farmer is $70,000 to $90,000 by the time he is established on his own farm and harvests his first crop. This investment includes a house and 120 acres served by water from the Navajo irrigation project, plus a $25,000 loan to the farmer for equipment.[20] The goal is eventually to train 1,000 farmers at a total cost of $60 million.

The tribe has also taken steps to encourage industrial development. In 1956 the Babyline Furniture Company of Gamerco, New Mexico, established a plant on the reservation. This factory, which received a $200,000 subsidy from the Navajo tribe, employs about forty workers.[21]

A new industrial park was developed by the Navajo tribe at Fort Defiance, Arizona, with an Economic Development Administration grant of $114,480, plus a small loan. The first plant located there is operated by General Dynamics Corporation and employs 200 Navajos. The building and much of the equipment was provided by the tribe at a cost of $820,000.[22]

Several tourist facilities are owned by the tribe and operated by non-Indian lessees. The most elaborate is the Monument Valley Inn at Kayenta, Arizona, with swimming pool, lounge, gift shop,

[19] Robert W. Young (comp.), *The Navajo Yearbook* (Window Rock, Ariz.: Navajo Agency, 1961), pp. 195–96.
[20] Hough, *Indian Resources,* pp. 87–88.
[21] Young, *Navajo Yearbook,* p. 192.
[22] Hough, *Indian Resources,* p. 200.

and an eighty-unit motel. The tribe also has lodges at Window Rock and Shiprock.

The tribe has established a $10 million fund to be used for the higher education of Navajos.

Although the Navajos have used their income for economic development purposes, future funding requirements to produce a viable reservation economy seem in excess of present trust fund balances ($70 million) plus current income ($6 to $10 million).[23] To complete the irrigation project by 1981 will require $140 million,[24] and to bring the present road system up to an adequate standard by 1985 will require an estimated $200 million. An additional $50 million may be needed to fund the farm training project. Thus, in spite of the Navajos' willingness to devote income and trust funds to development purposes, other sources of capital will be needed to sustain reservation development.

TRIBES WITH MEAGER RESOURCES

Other tribes with trust funds smaller than the Navajos' (Appendix Table A-17) are forced to rely on other sources of development capital. The situation of the Pine Ridge Sioux in South Dakota is an example. This tribe of 11,000 members is one of the poorest. The median family income in 1964 was $1,335, one-half of the male labor force was unemployed, and one-third of reservation families had to depend on some form of welfare assistance during the year.[25]

This tribe, with only $58,000 in trust fund balances and hardly enough current income to pay tribal officials, is totally dependent on outside sources of development funding. The Wright & McGill fishhook snelling plant, the only sizable factory located on the reser-

[23] On a per capita basis the Navajo trust funds amount to a relatively modest $800.

[24] Bureau of Indian Affairs, "Indian Irrigation Projects" (July 1967; processed), Table F.

[25] Bureau of Indian Affairs, "Selected Data on Indian Reservations Eligible for Designation under Public Works and Economic Development Act" (December 1966; processed); Human Sciences Research, Inc., "A Comprehensive Evaluation of OEO Community Action Programs on Six Selected American Indian Reservations" (McLean, Va.: HSR, September 1966; processed), p. 168.

vation, closed permanently in mid-1968. Feasibility studies show that the reservation is a poor location for industry. Even if the inadequate infrastructure were improved, the reservation would remain a poor industrial site simply because it is too far from potential markets.

Two possible avenues of development for the Pine Ridge Reservation are greater participation in, and development of, reservation agriculture, and the discovery of minerals. The oil and gas potential is judged good by geologists, but no important discoveries have yet been made.

While 90 percent of the reservation land is suitable for grazing, less than 50 percent is used by the Indians themselves. The remainder has been sold or leased to non-Indians. The scanty Indian participation in cattle ranching (only about fifty families derive an adequate income from ranching) is partly due to lack of training. Vocational agriculture is no longer taught in bureau schools, and few Indians have an opportunity to acquire the skills needed to operate an economically sized family farm. Nor are the inhabitants able to raise enough capital to develop herds of an economic size—350 cattle. A 1959 study indicates that currently about 40 percent of all families on this reservation could be accommodated on economically sized ranches (net income $3,000 a year) for an investment of $18 million in managerial training, cattle, irrigation, and land consolidation.[26]

Even with an expanded agricultural program, a large portion of the adult tribal members would remain unemployed or underemployed. Thus opportunities for training and relocation should be pursued. However, to raise the economic levels of those Indians wishing to remain on the reservation, the government would have to become the employer of last resort. It is estimated that over a ten-year period $20 million would be needed to bring reservation roads up to an adequate level and $3 million to bring electricity to all sections of the reservation. The maximum possible use of Indian labor in these and other development projects would sig-

[26] Peter P. Dorner, "The Economic Position of the American Indians: Their Resources and Potential for Development" (Ph.D. dissertation, Harvard University, 1959), pp. 157–58.

nificantly diminish the reservation unemployment rate, at least for the intermediate future.

THE CROW FAMILY PLAN

One of the more enlightened distributions of an award from the Indian Claims Commission was made by the Crow tribe in Montana. A total of $10,242,985 was awarded to the tribe in 1961, with $9,238,500 remaining after attorneys' fees were deducted. The Crow Tribal Council, with the approval of the secretary of the interior, allocated the money as shown in Table 7-2, assigning nearly 50 percent to members of tribal families.[27]

TABLE 7-2

Allocation of Land Compensation Funds by Crow Tribe, under the Family Plan Program, 1962

Type of allocation	Amount (thousands of dollars)	Percentage
Per capita payment (winter relief measure)	1,194	12.9
Family plan, $1,000 to each enrolled Crow	4,336	46.9
Tribal land purchase plan	1,000	10.8
Expansion of tribal credit program	275	3.0
Competent lease loans	1,000	10.8
Economic development of Crow tribe	1,000	10.8
Educational purposes	200	2.2
Law and order activity	100	1.1
Construction of tribal headquarters	120	1.3
Unobligated funds as a reserve	14	0.2
Total	9,238	100.0

Source: Bureau of Indian Affairs, Missouri River Basin Investigations Project, "Family Plan Program, Crow Reservation, Montana" (May 1967; processed), p. 1. Figures are rounded and may not add to totals.

Under the plan, each family received an average of $3,019, with the requirement that money be spent only for capital goods or durable consumer goods, or for personal improvement through, for example, expenditures on health and education. Each family was

[27] See Bureau of Indian Affairs, Missouri River Basin Investigations Project, "Family Plan Program, Crow Reservation, Montana" (May 1967; processed), pp. 1–3.

required to submit a detailed proposal for its use of family plan funds to the Bureau of Indian Affairs before moneys could be released. Funds could not be used for automobiles, vacations, daily living expenses, or to pay debts incurred before approval of the plan.

Virtually all of the expenditures were limited to goods permitted under the plan. Four-fifths of the funds were used for durable consumer goods, such as additions to or renovation of houses, household furnishings, and water and sanitation facilities. Occupancy decreased by 40 percent, from an average of 2 persons per room to 1.2 persons. Most of the remaining outlay was for capital goods, purchased mainly by ranchers and including livestock, machinery, and equipment. A relatively small part of the money was spent for education, health, medical, and other personal improvement purposes. From all indications this program worked well and could be emulated where there is strong pressure for per capita payments. It should be noted that a few families evaded the intent of the plan by purchasing durable goods and then, after a short period, selling them and using the money for unapproved purposes.

Individual Money Problems

The Bureau of Indian Affairs maintains individual bank accounts on behalf of some 60,000 reservation Indians. In 1968 these accounts held about $50 million (they totaled $45 million in 1926 and $67 million in 1944).[28] In recent years the BIA has invested this money as it does tribal trust funds, in certificates of deposit paying 5 to 6¼ percent annual interest and in U.S. Treasury securities.

The accounts are of five kinds. By far the most numerous are unsupervised individual accounts containing unearned income assigned by the Indians to the BIA from various sources—per capita payments, from either an Indian Claims Commission award or current tribal income; income from the lease or sale of individually

[28] Bureau of Indian Affairs, "Amount of Tribal Funds Deposited in Banks, August 30, 1968" (unpublished tabulation); Schmeckebier, *Office of Indian Affairs*, p. 315; *Remove Restrictions on Indian Property*, Hearings before the Subcommittee of the Senate Committee on Indian Affairs, 78 Cong. 2 sess. (1944), p. 54.

owned land; and proceeds of estates. Income from other sources usually cannot be accepted. The depositors in this category choose voluntarily to use BIA facilities because few commercial banks operate on the reservations and because the BIA encourages the practice. (Even Indians who have left the reservation are discouraged from investing unearned income themselves because the BIA fears they would lose it.)[29]

But a minority of the depositors are not legally free to spend or save their unearned income as they wish. For them there are four classes of supervised accounts. The first and largest is that of the so-called restricted Indians, persons who, because of a lack of education or intelligence, are deemed by the BIA to be incompetent to manage their financial affairs. They receive either a monthly or a quarterly stipend (from current income or an individual account) to cover living expenses for themselves and their families. The purchase of a durable item such as a house, a car, or land by a restricted Indian is a complicated procedure:

When automobiles are purchased under supervision, the applicant is furnished an individual money purchase order for delivery to the dealer. Prior to payment the dealer is required to file with the Agency the following: a certificate executed by the county clerk . . . showing there are no liens or encumbrances against the automobile; a bill of sale vesting title to the automobile in the United States in trust for the individual; a state motor vehicle registration certificate, showing title in the United States in trust for the individual; a policy of complete insurance coverage on the automobile; and the purchase order executed by the Indian acknowledging receipt of the car and authorizing payment from his account. Upon receipt of these documents, the Agency files the bill of sale with the county clerk for recording and mails a check to the dealer.[30]

The number of restricted Indians has declined greatly in recent years; in 1944 there were 37,000 in Oklahoma alone; in 1968 there were only 6,000 in the entire United States.[31] Most of them are full-blooded and more than fifty years of age. The BIA has no

[29] Interview with Frank Limpouch, chief, Finance Section, Bureau of Indian Affairs, January 1969.

[30] Bureau of Indian Affairs, "The Osage People and Their Trust Property," pp. xxxiv–xxxv.

[31] Data for 1944 from *Remove Restrictions on Indian Property*, Hearings, p. 8. Data for 1968 from interview with Frank Limpouch, January 1969.

authority to control the earnings of a restricted Indian; its control is limited to the income from the sources listed above.

The second class of supervised accounts is that of Indians who, while not held legally incompetent (restricted), are considered by the Division of Social Services of the local BIA office to be unable or unwilling to spend their income for the benefit of themselves or their families. These persons, who squander their money on liquor, gambling, or luxuries, may have their savings and expenditures supervised. For example, an Indian who receives $800 a month by leasing his lands may be allowed to spend only $400 a month, the other $400 being deposited in his individual account. No clear guidelines determine when a legally competent Indian requires the supervision of the Division of Social Services to prevent wasteful expenditures. Thus, the rules on what patterns of conduct indicate a need for supervision vary from reservation to reservation.

The third class of supervised accounts is that of minors. It has been bureau policy to deposit funds belonging to minors in supervised accounts whether the parents are competent or not. As a rule these funds are paid only to those parents who are appointed legal guardians, but an exception is made if the parent spends the money for the benefit of the minor. Such expenditures are restricted to such purposes as education, medical care, or investments in livestock and other property.[32]

A final class of supervised accounts is that of Indians who voluntarily request that their expenditures as well as their savings from the income sources listed above be supervised. These persons, in consultation with the bureau's Division of Social Services, work out a monthly or bimonthly budget and receive a check to cover their needs. This arrangement permits the Indian to save regularly, but also eliminates his responsibility for the management of his property.

The bureau's creation and handling of individual Indian accounts raise two basic questions. Should the government assume responsibility for investing $50 million in private funds? And should the government supervise the expenditures of certain Indians? If so, what are the proper limits?

The policy of discouraging individual Indians from investing

[32] These restrictions do not apply to the earnings of minors.

their own money is paternalistic and insulting. Many well-edu-
cated reservation Indians could manage their funds and should be
encouraged to do so. Since the BIA has recently shown a willingness to permit tribes to seek the advice of private investment consultants, it is inconsistent to continue to discourage Indians from
making their own investments. While some individuals might
make bad investments, in the long run most Indians would become
more responsible managers of their money. The experience of
opening a savings or checking account, of making regular deposits
and withdrawals, and perhaps of obtaining loans through a bank
would be preferable to having the government perform banking
and investment services.

No doubt the elimination of unsupervised individual accounts
would be bitterly resented by many Indians. They are accustomed
to going to the agency to receive checks or inquire about other
money-related matters. For some, this event is a social occasion—
an opportunity to meet their friends from other parts of the
reservation.

One difficulty of encouraging Indians to invest their unearned
income themselves is the dearth of banks or financial institutions
on very isolated reservations. Many of them would have to drive a
great distance from the reservation to deposit or invest funds.
However, if the BIA gave up its responsibility for investing the
funds, private financial institutions might find it worthwhile to
locate on the reservations.[33]

The second question concerns the four classes of supervised accounts enumerated above. Are these justifiable? Can an American
citizen be told by the federal government how to spend his own
money? The answer definitely is yes. The Supreme Court has
held that "citizenship is not incompatible with tribal existence or
continued guardianship, and so may be conferred without completely emancipating the Indians or placing them beyond the
reach of Congressional regulations adopted for their protection."[34]

This decision is not in conflict with the general application of

[33] Most of the individual Indian money is placed in banks in metropolitan areas
located some distance from the reservation.

[34] United States v. Nice, 241 U.S. 598 (1916), cited in The Problem of Indian
Administration, Report of a Survey made at the request of Honorable Hubert
Work, Secretary of the Interior, and submitted to him, Feb. 21, 1928 (Johns Hop-
kins Press for Institute for Government Research, 1928), p. 753.

the law. Among non-Indians, citizenship does not preclude guardianship, nor does it give unlimited control over property. Although minor children are citizens, they are not able to dispose of property or make contracts. Some adult citizens are deprived of control of their property for a variety of reasons, usually following court action. "The status of the restricted citizen Indian with respect to his property secured through the government is like that of a citizen child with respect to his, except that under existing law the Indian may be declared competent and thereby be given full control."[35]

While it may be justifiable to supervise the property of restricted Indians for their own protection, the BIA should encourage them, whenever possible, to work toward unrestricted status. In some cases attending adult education courses would suffice; in others, simply demonstrating to a competency board the individual's ability to handle his own affairs would be enough. It seems vitally important that no one be kept in a restricted status unnecessarily.[36]

While one may agree that Indians who are legally incompetent need close supervision of their property, does this justify supervision of a person who, while legally competent, dissipates his funds on drinking and gambling or on spending sprees? It can be argued that the bureau, as guardian of these funds, not only must seek to obtain the highest rate of return on their investment, but must seek to prevent their dissipation. By supervising a man's expenditures of unearned income, the government is acting in the interest of his family. But if an Indian is legally competent, does he not have the right to spend the money as he wishes even if his choices appear foolish to others? An Indian living off the reservation who received unearned income could squander it far from the watchful eyes of the bureau's welfare employees. Ideally, this type of restriction should be temporary and combined with counseling and rehabilitation, if alcoholism or a similar diffi-

[35] *The Problem of Indian Administration*, p. 754.

[36] When Commissioner Robert L. Bennett took office in 1966, he made a determined effort to have the number of supervised Indian money accounts reduced. As a result, the number of such accounts (belonging mainly to restricted Indians) declined by one-third between 1966 and 1968. In the long run the question whether the property of the so-called restricted Indian should be supervised is academic, since in thirty years there will be very few restricted Indians.

culty is the problem. In any event, the supervision should be minimal, and clear guidelines should be established to determine when a legally competent Indian needs supervision of his unearned income.

Finally, the bureau should discourage those who, while legally competent and reasonably able to manage their money, prefer to give the responsibility to the agency. Although they may need counseling on how to manage their funds (or adult education courses that would serve the same end), it seems blatantly paternalistic for the bureau to handle their money problems for them.

Termination

Perhaps the most controversial issue on the reservations for two decades has been termination—"the legal process of depriving an Indian of his Indian-ness, divesting him of all of his inherited treaty rights, usually in exchange for a cash settlement representing his per capita share of his tribe's liquidated assets."[37]

Advocates of termination argue that past federal support of the reservations has kept the Indian in a dependent wardship status. A leading proponent of termination has said:

Secluded reservation life is a deterrent to the Indian, keeping him apart in ways far beyond the purely geographic. . . . Self-reliance is basic to the whole Indian-freedom program. Through our national historic development the Indian was forced into a dependent position with the federal government . . . tending to sublimate his natural qualities of self-reliance, courage, discipline, resourcefulness, confidence, and faith in the future. . . . But self-reliance demands opportunity to grow. The Indian must be given the conditions under which . . . self-reliance can be wholeheartedly regenerated.[38]

The other principal argument advanced by those who favor termination is that it would result in a substantial saving for the federal government. Recognizing that treaties obligate the government to provide health, education, and other specified assis-

[37] Hough, *Indian Resources*, pp. 160–61.

[38] Arthur V. Watkins, "Termination of Federal Supervision: The Removal of Restrictions over Indian Property and Person," in George E. Simpson and J. Milton Yinger (eds.), *American Indians and American Life, Annals of the American Academy of Political and Social Science*, Vol. 311 (May 1957), p. 51.

tance, some advocates of termination contend that the government would save money by "paying off" Indians who could be persuaded to accept a cash settlement in exchange for giving up their rights under the old treaties.

Opponents of termination point to the Indians' desire to keep reservation lands intact, to preserve the reservation area not merely as real estate but as a homeland and refuge. An Indian takes pride in belonging to a specific tribe. With termination, the tribe lacking common property would probably break up and lose its identity. Moreover, as mentioned earlier, some Indian lands are rich in as yet undeveloped resources. A forced sale would result in liquidation of the assets for a fraction of their potential value. Since the Indians' development of their own resources is still in the early stages, it is argued that now "is a poor time to disrupt a long-suffering people who have made a good beginning at last."[39] Finally, the poverty of most reservation Indian families is poignant evidence that the health, education, and welfare benefits guaranteed by the federal government under existing laws and treaties should be continued.

While, a priori, there appear to be defensible arguments on both sides of the termination issue, the results of termination have been disastrous for the individual members of the major tribes that have been terminated.

In 1953, the Congress resolved that,

at the earliest possible time, all of the Indian tribes and the individual members thereof located within the States of California, Florida, Iowa, New York, and Texas, and all of the following named Indian tribes and individual members thereof, should be freed from Federal supervision and control and from all disabilities and limitations specially applicable to Indians: The Flathead Tribe of Montana, the Klamath Tribe of Oregon, the Menominee Tribe of Wisconsin, the Osage Tribe of Oklahoma, the Potowatamie Tribe of Kansas and Nebraska, and those members of the Chippewa Tribe who are on the Turtle Mountain Reservation, North Dakota. . . . the Secretary of the Interior should examine all existing legislation dealing with such Indians, and treaties . . . [with] each such tribe, and report to Congress . . . not later than January 1, 1954, his recommendations . . . to accomplish the purposes of this resolution.[40]

[39] Hough, *Indian Resources*, p. 162.
[40] H. Con. Res. 108, *Congressional Record*, Vol. 99, Pt. 8, 83 Cong. 1 sess. (1953), p. 10933.

Bills were enacted in 1954 to terminate federal supervision of six groups: the Menominee tribe, the Klamath tribe, miscellaneous small tribes and bands of western Oregon, the Alabama and Coushatta Indians of Texas, the Utes of Utah, and the Paiute of Utah.[41]

The Paiute, a small tribe of 200 members, were among the first to be terminated, with termination commencing on February 28, 1957.[42] The tribe was not competent to meet the situation. Within a short time responsibility for the administration of reservation land was transferred from the Bureau of Indian Affairs to a bank in Salt Lake City, 160 miles from the reservation. The Indians had difficulty getting to the bank and discussing their problems with the trust officer. An attorney appointed by the bank and paid with tribal funds proved unsatisfactory. Without tribal consent, the trustee leased tribal lands to a non-Indian cattleman at one-fifth the going price per head. In addition, the land was overgrazed. Extra charges connected with public education placed additional burdens on the Paiutes. Each child was required to pay $15 a year to the school activity fund as well as $1 a week for school lunches. Many Paiute children went home for lunch as they had no money.[43] Health services formerly provided free of charge by the Public Health Service became a burden. Welfare payments and old-age assistance were difficult to obtain from state agencies because most Paiutes had no birth certificates and could not prove their age.

The Klamath Termination Act gave members of that tribe a choice of taking a pro rata share of the assets or keeping the property in one block held in trust for the group. The tribe held an election to decide what to do with the assets; 1,660 members voted for a per capita distribution while 84 voted to continue as a group.[44] The members receiving per capita shares obtained $44,000 each, or 78 percent of the entire property. While some used the money wisely, others dissipated their funds in spending sprees and ended up on state relief rolls. The 84 who voted to pool their assets and

[41] Public Laws 83-399, 83-587, 83-588, 83-627, 83-671, and 83-762.

[42] William A. Brophy and Sophie D. Aberle (comps.), *The Indian: America's Unfinished Business* (University of Oklahoma Press, 1966), p. 194. Because of lack of education, low income, poor knowledge of English, and lack of understanding of financial transactions, this tribe was not ready for termination. This is confirmed by subsequent experience.

[43] When the BIA operated schools for the tribal members, lunches were provided free of charge.

[44] Brophy and Aberle, *The Indian*, p. 196.

389 others who did not take part in the election (473 in all) were organized as a nonprofit trusteeship under state law.[45] The assets of the trust are administered by a Portland, Oregon, bank. The trust operates on a paternalistic basis. Its aims are to produce the maximum income for the beneficiaries, but it does not concern itself with helping the Indians learn how to handle their own property. Since the bank is operating in a manner similar to the BIA, the traditional Indian hostility toward BIA is now aimed at the bank. For example, the bank's failure to hire Indians to manage the forest or cattle herds owned by the trust has caused resentment, especially among unemployed Indians.[46]

The Menominee Indians in Wisconsin voted for termination because the tribe was informed that Congress would act on a pending bill for a per capita payment of $1,500 from some $10 million of tribal funds on deposit in the Treasury only if the members accepted termination. After termination, they received a per capita payment of $778.[47] When termination became effective in 1961, it was obvious that the economic condition of these "ex-Indians" did not justify the action. One-half of the labor force was unemployed and one out of six Menominees was on relief, compared with one person in forty for the state as a whole.[48] After termination the one small tribally operated Catholic hospital was closed because it could not meet state standards, and hospital care was no longer available. With bureau services eliminated, most Menominees became more deeply mired in poverty than ever. The Menominees' original treaty with the federal government gave the tribe hunting and fishing rights on the reservation in perpetuity. Now that they must obey Wisconsin's fish and game laws, poor families who could once eat fish and venison go hungry during the closed seasons, while sportsmen deplete these food resources.

Since the late 1950s the pressure for termination has subsided, but the termination resolution has not been rescinded. As a result many Indian leaders still have a profound fear of termination. One of the recommendations from a series of meetings held in late 1966

---

[45] *Ibid.,* pp. 197–98.
[46] The bank argues that Indian employees have not been as efficient as non-Indians.
[47] Brophy and Aberle, *The Indian,* pp. 201–02, 206–07.
[48] Hough, *Indian Resources,* pp. 166–68.

by the commissioner of Indian affairs with tribal leaders in nine separate areas expressed "opposition to termination legislation of any sort" and urged that "termination take place only with the consent of the group involved."[49]

One kind of termination is not repugnant to those who believe Indians should be allowed to choose their own goals: ". . . the termination of Indian status of a tribe when its members have reached a point of competence at which they find that they will do better on their own, with full freedom to handle or dispose of their assets, than under established protections and restrictions."[50]

Although most persons familiar with the social and economic problems of reservation Indians do not advocate the prompt withdrawal of federal Indian programs, many of them contend that states should assume increased responsibility. President John F. Kennedy's 1961 Task Force on Indian Affairs recommended—and the BIA has the authority to effect—a gradual transfer of jurisdiction to states following agreements reached among tribes, the United States, and the states where reservations are located.[51] However, such action is not practical at present. Such a transfer would require state legislatures to enact laws providing for the integration of reservations into the structure of government. Many Indian leaders oppose transferring jurisdiction to states unless Indian consent is obtained through tribal elections and the states are willing to provide adequate services.

Since the 1920s and 1930s the federal government has attempted to transfer Indian services to states but has been unsuccessful. The legislatures of California, Nevada, and Wisconsin, when faced with the issue, have rejected state responsibility. The legislatures of New Mexico, Arizona, North Dakota, and Montana, by requesting additional federal aid for Indians, have indicated that they are not interested in assuming this burden.[52]

[49] Deward E. Walker, Jr., "An Examination of American Indian Reaction to Proposals of the Commissioner of Indian Affairs for General Legislation, 1967," *Northwest Anthropological Research Notes*, Vol. 1 (Fall 1967), Pt. 2, p. 168.

[50] Oliver La Farge, "Termination of Federal Supervision: Disintegration and the American Indians," in Simpson and Yinger (eds.), *American Indians and American Life*, p. 44.

[51] See Brophy and Aberle, *The Indian*, p. 131.

[52] *Ibid.*, p. 132.

While states do not appear willing to undertake a larger share of the responsibility for Indians, the tribes themselves are eager for increased responsibility. Some tribes, notably the Navajo, are providing services to their own people under contracts with the BIA. For other tribes, to begin performing services traditionally furnished by the BIA should be a goal of the highest priority, but it should not be attained by pressure on the tribes from the federal government.

CHAPTER VIII

Welfare Services

Because the annual incomes of most reservation Indian families are low, meager (or in some cases nonexistent) earnings are often supplemented by welfare payments from the Bureau of Indian Affairs (BIA) or state public assistance agencies. Indians may also receive other such transfer payments as unemployment compensation and social security benefits, subject to the same eligibility requirements as non-Indians.

Welfare Payments

The bulk of Indian public assistance comes from state programs, supplemented by the BIA, usually in the form of general assistance payments. During fiscal year 1968, this kind of assistance was given to an average of 21,000 Indians a month, with a peak of 28,900 in March.[1] Total expenditures were $0.7 million, or approximately $140 per case per month.[2] (Appendix Table A-21 shows the schedule of general assistance payments provided by BIA on the assumption of no other income.) The BIA states its policy on general assistance in these words:

When resources are unavailable, or are insufficient, and assistance from other public sources is not available, then general assistance will be furnished to meet unmet living needs or to supplement available re-

[1] During 1968 a total of 53,769 persons received general assistance. U.S. Bureau of Indian Affairs, "Social Services Program" (1969; processed), and memorandum from Bureau of Indian Affairs, Division of Social Services.

[2] This is much higher than the 1968 average of $90 per case under state general assistance programs. However, non-Indians are eligible for payments under other

sources. . . . Indians for whom general assistance is actually availabl\
from a state, county or local public jurisdiction are not eligible for
general assistance from the Bureau.[3]

The number of Indians receiving BIA general assistance has increased rapidly, doubling from 1962 to 1968, not because of a wors-
ening economic situation on the reservations but because a higher
proportion of eligible Indians have been applying for benefits.[4]

The BIA bears an important share of the relief load for several
reasons. Some states have refused to provide aid to dependent children if there is an able-bodied man in the household; many reservation families are headed by an unemployed male and hence are
ineligible for benefits. A few states with large Indian populations
have been very reluctant to assist them because Indian trust property is exempt from state taxes (although personal income is not)
and because the feeling persists that the federal government will
provide aid if the states do not. Even in states that do provide public assistance to Indians, the certification procedure is often slow
and the BIA must provide interim assistance until the state has completed the necessary investigation.

Despite the unwillingness of a few states to give Indians public
assistance on the same basis as non-Indians, state programs furnish
a preponderance of welfare assistance (Table 8-1). During June
1968 nearly 64,000 reservation Indians (about 75 percent of the
total given assistance) received state public assistance, compared
with about 21,000 who received BIA general assistance payments.
The total costs of state assistance programs were estimated at $2.8
million,[5] or four times the BIA expenditure of $0.7 million.

Increases in the number of Indians receiving public assistance, as
shown in the table, have come about in two ways. First, the num-

programs, such as old-age assistance or aid to dependent children, for which many
reservation Indians cannot qualify.

[3] Bureau of Indian Affairs, "General Assistance and Social Services" (1965; processed).

Some states limit the aid provided under categorical assistance programs. If
these limitations work a hardship on the Indian recipient, the BIA can supplement
the public assistance payments.

[4] Interview, Bureau of Indian Affairs, Division of Social Services, October 1969.

[5] The estimate of $2.8 million was derived from data in U.S. Bureau of the Cen-
sus, *Statistical Abstract of the United States: 1969*, p. 299, and population data from
Bureau of Indian Affairs, Office of Program Coordination, "Estimates of the Indian

TABLE 8-1

State Public Assistance to Indians Living on Reservations,
by Category, 1965–68

Category	Number of persons				Percentage increase, 1965–68
	1965	1966	1967	1968	
Old-age assistance	7,823	9,000	10,192	9,791	25
Aid to the blind	627	699	719	670	7
Aid to dependent children	34,520	39,570	45,828	49,379	43
Aid to the permanently and totally disabled	2,285	3,119	3,924	4,058	78
Total	47,555ᵃ	53,862ᵃ	60,663	63,898	34

Source: U.S. Bureau of Indian Affairs, "Public Assistance to Indians Living on Reservations" (1965, 1966, 1967, 1968; unpublished). Figures are for the month of June in each year.
a. Total includes aid to aged, blind, and disabled in New Mexico (2,300 in 1965 and 1,474 in 1966) for which a breakdown among the categories is not available.

ber of Indians applying for assistance has increased markedly in recent years. Second, a number of states with sizable Indian populations have become more receptive to meeting Indian needs. In June 1968 some 20 percent of the reservation Indian population was receiving welfare payments—about four times the percentage of non-Indians.[6]

Other Transfer Payments

No data are available on the other kinds of transfer payments to Indians, such as social security, unemployment compensation, and veterans' benefits.[7] However, some qualitative statements can be

Population Served by the Bureau of Indian Affairs: September 1968" (March 1969; processed). The estimates are based on the assumption that the average state categorical assistance payment to an Indian is the same as that to a non-Indian. Average state payments are obtained by weighting the individual state payments for the particular assistance category by the number of Indians in that state. The weighted average payment per case is multiplied by the number of cases (see source to Table 8-1) to obtain total cost for each benefit category. By adding the costs for the four types of public assistance, an estimate of total costs is obtained.
[6] Data for non-Indians from *Statistical Abstract: 1969*, p. 296.
[7] During 1970 the BIA, with the cooperation of the Social Security Administration, received for the first time data on the amount of social security payments to reservation Indians. This data is not yet available.

made about the level of these payments. Probably few reservation Indians receive unemployment insurance. Much reservation employment is seasonal, and many workers are not employed long enough to be eligible for benefits. Also, many Indians still earn their living in agriculture or as nonagricultural laborers, occupations generally not covered by unemployment compensation.

The average level of social security payments to reservation Indians over sixty-five is probably far lower than for non-Indians. Most elderly Indians had agricultural occupations and did not make contributions to the social security system. Others, although they were in covered employment, received such meager earnings that their social security payments are minimal.[8]

About 25,000 Indians served in the armed forces during the Second World War, and thousands more served in Korea and Vietnam. They are eligible for veterans' benefits and should be receiving them at the same average level as non-Indians.

Because of isolation and their low level of schooling, however, Indians may be unaware of veterans' and social security benefits to which they are entitled. Only if an Indian applies for welfare is a conscious effort made by the BIA to obtain benefits that should be coming to him from other programs.

Office of Economic Opportunity Programs

The goals of Indian community action programs under the Office of Economic Opportunity (OEO) are not very different from those of programs operated in non-Indian poverty areas; that is, development of remedial programs, more efficient delivery of health, legal, and other services to those in need, and—of greatest importance—enhancement of the beneficiaries' economic status.

Tribal governments provide an efficient vehicle through which to create community action agencies (CAAs), and Indian tribes were quick to establish them. Tribal councils often designated

[8] Amendments to the Social Security Act in 1965 and later years provide payments to noninsured persons over seventy-two ($46 for an individual and $69 for a husband and wife if both are eligible) who reached that age before 1968 or have three quarters of coverage for each year after 1966 and before the age of seventy-two.

themselves as the CAA boards so that separate boards were seldom chosen by the tribal members.

Although the tribes availed themselves of OEO programs, many Indians were skeptical of the Economic Opportunity Act. After years of exposure to federal programs, some leaders assumed that this was "just another program," which would be terminated when the federal government decided to restrict outlays on social welfare.[9] However, the fact that Indians were permitted to initiate projects themselves, instead of having them developed by outsiders (such as the BIA or the Public Health Service), raised their expectations about OEO. The tribes' lack of experience in drafting project proposals and the severe time constraints imposed by the Washington headquarters of OEO resulted in the rewriting of many proposals and the rejection of others for lack of requisite supporting documents.

To facilitate the initiation of reservation-based OEO programs, as well as to provide assistance in writing proposals and choosing among alternative programs, OEO in 1965 created a consortium of three state universities in Utah, South Dakota, and Arizona. This step was a realistic attempt to bring the benefits of the Economic Opportunity Act to members of an ethnic group whose limited education and inexperience made it very difficult for them to conform to the bureaucratic procedures required for obtaining OEO programs.

By June 30, 1968, there were 63 CAAs serving 129 reservations where 80 percent of the reservation Indians lived (some CAAs served several reservations).[10] The programs included provision of legal services, Neighborhood Youth Corps (operated in the same manner as for non-Indians), recreational activities and field trips, adult education, Head Start, and a number of job-training programs.

The appropriations for Indian OEO programs have increased rapidly (Table 8-2). Grants for projects initiated locally (as op-

---

[9] On some reservations, inhabitants could not distinguish between OEO and BIA programs. For example, on the Papago Reservation, the OEO community action program was similar to the BIA ten-year development program, and considerable confusion resulted.

[10] Sar A. Levitan, *The Great Society's Poor Law: A New Approach to Poverty* (Johns Hopkins Press, 1969), p. 266.

TABLE 8-2

OEO Community Action Obligations for Indian Reservations, by Program, Fiscal Years 1965–68

(*In millions of dollars*)

Program	1965	1966	1967	1968
Local initiative	3.6	10.5	11.7	14.4
Community organization	—	—	3.7	3.6
Home improvement	—	—	3.6	4.3
Educational development	n.a.	n.a.	2.2	2.5
Health	—	—	1.0	0.9
Special programs	—	—	0.7	2.4
Economic development	—	—	0.5	0.7
National emphasis	—	1.5	8.4	7.9
Head Start	—	1.5	7.7	6.7
Comprehensive health centers	—	—	0.4	0.5
Legal services	—	—	0.3	0.7
Total	3.6	12.0	20.1	22.3

Source: Sar A. Levitan, *The Great Society's Poor Law: A New Approach to Poverty* (Johns Hopkins Press, 1969), p. 267.
n.a. Not available.

posed to such nationwide programs as Head Start) accounted for 65 percent of all OEO reservation funding from 1965 to 1968. Among the national emphasis programs, Head Start received the bulk of the funds; expenditures for this program were larger than for any other. All reservations with OEO projects had Head Start programs in 1968, serving 8,000 four- and five-year-olds at a cost of $1,000 per child.[11]

Expenditures for home improvement were second in size in 1968, reflecting the critical housing situation on the reservations. (As mentioned, a 1966 survey indicated that 75 percent of all reservation homes were substandard.) However, since more than 50 percent of all reservation housing is dilapidated beyond repair, those in greatest need of improved housing will not benefit from this program.

One concrete benefit of the OEO reservation-based programs has been to provide jobs. At the end of fiscal 1968, OEO was employing about 760 professionals and 3,000 nonprofessionals. How-

[11] *Ibid.,* p. 268.

ever, some of the latter were receiving stipends while in training and were in a sense only "temporary employees" of OEO.[12]

Criticisms of the OEO Programs

Although the Indian reaction to OEO programs is more favorable than it usually is to BIA programs, grumbling has arisen about several aspects. There is evidence of nepotism in the distribution of jobs created by the poverty programs. For example, on the White Earth Reservation in Minnesota 20 percent of the 109 community action program employees were related to members of the governing council.[13] This problem may be very difficult to solve. On some reservations the population is divided into factions, based on the extended family, which show varying degrees of animosity toward each other. While the person responsible for hiring may be quite willing to help a relative, he may be reluctant to help a member of an opposing faction, and the best qualified person thus may not be hired.

As has been the case with the staffing of programs funded under Title II of the Elementary and Secondary Education Act, it is often difficult to recruit competent professionals. On the Pine Ridge Reservation, difficulty in finding a qualified director and teachers delayed the opening of OEO-sponsored nursery schools. Teacher aides were hard to recruit because most Sioux women over twenty-one (the minimum hiring age) had children of their own. Partly because of recruiting problems, three teachers were hired in early May to teach remedial reading on the Papago Reservation and worked only two weeks before the school year ended. Recruiting personnel to run the Pima recreation program proved particularly troublesome. Eight local residents were hired, but several had to be replaced because of inadequate performance. The newly appointed director quit two days before he was to report for work, claiming that family illness prevented his accepting the posi-

[12] *Ibid.*, p. 268. No data are available showing what proportion of the professional jobs were filled by Indians. Virtually all of the nonprofessional jobs were held by Indians. Moreover, there is no information on the prior employment status of these employees.

[13] Human Sciences Research, Inc., "A Comprehensive Evaluation of OEO Community Action Programs on Six Selected American Indian Reservations" (McLean, Va.: HSR, September 1966; processed), p. 330.

tion. His replacement quit after two weeks because of "a disabling personal illness." One of the recreation aides was then promoted to director.[14]

A criticism heard on many reservations is that most of the OEO programs benefit primarily the young. The Neighborhood Youth Corps, Head Start, day care centers, and remedial education programs were seen by the adults as inapplicable to their special needs. The Neighborhood Youth Corps was criticized particularly because it provided money for young people while many of their fathers remained unemployed. Adults complained that it was hard to command the respect of their children when they were the only ones in the household earning money.[15] While it is true that a large part of the expenditures has benefited young people most directly, the home improvement program, which is one of the larger OEO efforts, benefits the whole family. Given the great need for adult education, it is unfortunate that such a program usually has not been incorporated in the reservation poverty programs.

The most widespread complaint against OEO is that the number of jobs created is inadequate to meet the needs. For example, on the Pine Ridge Reservation a Ranger Corps was established, which called for the hiring of 10 men; there were 127 applicants. From 150 applicants for the Homemaker Aide Program, 5 were chosen.[16]

The task of lifting appreciable numbers of Indians out of poverty is clearly beyond the scope of present OEO reservation programs. An effective attack calls for coordinated efforts by all the federal agencies working with Indians, at levels of funding significantly higher than the present ones.

The Family Assistance Plan

Any examination of reservation income maintenance programs should include a discussion of the impact on Indian income of the

[14] *Ibid.*, pp. 61, 121, 185–86.

[15] Other complaints concerned the lack of supervision of the Neighborhood Youth Corps, which resulted in unproductive activities; a rise in drinking by corpsmen, attributed to their extra income; and the fact that the program benefited only those who left school.

[16] Human Sciences Research, "Evaluation of OEO Programs," pp. 182, 191.

family assistance plan proposed by President Richard M. Nixon in August 1969 and later introduced into Congress.[17]

Under the proposal the basic benefit for each family with no income would be $500 for each of the first two members and $300 for each additional one. Thus a family of four without income would receive federal payments of $1,600 annually. The first $60 a month (up to $720 a year) of other income, earned or unearned, would not cause a cut in the basic payment. For each dollar of income above that level the payment would be reduced, but by only fifty cents; assistance to the family would continue until its total income rose to $3,920. The plan thus provides a modest incentive to get and hold a job, since earning an income would not bring a sudden end to welfare payments.

The adoption of such a plan would have an important effect on the family income of reservation Indians. For example, in 1960 their median family income was estimated at $1,800.[18] If the provisions of the family assistance plan had then been in effect, the median income would have been an estimated $3,100, or 72 percent higher (Table 8-3).[19] The total cost of the program for Indian reservations, based on 1960 income distribution, would be about $50 million.

Enactment of the plan would undoubtedly improve the quality of life for most reservation Indians. Sharply increased incomes would permit families to improve their housing, even without an accelerated housing program. Higher incomes would increase family stability, and, to the extent that school achievement and attendance are related to family income, adoption of the plan would improve the children's educational achievement. However, larger incomes might encourage many persons to remain on the reserva-

[17] H.R. 14173, 91 Cong. 1 sess. The plan was not enacted by the 91st Congress and was resubmitted by the President to the 92d Congress (see his Budget Message for fiscal year 1972).

[18] Calculated from data in U.S. Bureau of the Census, *U.S. Census of Population: 1960, Subject Reports, Nonwhite Population by Race,* Final Report PC(2)-1C (1963), p. 26.

[19] In 1960 the median Indian family consisted of four persons. It is assumed here that the average-sized family in the two lowest income classes (60 percent of the families) is four persons and that earnings are uniformly distributed within each income class. It is also assumed that all eligible Indians would take advantage of the provisions of the plan.

TABLE 8-3

Distribution of Reservation Families by Income Class before and after Implementation of Family Assistance Plan Proposed by President Nixon

Number of families	Income class (in dollars)	
	Before implementation	After implementation
18,025	0– 1,000	1,600[a]– 2,460[a]
22,085	1,000– 2,999	2,460 – 3,460[a]
12,391	3,000– 4,999	3,460 – 5,000
6,557	5,000– 6,999	5,000 – 6,999
3,659	7,000– 9,999	7,000 – 9,999
1,290	10,000–14,999	10,000 –14,999
354	15,000 and over	15,000 and over
Median[b]	1,800	3,100

Sources: Cols. 1 and 2, U.S. Bureau of the Census, *U.S. Census of Population: 1960, Subject Reports, Nonwhite Population by Race* (1963), Final Report PC(2)-1C (1963), Table 15, p. 26. Col. 3, author's estimates based on family assistance plan proposed in H.R. 14173, 91 Cong, 1 sess.
a. End points were determined by applying provisions of the family assistance plan as introduced.
b. The medians are estimates based on 1960 census data.

tion who might otherwise migrate in search of employment. Since most reservations cannot provide permanent jobs for even a majority of the labor force, the unemployment problem might become even more acute.[20] Another consequence of slackened migration would probably be a lessening of interest in the BIA employment assistance programs. On the other hand, the effect on migration might be small, because migrants are young and fairly well educated and steady off-reservation employment would yield earnings in excess of payments under the plan. Among older Indians, who make up a small proportion of participants in employment assistance programs and who have more trouble adjusting than younger migrants, interest in relocation might decline if the Nixon proposal or some variation becomes law.

In any event, passage of the family assistance plan would not alleviate the poverty of many Indian families. Thus, expansion of the health, education, and economic development programs would still be needed to make the reservations economically viable.

[20] It is also conceivable that a number of off-reservation Indians would return, since there would be a guaranteed income even in the absence of employment.

Housing Programs

A number of federally sponsored housing programs have been instituted for reservation Indians. Several agencies are participating in them—the Bureau of Indian Affairs, the Housing Assistance Administration, and the Office of Economic Opportunity—and close coordination is required for maximum effectiveness.[21]

THE BIA HOUSING IMPROVEMENT PROGRAM

The Housing Improvement Program is the only housing program that is funded directly by the BIA. From fiscal year 1964 through 1967, 333 houses were built at an average cost of about $11,000 each. During fiscal years 1964–68, some 2,600 dwelling units were either improved or constructed. The pace accelerated in 1969, when more than 2,500 units were renovated or built.[22] The program has operated on several northern reservations where unemployment rates are very high and a great many Indians live in dilapidated or makeshift housing. Bureau welfare workers first identify elderly families and those with large numbers of children that have critical housing needs; then, as funds become available, houses are built for them. This program has been devoted almost entirely to new house construction rather than home improvement.

Funding limitations have restricted the number of units built. Many persons disappointed at not receiving new houses have envied those who did, and community tensions have increased. Moreover, since the dwellings are provided free of charge, some Indians have been reluctant to participate in other housing programs that require payment.

MINIMUM SHELTER PROJECT

The Office of Economic Opportunity, through its Demonstration Section, built 375 minimum shelter type houses on the Rose-

[21] The OEO home improvement program has already been mentioned and is not treated in this section.

[22] Task Force on Indian Housing, "Indian Housing: Need, Alternatives, Priorities and Program Recommendations," Bureau of Indian Affairs (December 1966; processed), p. 25; Bureau of Indian Affairs, *Answers to your questions about American Indians* (May 1968), p. 21.

bud Reservation in South Dakota. These are prefabricated structures, containing 400–560 square feet of living space and costing about $5,000 each.[23] The ownership originally is tribal, but after six years, if the houses are maintained properly, ownership is transferred to the occupant. The program was experimental, and OEO is not repeating it elsewhere.

Several criticisms can be made of this project. First, the houses are very small. In addition, they lack indoor plumbing, which is one of several factors that make them substandard, according to Bureau of the Census criteria. Finally, the Indians who built the houses were not the ones who were to live in them.[24] Nevertheless, they do offer shelter and can be built more cheaply than any others being built on the reservations. For Indians who live in tarpaper shacks, tents, or abandoned automobiles and trailers (and there are many who do), these houses are far better than their present homes.

CONVENTIONAL LOW-RENT HOUSING

The low-rent program operates on reservations much as it does in other parts of the nation. Indian tribes have established tribal housing authorities (similar to municipal housing authorities), paying for the construction with funds from the Housing Assistance Administration (HAA) of the U.S. Department of Housing and Urban Development. Between 1964 and 1968, 2,238 units were built at an average cost of $17,500 each.[25]

The cost per unit of low-rent housing has been higher than that of any other housing program. Factors in the cost have included HAA's intent to hold reservation housing to the normal standards for urban housing projects; the Indians' desire for separate dwellings, with resulting higher costs for utilities; and the high wages paid to construction workers.[26] The maximum annual income for eligibility for the low-rent program ranges between $3,000 and $5,000. Rents are $40 to $70 a month, depending on income and number of dependents.

[23] Task Force, "Indian Housing," p. 26.

[24] This criticism is significant only if participation in construction generates enough pride in one's home to encourage proper maintenance.

[25] See Task Force, "Indian Housing," p. 27.

[26] The U.S. Department of Labor determines the wages paid construction workers on government contract under the terms of the Davis-Bacon Act—that is, union

Indian leaders indicate that dissatisfaction centers on two aspects of this program. First, because these houses cannot be owned by the occupant, some Indians have preferred to stay in their present homes, even though these are much more modest, because they own them. A number of the low-rent projects are deteriorating quite rapidly because of a lack of maintenance by the inhabitants.[27] Perhaps if the units were owned rather than rented, upkeep would be improved.

The second major complaint is that the rents are too high. While they are not as high as those in urban housing projects, the annual incomes of the Indian occupants are very small, and the monthly charges are beyond the means of some.[28] Lack of experience in budgeting prevents some from keeping up payments. In a large number of the housing projects visited many renters had been evicted or were in arrears. For example, at the Navajo low-rent project in Chinle, Arizona, twenty-five of fifty-six families were behind in their rent.[29]

MUTUAL HELP

The mutual-help program was jointly conceived and is administered by the Housing Assistance Administration and the Bureau of Indian Affairs. Tribal members contribute their labor and thus acquire a "sweat equity" in a home, which is otherwise financed

---

scales prevailing for commercial construction in urban areas, rather than prevailing wages for housing construction on or near the reservations, are the standard. For example, wage rates for construction on the Cuyona portion of the Navajo Reservation are based on the Phoenix wage rate plus a travel increment, bringing the total hourly wage for common labor to $3.74 in 1968, or more than double the prevailing rate on the reservation. While this inflates the cost of Indian housing, it is beneficial to the extent that Indians are employed in the construction process. However, because few Indians are skilled in the construction trades, they do not benefit from the high wages paid to skilled construction workers. If the Davis-Bacon wages (plus a travel increment) were not paid, it might be extremely difficult to recruit an adequate supply of skilled construction workers.

[27] This problem is also encountered on public housing projects in urban areas.

[28] Funds obtained from renters are intended to provide for the administrative costs of the tribal housing authority and for utilities and maintenance. They are not intended to repay the cost of construction.

[29] Interview with project manager, Chinle, Arizona, June 26, 1968.

from funds of the HAA. Houses usually are built in groups of ten to fifteen, with all beneficiary families expected to continue working until a set of dwellings has been completed. Only families with incomes below the $3,000–$5,000 range are eligible. The title to a finished house remains with the tribal housing authority until the original loan from HAA has been repaid. It is estimated that an average of about seventeen years will be required for repayment. Between 1965 and 1969, 1,930 mutual-help units were constructed, at an average cost of $8,500 each.

Families who move into mutual-help houses make monthly payments to the tribal housing authority ranging upward from $7, depending on family income and number of dependents (Appendix Table A-22). While these amounts are sufficient only to cover the administrative costs of the housing authority and insurance payments, some families, as they become more affluent, will make larger payments and thus help to repay some of the principal and interest on the original HAA loan. Unlike the low-rent program, which makes ineligible anyone whose income rises above the maximum level, the mutual-help program permits a person with increasing income to remain in his house so long as he is willing to meet added monthly payments.

While this program has the advantage of enabling the occupant to gain title to his house (with monthly payments lower than those required from occupants of low-rent units), it has several disadvantages. Because most beneficiaries of the program are inexperienced in house construction, it sometimes takes as long as seventeen months to complete a group of homes.[30] In some cases the Indian men lose interest after one or two houses are completed, and the women often have to do the bulk of the additional work. While an Indian is required to devote a minimum number of hours to construction before he is eligible for a house, the program permits him to let friends contribute time in his behalf. This limits the training in carpentry, bricklaying, and general construction that the original participant is supposed to acquire. Also, it is difficult for an employed Indian to find time to take part in house construction, except on weekends. Only those who are unemployed can contribute enough man-hours to build up the necessary "sweat

[30] Task Force, "Indian Housing," p. 29.

equity" within a reasonable period. However, many of them will probably have difficulty making the minimum payment of $7 a month if they remain unemployed.

TURNKEY HOUSING

A relatively new approach to public housing is the turnkey method, which has been used in constructing some 10,000 units throughout the country. It allows private developers great latitude in project formulation and development. The developer supplies the site and the plans and builds the development, which is then sold to the housing authority. This procedure is quite different from the usual public housing construction process, in which the housing authority acts more or less as its own general contractor. Early evidence indicated that turnkey units could be built for about $3,000 less than conventional public housing units and in about one-third less time.[31] Under a variant of the turnkey program, known as Turnkey III, the local housing authority is permitted to turn the property over to the renting occupant after twenty-five years, provided the occupant has performed his own maintenance during that period. Thus turnkey housing can be built more quickly than conventional low-rent housing and much more quickly than mutual-help housing, and, unlike the low-rent program, eventually it permits individual ownership.

In 1966, BIA estimated that 57,000 dwellings on Indian reservations were substandard, 42,000 of them so dilapidated as to be beyond repair.[32] Between 1965 and 1968, slightly fewer than 5,000 units were constructed, or about 10 percent of the number needed. More housing units will be needed in the future to take care of a growing population and to relieve overcrowding. An accelerated housing construction program flexible enough to meet the housing needs of each reservation is badly needed.

[31] Joseph Burstein, "Doors to Profit Opened through Turnkey Program," *National News* (National Lumber and Building Material Dealers Association, April 1967).
[32] Task Force, "Indian Housing," p. 3.

CHAPTER IX

A Program for Improvement

The economic status of the American Indian, particularly the reservation Indian, is one of abject poverty. On some of the reservations more than half of the male labor force is unemployed. Indian income, although rising at a more rapid rate than non-Indian income, is still only a small fraction of the latter. One-fifth of all reservation Indians receive welfare payments, about four times the proportion of the total population. The family assistance plan, if it is adopted, will sharply increase the average reservation family's income but will not by itself succeed in making the reservations economically viable. There is a housing crisis—more than three-quarters of reservation housing is substandard; half of it is beyond repair. Educational achievement and levels of health are far below those of the general population. Agricultural productivity of the reservations is low; industrial development is proceeding too slowly. The Bureau of Indian Affairs (BIA) employment assistance programs are efficient but too small to have a major impact on the reservation economy. Tribal trust funds are unevenly distributed, but even tribes with fairly ample funds are not encouraged by the BIA to use them for reservation development. Forced termination of federal responsibility for Indian tribes is opposed by the Indians and has been shown to be an unwise policy; but states with large Indian populations are unwilling to take on responsibility for their affairs. To improve the lot of the Indians in all these respects will require new policies and changes in old policies as well as larger funds.

To make recommendations that appear feasible and logically

177

consistent, several assumptions about the proper goals of federal Indian policy must be made. Three points underlie the recommendations and program cost estimates that follow.

1. The individual Indian should have maximum freedom to determine where he will earn his livelihood. The federal government should not as a general policy try to encourage or discourage migration from the reservations.

2. The services now provided by the federal government need to be continued for the intermediate future (twenty-five to thirty years) until the economic position of the Indians is less precarious.[1] The forced termination of Indian tribes therefore should not be a part of federal policy.

3. The federal government should encourage Indians, in every way possible, to acquire the necessary skills and abilities to manage their own economic resources and development.

Education

The record of accomplishment in the field of Indian education is unsatisfactory. Achievement tests show that Indian high school students are two to three years behind non-Indians in basic subjects. Only about half the reservation pupils complete high school. While more Indians are entering college than ever before, only a small minority graduate. The adult education program is inadequate. There is a severe shortage of skilled nonteaching personnel. The teacher turnover rate in bureau schools is unacceptably high.

The lack of education of American Indians has limited them to jobs that require little skill or training. Moreover, low educational attainment has discouraged many from leaving the reservation because they believe they cannot effectively compete for jobs with better educated non-Indians.

[1] Persons unfamiliar with Indian problems often suggest that if the total amounts spent in Indian programs were simply distributed directly to the Indians (about $1,000 per person), they would confer as many, or more, benefits as does the present system. This viewpoint is incorrect. Some of these programs create investments, both human and physical, that will yield a continuing return in the future and allow the individual a chance to become a productive member of society. Moreover, with no federal education expenditures many Indians would not have any schools; and with no Indian health program, Indian health care would be minimal.

To raise the quality of education for elementary and secondary students, an immediate survey should be made of the factors that prevent federally operated high schools from being properly accredited, and detailed proposals should be developed to remove these deficiencies. An intermediate goal should be to raise the quality of education to that of the states with the highest achievement. It is difficult to estimate the total cost of such an effort, but New York State (which has the highest current expenditures per pupil) spends about $300 more per pupil than the BIA. To bring bureau expenditures to the New York State level would require increased appropriations of $15.7 million a year.[2]

Extensive remedial programs should be begun in federal Indian schools, operating on a year-round basis and using the Yakima Reservation program as a model. Every Indian child who can profit from remedial education should have the opportunity, but if budgetary limitations preclude this ideal, priority should be given to the older students who will soon enter the labor market and who, because Indian education is progressively less effective, are probably in greatest need of remedial help.

Improvements in education will be of little value unless the students obtain jobs commensurate with their levels of education and training. On some reservations this may require a link between the secondary schools and the relocation program. On others, schooling will need to be adjusted to meet the demands of existing and potential reservation industry.

The BIA should moderately expand the high school vocational education programs to meet at least part of the demand, not only adding courses in schools where programs exist, but initiating programs in schools that lack them. Antiquated equipment should be replaced. A benefit-cost study should be made of the present programs; if a favorable ratio is indicated, vocational offerings should be expanded.

All Indian communities (instead of 51 percent, as at present) should have adult education programs. Improvement in quality is also needed. Achievement standards should be extended up to the twelfth grade level, instead of the present eighth grade level. More adult educators are needed, one for each reservation rather than

[2] It is assumed that an increase in expenditures per pupil would improve the quality of education offered.

one for every four reservations as at present. An adequate adult education program calls for a minimum expenditure of $100 per pupil (four times what is now spent) and a quadrupling of the number of students, requiring an additional expenditure of $16 million annually.

More than a fourfold increase in skilled nonteaching personnel (such as psychologists) is necessary for a more effective attack on the mental health and adjustment problems of students, as well as on their purely academic difficulties. Assuming the average salary needed to attract competent personnel is $12,000, the estimated increase of some 697 would raise annual expenditures by $8.4 million.

Because many Indian students have difficulty relating to non-Indians, increasing the number of Indian teaching and nonteaching personnel would help. Perhaps bureau-sponsored college scholarships could be offered, and students receiving them be required to teach or work for a specified period in the BIA school system after graduation.

To reduce the high rate of teacher turnover in BIA schools, the following steps are recommended. Teachers with little or no experience in rural living or working with Indian people should not be sent to the most isolated reservations. The salary structure should reflect differences among reservations, and teachers on the most isolated reservations should receive higher salaries and larger increments than those on reservations reasonably close to urban areas. The BIA should give its teachers summer vacations of the same length as those enjoyed by public school teachers, or if this is not possible, they should receive extra pay for the additional time they are required to be on duty. An orientation program should be instituted to make prospective teachers aware of the realities of reservation life before they accept a position. While this last approach might discourage some potential applicants, it would probably reduce the turnover among those who do accept positions.

It is not possible to determine the cost of this turnover-reduction program, but its net cost would probably be small because of offsetting savings in recruiting and administrative costs resulting from decreased turnover.

Because the focus of this volume is on federal programs for American Indians, these recommendations apply to BIA schools.

However, the majority of Indian children are educated in public schools with predominantly Indian enrollment, and many of the suggestions made apply equally to them. For example, most public schools visited did not offer vocational education or adult education. Moreover, these schools are often located in isolated areas and undoubtedly suffer from high teacher turnover. Finally, such public schools are less likely to be accredited than public schools enrolling non-Indians. State boards of education should recognize their responsibility to provide the same quality of education for all their citizens.

Health

Although there has been considerable progress in reducing the mortality and (to a lesser degree) the disease levels of reservation Indians, largely through additional health manpower and facilities, conditions on the reservations are far below those of non-Indian areas. To accelerate the drive to bring the level of Indian health up to parity with that of the non-Indian population, the following proposals seem most important:

1. Increase the number of physicians, dentists, nurses, and pharmacists so that the number of Indians served by each health professional is the same as for non-Indians. To achieve this in 1971 would mean adding 165 physicians, 100 dentists, 120 nurses, and 270 pharmacists to the Division of Indian Health staff, at a total cost of $6.4 million.[3]

2. Expand the health education program. At present there are only forty-eight medical social workers, nine health education specialists, and forty community health workers—less than one worker for each reservation. The number should be trebled. At an estimated average salary of $9,000 per employee, the additional appropriation would be $1.8 million.

3. Initiate a mental health program. The pilot project at the Pine Ridge Reservation has a staff of one psychiatrist, one psychologist, one anthropologist, three social workers, and two aides, with

---

[3] This assumes that base pay would be $13,400 annually for doctors and dentists, $7,500 for pharmacists, and $7,000 for nurses.

total expenditures of approximately $200,000. As a first step toward meeting the mental health needs of the Indian population, projects similar to that developed for Pine Ridge should be initiated on all reservations. The estimated total cost would be $32 million.

4. Undertake a major research program on the causes of alcoholism among reservation Indians. There is little point in making recommendations for dealing with the situation until more is known about the subject. A two-year study, funded at a level of $250,000 a year and covering the reservations where the problem is most acute, should produce enough information to make useful recommendations possible.

No estimates are made here for the cost of additional health facilities, since current expenditures of the Division of Indian Health provide for a ten-year program of construction and improvement of such facilities.

Agriculture

Indians have not developed the agricultural resources of their reservations. The most productive land is usually leased to whites, while other tracts lie idle. Only one-third of the gross income from agricultural production on Indian reservations accrues to Indians.

An important drawback is the fragmentation of heirship land. Legislation should be passed that would permit the tribes to undertake a massive land consolidation program, as well as to limit the further fragmentation of land; an appropriation of $10 million would be a good beginning.

Other actions, such as the reintroduction of vocational agriculture in Indian schools, an increase in the number of extension agents, and expenditures on irrigation projects and development of grazing lands, must be held in abeyance. Tentative evidence indicates that Indian participation in agriculture is declining rapidly. The Bureau of Indian Affairs, working in cooperation with the tribes, should make extensive surveys to determine whether there is enough interest in agriculture to merit large expenditures. On reservations where the people have considerable interest in agriculture and significant potential resources exist, the actions mentioned should be taken.[4]

Industrial Development

While reservation industrialization is increasing fairly rapidly, only about 3 percent of the Indian labor force is employed in reservation industry.

An important factor limiting the growth of reservation industry is a lack of knowledge on which to base decisions about plant location. This problem should be ameliorated by a doubling or trebling of the professional staff of the BIA Division of Industrial Development, which would prepare a prospectus for each reservation, with data on such items as level of wages and employment, cost and availability of water or electric power, adequacy of transportation and communication facilities, skills and abilities of the potential labor force, and the proximity and possible effective demand of the market.

The present appropriation for the Division of Industrial Development and Tourism is $800,000, and the proposed additional staff would raise it to $2 million. A staff of professional economists (not necessarily employed by the BIA) should undertake feasibility studies of the kinds of industries that could locate on various reservations. It should also prepare, with the help of tribal leaders, an inventory of social overhead capital projects that would increase the possibility of attracting industry to specific reservations. The results of the feasibility studies should be widely distributed so that businessmen could have ready access to the findings.

A staff of twenty economists employed for a five-year period should be able to complete both the feasibility studies and the inventory of social overhead capital projects. The total budget (including costs of travel and supporting staff) would be $2.6 million.[5] After the inventory has been developed, a long-term expenditure

[4] For example, on the Yakima Reservation in Washington State, there is great potential for irrigation farming, and the tribal members appear to be interested in this type of agriculture. Moreover, BIA analysis indicated that a proposed irrigation project would have a benefit–cost ratio of 6.7.

[5] This assumes an average economist's salary of $18,000 a year and $6,000 for sup

program should be formulated by the federal government to meet these needs. Tribes with multimillion dollar trust funds should be encouraged to help meet the cost of the projects. The government should insist that as many Indians as possible—consistent with efficiency requirements—be employed in constructing and operating projects.

Because such an inventory has not yet been developed, it is not possible to estimate the costs of the projects. However, some idea can be obtained by examining the estimated cost of an adequate reservation road program prepared by the BIA Branch of Roads: to bring the reservation road system up to "adequate standard" would require a total expenditure of $653 million, including $531 million for 11,166 miles of "intermediate" roads and $122 million for 8,439 miles of "low type" roads (trails, limited access roads, and so forth).[6]

One step taken by the Bureau of Indian Affairs to impart knowledge of the industrial potential of reservations was to sponsor a conference in 1968 attended by government officials, Indian leaders, and industrial executives. Such a conference should be held annually, featuring displays of items produced in reservation plants. Not only would this indicate the kinds of goods that could be profitably produced, but it would dispel the notion that Indian skills are restricted to basketry, rug weaving, and the making of pottery and jewelry.

To encourage Indians to invest their funds in industrial development (on an individual or a tribal basis) by making them aware of existing opportunities, as well as to prepare them for management positions in non-Indian-owned reservation industry, residential training centers should be established on several reservations to provide training in business and financial administration. Retail establishments, which would be part of the training center, would be staffed by trainees to give them practical experience in effective management and to develop entrepreneurial skills.

---

porting staff, with a ratio of two professional employees to one nonprofessional; $2,000 per man per year for travel expenses; and $300,000 for research tools, such as a computer.

    [6] U.S. Bureau of Indian Affairs, Branch of Roads, "20 Year Study, 1965–1985" (July 1965; unpublished).

Dr. Mayland A. Parker of Arizona State University has developed a detailed proposal for a residential manpower training and development center, with a capacity of 2,500 students and annual operating costs of $2,500 per student.[7] Construction costs would amount to $3 million to $5 million and operating costs would average $6.25 million a year for such a center.

For tribes whose resources are inadequate to finance their economic and industrial development projects, federal loans should be provided. This could be accomplished most readily by a $50 million expansion in the revolving credit loan fund established as part of the 1934 Indian Reorganization Act. Increased subsidies should not be given reservation industry unless there is a general federal policy of encouraging the relocation of industry to depressed areas (including city ghettos as well as reservations).[8] The Defense Department should consider locating defense plants on reservations if it has a policy of extending indirect aid to areas of substantial unemployment.

Not all tribes are interested in economic development, and their position must be respected by the federal government. However, a forthright statement by Congress and the Bureau of Indian Affairs indicating that forced termination is not a part of existing Indian policy would probably be of great importance in reducing the more traditional tribes' opposition to development. These tribes would then have less reason to fear that modest progress toward self-sufficiency would result in the termination of federal responsibility.

Even if most of these recommendations were carried out, some reservations would remain unattractive as locations for industry.[9] Special efforts must be made there to acquaint the residents with training and relocation opportunities. To improve the level of

[7] See Arizona State University, "Model 'Demonstration Community' for a Manpower Training and Resource Development Center" (October 1968; processed).

[8] It could be argued that the tribes that value cultural separatism (maintenance of the reservation) most highly should receive added subsidies to attract industry. In practice, however, it would be impossible to determine objectively which tribes were most interested in cultural separatism. Moreover, this would place the government in the position of openly encouraging some Indians to remain on the reservations.

[9] This would be true even if Congress voted to increase the available subsidies as proposed by Herbert Striner. See Chap. 5.

skills of the community and the quality of life on the reservations, the federal government, as the employer of last resort, should undertake a number of employment-creating public works projects to improve the reservation's roads, recreation facilities, or community buildings. An appropriation of $50 million annually is recommended for this purpose.

Manpower Programs

It should be clear, even to those skeptical of federal manpower efforts, that the manpower programs operated by the Bureau of Indian Affairs are successful. Existing evidence, although tentative, indicates that they should be expanded. More specifically, enough funds should be made available so that every Indian who wishes to leave the reservation could participate in the adult vocational training or direct relocation program.[10] This would cost an additional $12 million to $15 million annually.[11]

The following steps are recommended to overcome weaknesses observed in the programs and make them more effective:

As a first step toward lowering the returnee rate for participants in the off-reservation employment assistance programs, detailed information should be kept on those relocated, as well as on the returnees. These data should include tribal affiliation, educational attainment, size of family, age, occupation, proportion of Indian blood, and earnings. The information could be used to identify potentially high risks, and extra resources could be applied to them to ease their adjustment to off-reservation life. The one-year limitation of follow-up services for persons relocated and/or trained should be modified to allow a flexible approach more com-

---

[10] This recommendation is not inconsistent with the first assumption on the goals of federal policy for Indians (p. 178), since the program would still be on a voluntary basis. Expansion would simply allow all Indians to exercise the option of living on or off the reservation. Increasing the Indian's potential mobility would enhance his opportunities.

[11] This estimate assumes a 40 percent increase in adult vocational trainees and a 20 percent increase in those relocated under the direct employment program. Total costs per trainee and/or migrant are assumed to remain the same. The cost figure also includes estimates of new staff needed in the employment assistance centers.

Because it is not certain that a major expansion of these programs will leave their efficiency (benefit–cost ratio) unchanged, further studies will be needed to judge their effectiveness.

patible with the individual needs of those leaving the reservations.

Anthropological studies indicate that a large percentage of Indians have serious adjustment problems when they are relocated to a large city. Pilot projects should be undertaken to settle vocational trainees and those in the direct relocation program in towns of moderate size with tight labor markets in order to determine whether it is easier for a reservation Indian to adjust to a city the size of Omaha, for example, than to Chicago or Los Angeles. To measure the effectiveness of such pilot projects, a control group of Indians similar in tribal identification, age, education, and other demographic variables should be sent to the urban centers where participants in these manpower programs have traditionally been sent. Comparison of the two groups in terms of economic success and psychological adjustment should prove revealing.

To reduce the high proportion of women in the on-the-job training programs, the BIA could urge some of the firms operating these subsidized programs to hire more men, especially heads of families. The pressure could range all the way from moral suasion to cancellation of the firm's subsidy for flagrant noncompliance. However, the bureau should not establish a rigid ratio of men to women.

If funds for the adult vocational training or direct employment programs are in short supply, single or married men should have priority over single women in the employment assistance programs, since a large proportion of single female trainees leave the labor force soon after training or after placement and obtain few economic benefits from the programs.

Financial Resources

Although the vast majority of reservation Indians are poverty-stricken, tribal trust funds from Indian Claims Commission awards and mineral resources have grown rapidly since the end of the Second World War to a total of more than $300 million. The Bureau of Indian Affairs should continue, with tribal approval, the present policy of withdrawing trust funds from the Treasury, where they earn only 4 percent interest, and investing them in certificates of deposit and Treasury securities, which have a better rate of return. Tribes should be encouraged to develop their own plans for the investment and expenditure of their trust funds, using the services of private investment consultants. Courses should be given at the proposed residential manpower training and development center to acquaint tribal officials with the fundamentals of individual and corporate investing. The federal government should discuss with the tribe possible uses of the funds for economic or industrial development. Projects wanted by the tribe could be planned either jointly or by the tribe exclusively, but not solely by the government, which should not tell the Indians how to invest their money.

Although it is evident that per capita payments eliminate the possibility of using income for development purposes, the Bureau of Indian Affairs should not openly discourage these payments. The federal role in this instance should be limited to advising the tribe about alternative uses of the funds.

The Bureau of Indian Affairs should, as an intermediate goal, discontinue handling individual Indian accounts, which totaled almost $50 million in 1968, and encourage Indians to invest income from trust property themselves. Counseling and courses in financial management should be given as part of the adult education program, as well as to secondary school students. Persistent efforts should be made to minimize the number of supervised accounts. Many restricted Indians must be capable of becoming legally competent through counseling and should be encouraged to seek such help; clear guidelines should be established by the Division of Social Services for supervision, combined with rehabilitation efforts, for Indians who are alleged to have spent their incomes foolishly; requests by individual Indians for supervised accounts should be discouraged, and self-reliance in personal finances should be encouraged, especially in the case of younger Indians.

Welfare Plans

Although state categorical assistance payments account for 70 percent of the welfare payments made to Indians (BIA general assistance payments account for the rest), some states have been unwilling to provide assistance to Indians. The federal government should insist that, as a condition for receiving the federal contribution to state public assistance payments, the states provide services to Indians on the same basis as to other citizens. Employees of BIA Social Services offices on the reservations should be more diligent about informing needy Indians of the welfare benefits to which they are entitled. With such a high proportion of the reservation population living in poverty, it is not enough to wait for Indians to apply for assistance; they should be encouraged to apply for aid, which in far too many cases they do not know is available.

Indians have generally been more receptive to the reservation programs financed by the Office of Economic Opportunity than to those provided by the BIA, because 65 percent of OEO funding has been for "local initiative" projects that have given the Indians an important part in planning and implementation. There is little point in recommending appropriate levels of funding for the local initiative programs, since this depends on the types of programs desired by the Indians themselves. However, in deciding which programs to approve for funding, OEO should try to give more emphasis to programs that benefit adults.[12]

The major OEO program with a national emphasis on the reservations—Head Start—should be expanded to include all four- and five-year-old children, instead of one-third of this group, as at present. With expenditures at $1,000 per pupil, this would mean an increase of $15 million. The vast number of Indians who begin school with no knowledge of English would be greatly reduced by a Head Start program that included all children of the appropriate age.

The family assistance plan, if enacted, would have a great impact on the standard of living of most reservation Indians, although one negative effect might be a slowdown of migration from reservations that cannot provide a livelihood for the present population. If it becomes law, tribal officials and government agencies will have the responsibility of seeing that all eligible Indian families are aware of the benefits available.

To meet the housing crisis, a variety of new projects have been developed by BIA, OEO, and the Housing Assistance Administration. While in terms of cost and efficiency turnkey housing, which

[12] Older Indians rightfully complain that they have been left out of OEO programs.

provides for eventual ownership, appears superior to the others, the Indians themselves should decide which kind meets their needs. Building twice as many new houses as at present could eliminate substandard housing in six years. This would mean an increase in expenditures of between $7 million and $10 million, depending on the type of houses constructed.

Application of Programs to Specific Reservations

Because of the diversity among tribes in culture, development potential, and interest in change, these programs will have differing degrees of success among reservations. A few tribes may not be interested in some of the programs, and their wishes should be respected. Nothing would be more paternalistic than for the BIA to press a tribe to accept a program the members do not want.

To increase the flexibility of the programs to meet the needs of the various tribes, the BIA should consult with the officials of each tribe and develop a statement of the tribe's long-term goals with respect to outmigration, political evolution, and economic and social development. For the last goal, some tribes may want a pastoral or agricultural economy. The review should indicate what assets (for example, trust funds or mineral income) are available and what additional funds would be needed to meet the tribe's stated goals over a specified period, such as twenty-five to thirty years.[13] These reports should be made available to Congress and the public. They would make it possible to assess the year-by-year accomplishments of each tribe in relation to its own goals, and the Bureau of Indian Affairs should be required to report annually on such progress in its budget requests.

Unfortunately, the data needed to determine the socioeconomic status of a tribe, as well as its future needs and potential, are not available at present. To develop the necessary information with greater precision should be a task of the highest priority.

[13] For example, a tribe with few natural resources, little prospect of industrialization, and heavy outmigration (including participation in employment assistance programs) may prefer a special program to ease adjustment to off-reservation living, thus lowering the proportion of relocated Indians who return to the reservation. A reasonable goal for such a program might be to lower the returnee rate from 50 percent of participants to 25 percent.

TABLE 9-1

Annual Increase in Cost for Proposed Federal Indian Programs,
and 1969 Level, by Type of Program

Program	Fiscal year 1969 level (millions of dollars)	Increase in cost (millions of dollars)	Percentage increase
Education			
Elementary and secondary			
(improved quality)	n.a.	15.7	
Adult	n.a.	16.0	
Skilled nonteaching personnel	n.a.	8.4	
	100.0	40.1	*40*
Health			
Health professionals (increased staff)	n.a.	6.4	
Health education	n.a.	1.8	
Mental health	n.a.	32.0	
Alcoholism (research)	n.a.	0.2	
	100.0	40.5	*41*
Agriculture			
Land consolidation	n.a.	10.0	
	25.0	10.0	*40*
Industrial development			
Division of Industrial Development and Tourism (increased staff)	0.8	1.0	*125*
Professional economists (feasibility and other studies)	0	0.5	
Adequate road system[b]	22.0	75.0	*341*
Resident manpower training and development center	0	10.0	
Revolving loan fund[c]	18.0	50.0	*278*
Public works projects	5.0	50.0	*1,000*
	45.8	186.5	*407*
Training and relocation	24.0	13.5	*56*
Other			
Head Start	7.0	15.0	*214*
Housing	5.0	8.5	*170*
	12.0	23.5	*196*
	306.8	314.1	*102*

Sources: Col. 1, author's estimates; col. 2, letter from Roderick H. Riley, assistant to commissioner of Indian affairs, Oct. 31, 1969.

n.a. Not available.

a. Total expenditures.

b. Assumes that an adequate road system would be completed in ten years, at an approximate cost of $75 million a year (includes maintenance).

c. First year only; in subsequent years appropriation should be virtually zero, since new loans would be made with repaid funds.

Total Costs

The total increase in annual costs that would result if these recommendations were followed is summarized in Table 9-1, which shows that the costs would approximately double. Two limitations should be noted. First, the figure is low, since it does not include estimates of needed social overhead capital expenditures on the reservations, with the exception of roads. Second, it does not include possible increased outlays on agricultural development (for reasons noted above), except the cost of land consolidation. Also, outlays on Indian-initiated OEO programs are not included.

Authorization of the expenditures recommended would not solve the "Indian problem," nor are the benefits of such expenditures likely to reach all reservation Indians. However, it would be an important beginning toward bringing the promise of America to the first Americans.

APPENDIX A

Statistical Tables

Comparison of Indian and White Students by Grade Level Equivalent, Reading, Verbal, and Mathematics Tests, 1965

Grade	Reading		Verbal		Mathematics	
	White	Indian[a]	White	Indian[a]	White	Indian[a]
6	6.7	4.6	6.6	4.9	6.7	4.6
7	7.7	5.6	7.6	5.9	7.7	5.5
8	8.7	6.6	8.6	6.8	8.7	6.5
9	9.8	7.6	9.9	7.8	10.1	7.5
10	10.8	8.3	10.8	8.3	11.3	8.1
11	11.7	9.0	11.7	8.9	12.3	8.5
12	12.6	9.9	12.6	9.6	13.0	9.0

Source: U.S. Office of Education, "Dynamics of Achievement: A Study of Differential Growth of Achievement Over Time," Technical Note No. 53, Equal Educational Opportunity Study (1966; processed), Table 3.
a. The Indians taking these achievement tests were enrolled in public schools and generally lived in urban areas.

Rank Correlation Coefficients, Income and Educational Achievement of Indian Children in Selected Areas, Based on Various Tests

			Rank correlation coefficient	
Year	Name of test	Skill tested	Grade 8	Grade 12
1950 Pressey		Vocabulary	0.12	0.33
Gates		Basic reading	−0.15	0.38
Pressey		English usage	0.20	0.72
Pressey		Sentence structure	0.69	0.64
BIA arithmetic		Factor abilities	−0.03	0.004
			Grades 4–12	
1952 California achievement		Reading vocabulary	0.31	
		Reading comprehension	0.31	
		Language	0.43	
		Spelling	−0.43	
		Arithmetic fundamentals	−0.44	
		Arithmetic reasoning	−0.14	
			Grade 9	Grade 12
1966 California mental maturity		IQ	0.18	0.12
California achievement		Reading	0.08	0.22
		Mathematics	0.08	0.18
		Language	0.18	0.18

Sources: For 1950 tests, Kenneth E. Anderson, E. Gordon Collister, and Carl E. Ladd, *The Educational Achievement of Indian Children*, U.S. Bureau of Indian Affairs (1953), pp. 35, 37, 39, 41, 42, 48, 50, 52, 54, and 55. For 1952 tests, L. Madison Coombs, Ralph E. Kron, E. Gordon Collister, and Kenneth E. Anderson, *The Indian Child Goes to School*, Bureau of Indian Affairs (Lawrence, Kans.: Haskell Press, 1958), p. 20. For 1966 tests, Willard P. Bass, "An Analysis of Academic Achievement of Indian High School Students in Federal and Public Schools, 1966–67," Bureau of Indian Affairs (January 1968; processed).

Income rankings were calculated from U.S. Bureau of the Census, *U.S. Census of Population: 1950*, Vol. 4, *Special Reports*, Pt. 3, Chap. B, *Nonwhite Population by Race* (1953), pp. 72–77, and Vol. 2, *Characteristics of the Population*, Pts. 51–54, Territories and Possessions (1953), pp. 51–52; *U.S. Census of Population: 1960*, *Subject Reports, Nonwhite Population by Race*, Final Report PC(2)-1C (1963), pp. 104–07, and *Detailed Characteristics, Alaska*, Final Report PC(1)-3D (1962), p. 210.

Number of Reservation Indian Students Enrolled
in Remedial Summer Courses, 1964–69

Year	Elementary	High school	Precollege
1964	2,540	1,265	—
1965	2,384	1,456	—
1966	1,602	667	—
1967	3,369	730	90
1968	5,738	2,140	241
1969	7,054	1,232	147

Source: Bureau of Indian Affairs, Office of Education, "Statistics Concerning Indian Education, Fiscal Year 1969" (Lawrence, Kans.: Haskell Institute, 1969), p. 35.

TABLE A-4

Increase in Achievement Levels, Selected Indian Schools,
Title I Remedial Education Programs, 1967[a]

School	Grade tested	Length of remedial instruction (months)	Gain in achievement level[b] (years)
Bullhead Day	5	2	0.22
Pierre Boarding	5	2	0.07
Standing Rock Community	8	2	0.10
Seneca Indian	6	3	0.13
Sequoyah High	9	3	0.43
Cibecue Day	5	2	0.33
Phoenix Indian	11	3	0.87
Roosevelt Boarding	5	2	0.25
Little Eagle Day	2	2	−0.17
Fort Totten Community	7	3	0.30[c]

Source: ENKI Corporation, "Evaluation Report, Bureau of Indian Affairs Title I Programs, Elementary and Secondary Education Act," Vol. 3, "Detailed Test Data" (San Fernando, Calif., 1967; processed).

a. Based on California achievement test scores. The tests were administered in late February and early March 1967.

b. Average gain on reading, arithmetic, and language tests.

c. Average gain on reading and arithmetic tests only.

TABLE A-5

Teacher Turnover, Bureau of Indian Affairs and Various Public Schools, Selected Periods, 1957–67

School system	Year of survey	Total teacher turnover per year (percent)
Bureau of Indian Affairs schools	1959–62	25.4
Bureau of Indian Affairs schools	1964–67	26.7
All public schools	1957–58	17.0
All public schools	1959–60	13.4
Great Lakes and Plains	1959–60	17.6
West and Southwest	1959–60	19.8
Alaska	1959–60	34.0
Nebraska	1959–60	34.0
New York	1959–60	12.6
Idaho	1958–63	17.0
Montana	1960–62	28.2
Montana (rural schools only)	1960–62	46.5
Tennessee	1960–62	11.0
Oregon	1961–62	17.0
Connecticut	1964–65	10.9

Source: Bureau of Indian Affairs, Division of Education, "Teacher Turnover Survey for 1964–67" (1968; processed).

Total Teacher Turnover per Year in Bureau of Indian Affairs Schools,
by Indian Agency Area, 1964–67

Area	States included	Total turnover per year[a] (percent)
Aberdeen	North Dakota, South Dakota	21.6
Albuquerque	Nebraska, Colorado	26.6
Anadarko	Kansas, Oklahoma	18.6
Billings	Montana, Wyoming	58.1
Juneau[b]	Alaska	38.4
Muskogee	Eastern Oklahoma, Mississippi	11.6
Navajo	New Mexico	32.4
Phoenix	Nevada, Utah, Arizona	17.5
Portland	Washington, Oregon, Idaho	11.7
Central office	North Carolina, Florida	15.3

Source: Bureau of Indian Affairs, Division of Education, "Teacher Turnover Survey for 1964–67" (1968; processed), p. 26.
a. Three-year average.
b. Teacher turnover per year in Alaska would undoubtedly be higher if teachers were not required to sign a two-year contract.

TABLE A-7

Teacher Turnover in Bureau of Indian Affairs Schools,
by Years of Experience, 1964–67

Years of teaching experience (BIA schools only)	Teacher turnover, 1964–67[a] (percent)
1	41.43
2	14.76
3	9.18
4	6.67
5	13.33
6–10	7.55
11–19	2.24
20 or more	4.83

Source: Bureau of Indian Affairs, Division of Education, "Teacher Turnover Survey for 1964–67" (1968; processed), p. 36.
a. Three-year average.

TABLE A-8

Personnel in the Division of Indian Health, by Profession,
Selected Years, 1955–66[a]

Profession	1955	1956	1960	1962	1963	1966	Percentage increase, 1955–66
Physician	125	195	216	256	270	315	*152*
Dentist	40	64	81	91	100	105	*162*
Dental assistant and technician	32	65	82	96	96	120	*275*
Graduate nurse[b]	783	790	809	875	890	909	*16*
Practical nurse	289	321	422	482	508	447	*55*
Sanitary engineer and sanitarian	14	24	46	60	72	96	*586*
Sanitarian aide	28	53	72	70	68	74	*164*
Pharmacist	7	20	45	58	61	77	*1,000*
Medical social worker	8	18	30	39	42	48	*500*
Educational specialist[c]	4	5	8	6	7	9	*125*
Community worker (health)	0	12	27	30	28	40	—
Community health aide	0	0	4	5	4	6	—
Dietitian	16	22	22	24	27	24	*50*
Nutritionist	1	2	9	11	11	8	*700*
Medical records librarian	4	5	9	12	13	18	*350*
Medical and X-ray technician	75	84	105	115	128	141	*88*
All other	2,148	2,454	2,833	2,974	2,881	2,933	*37*
Total	3,574	4,134	4,820	5,204	5,206	5,370	*50*

Sources: Data for 1955–63 are from U.S. Public Health Service, *Indian Health Highlights* (April 1964), p. 47; data for 1966 are from Public Health Service, "To the First Americans: A Report on the Indian Health Program of the U.S. Public Health Service" (1967; processed), p. 1.
a. Number of full-time filled positions.
b. Includes public health nurses.
c. Public health educators.

PHS Indian Hospital Statistics, Selected Years, 1955–65

Year	Admissions (excluding newborn)	Births	Outpatient medical visits	
			Hospitals	Health centers and field clinics
1955	42,762	6,685	355,000	110,000
1956	46,218	6,889	415,860	110,000
1961	54,313	8,437	628,657	389,000
1962	59,976	8,859	673,191	442,000
1963	64,749	9,192	721,678	550,000
1964	65,934	9,458	742,383	552,000
1965	67,744	9,514	757,726	572,000

Sources: Public Health Service, *Indian Health Highlights* (June 1966), pp. 46, 56; Public Health Service, Bureau of Health Services, "Charts on Health Trends and Services" (1967; processed).

TABLE A-10

Physician, Public Health Nurse, Dental, and Pharmaceutical Services Provided to Indian Service Population, 1955–66

Year	Physicians[a]	Public Health nurses[b]	Dental[c]	Pharmaceutical[d]
1955	400,000	n.a.	n.a.	83,870
1956	500,000	n.a.	181,000	123,328
1957	650,000	n.a.	212,069	326,029
1958	900,000	n.a.	244,975	495,119
1959	948,000	n.a.	291,542	529,066
1960	980,000	145,600	322,477	683,923
1961	1,018,000	166,889	349,997	892,990
1962	1,115,000	208,814	355,229	1,059,355
1963	1,272,200	n.a.	384,610	1,294,650
1964	1,294,000	255,525	446,010	1,351,325
1965	1,330,000	291,437	488,246	1,455,370
1966	1,367,000	n.a.	n.a.	1,480,000

Sources: Public Health Service publications: *Indian Health Highlights* (June 1966), pp. 56, 58–59; (April 1964), p. 63; *Dental Services for American Indians and Alaska Natives,* PHS Publication 1406 (1965), p. 24; "To the First Americans: A Report on the Indian Health Program of the U.S. Public Health Service," App. 1; "Charts on Health Trends and Services."
n.a. Not available.
a. Outpatient medical visits at hospital clinics, health centers, and field clinics.
b. Includes clinic visits and home and office visits. (The service visit is not defined.)
c. Total corrective dental services. (The unit of service is not defined.)
d. Service known as pharmacy workload units. One pharmacy workload unit is equivalent to the average time required to fill one prescription. Prescriptions, issues of drugs to nursing units, prepackaging of drugs, and bulk compounding are included in the total count of workload units.

Economic Development Administration Expenditures on
Indian Reservations, 1966–68

(Millions of dollars unless otherwise marked)

Type of expenditure	1966	1967	1968
Public works			
Grants	3,660	7,769	8,558
Loans	1,026	2,975	1,450
Business development			
Loans	2,301	3,797	2,081
Working capital guarantee	720	945	279
Planning grants (thousands of dollars)	45	98	299
Technical assistance (thousands of dollars)	212	357	181
Total	7,964	15,941	12,848

Source: U.S. Department of Commerce, *1968 Progress Report of the Economic Development Administration* (1968), pp. 37–123.

TABLE A-I2

Unemployment Rates before and after Participation
in Various 1963–67 Manpower Programs

Program	Median level of schooling (grade)	Median age (years)	Unemployment rate before entering program (percent)	Unemployment rate 2–3 years after leaving program (percent)
Indian programs				
Direct relocation	10.6	23	40–50	20
On-the-job training	10.5	26	40–50	6
Adult vocational training	12+	23	40–50	10
Programs for the disadvantaged population				
Job Corps	9.0	17	42[a]	29[a]
Neighborhood Youth Corps	9.5	17	—	20
Work Experience and Training[b]	8.0	34	70, or more	47
Manpower Development and Training Act[c]	11.0	26	85.2	20

Sources: Data for the three Indian manpower programs from Chap. 6 above, Tables 6-3 and 6-4, and Bureau of Indian Affairs, "A Followup Study of 1963 Recipients of the Services of the Employment Assistance Program" (October 1966). Data on the Job Corps and Neighborhood Youth Corps from Sar A. Levitan, *Antipoverty Work and Training Efforts: Goals and Reality* (joint publication of Institute of Labor and Industrial Relations and National Manpower Policy Task Force, 1967), pp. 29, 31, 51, 61. Data for work experience and training (except unemployment in col. 3, which is author's estimate), see *ibid.*, pp. 87, 96. Data for the MDTA program based on U.S. Department of Labor, *Manpower Report of the President, 1968*, pp. 205, 308–10.

  a. Corpsmen aged twenty and twenty-one only. Unemployment rate in col. 4 is for six months after leaving program.

  b. Trainees entering December 1966.

  c. Data for 1962–67 except for unemployment rate after leaving program, which was for 1967.

*Participants in Direct Employment Program Returning to Reservation within
Fiscal Year and Those Not Returning, by Fiscal Year of
First Relocation, 1953–57*

Fiscal year	Number relocated	Number returning	Percentage not returning	Percentage returning
1953	1,197	379	68	32
1954	1,263	362	71	29
1955	2,557	567	76	24
1956	4,191	1,113	73	27
1957	6,335	1,952	69	31

Source: *Indian Relocation and Industrial Development Programs*, Report of a Special Subcommittee on Indian Affairs of the House Committee on Interior and Insular Affairs, 85 Cong. 1 sess. (1958), p. 3.

TABLE A-14

*Dropout Rate, 1958–68, and Distribution of On-the-Job Trainees,
by Type of Product Manufactured or Training Given*

(*In percent*)

Field of training	Dropout rate[a]	Distribution, all 1968 trainees
Electronic parts	42.3	25
Furniture	61.8	12
Indian artifacts	53.6	4
Women's fashion specialty items	71.6	8
Garments, quilts	45.0	14
Wood	49.0	5
Fabricated metals	42.8	4
Snelled fishhooks	39.8	9
Sawmill	50.0	4
Plastics	45.8	2
Diamond processing	78.7	4
Nurse's aide	21.1	4
Miscellaneous	43.0	4
All trainees	49.0	100

Source: Computed from Bureau of Indian Affairs, Branch of Employment Assistance, "Annual Statistical Summary, 1968" (processed). Percentages in column 2 do not add to 100 because of rounding.
a. For all training programs operated from 1958 to 1967.

Length of Training, Educational Requirement, Total Enrollment,
Dropouts, Adult Vocational Training Courses, 1958–62

Course	Length of training[a] (months)	Educational requirement[a] (years)	Total number enrolled	Total	Partial completions[b]	Discontinuances	Percent
Accounting	24	12	141	73	18	55	52
Aircraft engine mechanic	14	12	57	15	2	13	26
Auto body and fender repair	4	8	295	128	30	98	43
Auto mechanic	7	8	277	98	13	85	35
Auto diesel mechanic	9	8	110	17	3	14	16
Barber	11	9	207	56	8	48	27
Bookkeeper	11	12	91	32	7	25	35
Carpenter	15	12	73	33	6	27	45
Clerk	8	12	260	77	20	57	30
Cooking	18	8	53	24	4	20	45
Cosmetology	11	10	456	191	24	167	42
Diesel mechanic	18	12	112	32	4	28	29
Draftsman	12	12	191	80	19	61	42
Dry cleaning	15	8	45	15	1	14	33
Electronics technician	14	11	135	41	9	32	30
Heavy equipment operator	3	8	40	5	0	5	12
Nurse (practical)	12	10	165	79	16	63	48
Radio-TV technician and repair	4	12	134	35	4	31	26
Secretary	11	12	352	149	28	121	42
Stenographer	8	12	248	83	27	56	34
Welding	4	8	655	146	32	144	22

Sources: Data for dropout rates from Bureau of Indian Affairs, "Summary of Results of AVT by Courses" (1963; unpublished tabulation). Data on length of training and educational requirement from Bureau of Indian Affairs, Pine Ridge Agency, "Adult Vocational Training Courses for American Indians" (Pine Ridge, S. Dak.: Jan. 2, 1968; processed).

a. Length of training and educational requirement varied among cities and towns. Figures shown here were selected as typical.

b. Trainees who have pursued enough training to allow them to accept employment in the field (or a related field) for which they have been trained.

Growth of Indian Tribal Trust Funds, 1840–1967

Fiscal year	Tribal trust funds[a]	Interest account[b]
1840	$ 4,477,322	—
1850	7,525,060	—
1860	3,396,242	—
1870	4,608,367	—
1880	15,675,140	—
1890	23,760,413	—
1900	34,317,955	—
1925	32,544,972	—
1947	28,497,081	$2,275,715
1950	42,224,130	3,335,822
1955	84,949,383	2,933,819
1960	157,717,238	2,875,979
1965	268,470,001	3,575,538
1966	257,657,380	4,212,687
1967	162,764,965	4,379,933

Sources: Data for 1840–1925 from Laurence F. Schmeckebier, *The Office of Indian Affairs: Its History, Activities and Organization* (Johns Hopkins Press for Institute for Government Research, 1927), p. 191. Data for 1947–67 from U.S. Treasury Department, *Combined Statement of Receipts, Expenditures and Balances of the United States Government for the Fiscal Year Ended June 30, 1947*, and following issues.

a. Tribal funds in Treasury only. From 1840 to 1966, this was the only depository of tribal trust funds. In 1967, approximately $150,000,000 was in banks.

b. Data for 1840–1925 not available.

TABLE A-17

Distribution of Treasury Deposits of Indian Trust Funds, by Tribe, June 30, 1966

Amount of deposit	Number of tribes	Percent of tribes	Percent of tribal funds
Less than $10,000	92	39	0.1
$ 10,000–$ 99,999	49	21	0.7
$ 100,000–$ 999,999	58	24	7.7
$1,000,000–$4,999,999	30	12	29.5
$5,000,000 or more	8	4	62.0

Source: U.S. Treasury Department, *Combined Statement of Receipts, Expenditures and Balances of the United States Government for the Fiscal Year Ended June 30, 1966*, pp. 450–64.

Per Capita Distribution of Treasury Deposits of Indian Trust Funds,
Selected Tribes, June 30, 1966

Amount of deposit	Number of tribes	Percent of tribes	Percent of Indians
Less than $300	54	62	56
$ 300–$1,000	8	9	35
$1,000–$5,000	20	23	8
Over $5,000	5	6	1

Sources: U.S. Department of the Treasury, *Combined Statement of Receipts, Expenditures and Balances of the United States Government for the Fiscal Year Ended June 30, 1966*, pp. 450–64; Bureau of Indian Affairs, "U.S. Indian Population (1962) and Land (1963)" (November 1963; processed).

TABLE A-19

Awards by Indian Claims Commission, Fiscal Year 1969

Tribe, band, or group	Award
Assiniboine	$3,108,506
Blackfeet and Gros Ventre	8,679,815
Delaware	457,980
Fort Berthold	1,850,000
Iowa	3,163,208
Kickapoo	273,250
Miami, Oklahoma	1,449,966
Peoria	1,139,533
Potawatomi, Citizen	797,509
Sac and Fox	4,474,378
Sioux, Cheyenne River	1,300,000
Sioux of Fort Peck	1,161,354
Sioux, Yankton	1,250,000
Skagit, Upper	385,471
Snoqualmie-Skykomish	257,698
Yakima	2,100,000
Yavapai-Apache	5,100,000

Source: Indian Claims Commission, *1969 Annual Report*, App. 2, p. 4.

Income from Oil and Gas, Selected Tribes, 1965

(In thousands of dollars)

Tribe	State	Amount
Wind River[a]	Wyoming	2,120
Navajo	Arizona, Utah, New Mexico	6,447
Five Civilized Tribes	Oklahoma	1,430
Jicarilla Apache	New Mexico	880
Southern Ute	Colorado	699
Fort Berthold[a]	North Dakota	191
Tlingit and Haida	Alaska	11,672

Source: Henry W. Hough, *Development of Indian Resources* (World Press, 1967), pp. 124–26.
a. Data are for 1966.

TABLE A-21

Schedule of BIA General Assistance Payments, 1968

Number of persons	Monthly payment[a] (in dollars)
1 alone	56
1 with others	51
2 adults	95
1 adult and 1 child	79
3 persons	105
4 persons	137
5 persons	169
6 persons	200
7 persons	232
8 persons	263
Each additional person	32

Source: Bureau of Indian Affairs, Branch of Welfare (October 1969; unpublished).
a. Under assumption of no other income.

Schedule of Payments, by Income, Family of Four, Mutual-Help Housing

(In dollars)

Annual income	Monthly payment
1,750	7.00
2,000	7.00
2,250	10.00
2,500	15.00
2,750	15.00
3,000	17.50
3,500	17.50
3,750	20.00
4,000	25.00
4,375	27.50
4,750	27.50
5,000	35.00
5,500	40.00
6,000 or more	45.00

Source: Bureau of Indian Affairs, "Income and Payment Chart" (1968; unpublished tabulation).

Recent Manpower Programs

In the mid-1960s the Bureau of Indian Affairs (BIA) realized that its adult vocational training program was not reaching the high school dropout. Since the educational requirement for most of the courses was high school graduation, nongraduates were generally ineligible for training. Three programs that combine basic education and prevocational or vocational training were established in 1967–68 to reach the less educated segment of the Indians. The first project was undertaken by the RCA Corporation, under contract with the Bureau of Indian Affairs, to give Indians on the Choctaw Reservation in Mississippi prevocational training and basic education. The other two projects combine vocational training with basic education; one is operated by the Thiokol Chemical Corporation at Roswell, New Mexico, the other by the Philco-Ford Corporation at Madera, California. Because these programs have been in operation for only a short time, evaluation is necessarily tentative and incomplete. It is hoped that future studies of Indian manpower programs will be able to evaluate these new efforts more intensively.

RCA Corporation Training Center

The RCA Corporation project for the Choctaw Indians of Mississippi is probably the most ambitious of all Indian manpower programs. In 1968 about seventy-five Indian families, most of whom were formerly sharecroppers earning $300–$400 a year, were taking prevocational training and basic education. Wives of breadwinners were being given training in homemaking, personal hygiene, and child care. The average age of family heads was thirty-one, and both men and women had about two years of formal education. Families had, on the average, five or six children.[1]

[1] Interview with Robert Murray, director, April 1968.

The participants are trained to take low-skilled positions in industry after graduation. Instruction in the use of tools, blueprints, and shop procedure is combined with education in communication skills and mathematics, with the goal of bringing reading and mathematics achievement up to sixth or seventh grade levels. As of mid-1968, fourteen families had left the project and twelve families had completed the twelve to fifteen months' training course and had been relocated, mainly in the South and Midwest.

The cost per trainee is $4,600 a year, not including subsistence,[2] approximately three times the training cost of the adult vocational program. One of the main factors in the relatively high cost is the low ratio of students to teachers (about six to one).[3]

Since the project has been in operation only a short time, with correspondingly few "graduates," it is impossible to make a precise assessment. One of the greatest problems the participants face is the barrier their limited formal schooling presents to employment and advancement in the urban areas to which they are relocated. Surveys of Indian participation in manpower programs show that participants tend to change jobs frequently. While RCA and the Bureau of Indian Affairs may be successful in placing the trainees initially, they may have difficulty when they seek jobs for themselves.[4] At present many of the graduates are not earning enough to support their families (their salaries are usually $1.60–$2.00 an hour), and the Bureau of Indian Affairs supplements their income.

Although the benefit–cost ratio is probably not as great as for other programs,[5] one of the main purposes of the RCA program is to remove the Indian from the economic and social limitations of sharecropping. The low level of schooling of the participants attests to the oppressiveness under which these people and their ancestors have lived for generations.

The training center is surrounded by a large number of trailers occupied by the participants and the staff. Reports indicate that the biggest problem affecting the trainees' progress is heavy drinking, especially on weekends. Since Neshoba County is a dry county, much of

[2] Interview with Joseph Lasalle, Branch of Employment Assistance, Bureau of Indian Affairs, July 1968.

[3] Interview with Robert Murray.

[4] Because this is a new program, it is not clear how long follow-up services will be available to graduates.

[5] For example, assume that the average trainee (including dropouts) earns $2,000 during the year after completion. This would mean, on a lifetime earnings basis and assuming a constant differential between earnings before and after "graduation," a benefit–cost ratio of 5 to 1 (at a 5 percent discount rate).

the liquor sold to the Indians comes from bootleggers, who come to the training center to sell their wares. It is difficult to understand why this traffic in illegal liquor cannot be controlled, but from all reports, if it is not controlled, the effectiveness of the entire program will be seriously jeopardized.[6]

The Roswell Employment Training Center

This center, which was established by the Thiokol Chemical Corporation in March 1968, combines job-related basic education with vocational training for semiskilled jobs. The educational program is made up of three component areas that include communication arts, mathematics, and personal development. Each area exposes all students to the rudiments of job-related skills in computation and mathematical concepts, paragraph meaning, language arts, vocabulary, verbal communication, social skills, consumer economics, and personal hygiene.[7] Special programs for those who do not read and speak English have been developed, and English is being taught as a second language. The education is related as closely as possible to the vocational training course selected by the student.

It is clear that most of the students come to the center with serious academic deficiencies. The achievement levels of entrants on various phases of the Stanford Achievement Test battery were as follows:[8]

Test	Mean grade level
Spelling	6.9
Paragraph meaning	5.5
Language	5.1
Arithmetic computation	5.0
Arithmetic concepts	5.2
Arithmetic applications	5.9
Years of school completed	8.4

The average student's achievement is two to three years below the highest grade level completed on language and mathematics subtests.

The vocational training department is composed of four major areas: (1) auto welding (body and fender, small engine, auto repair, tune-up,

[6] RCA Corporation, "Quarterly Progress Report" (July 1968; processed).

[7] Thiokol Chemical Corporation, "Quarterly Report, Roswell Employment Training Center" (June 30, 1968; processed), p. 14.

[8] *Ibid.*, p. 38.

and welding); (2) food processing (cooking, baking, and meat-cutting); (3) electronic assembly; and (4) government services (office-clerical, typing, stenography, surveying and drafting, and nurse's aide).[9]

The training and administrative costs of the program are about $5,600 a year per trainee, not including subsistence for him and his family.[10] Most trainees probably remain at the center for about a year.

Since there have been few graduates from this training program, it is impossible to apply any evaluative criteria. However, student progress reports point up certain problems that will have a profound effect on the benefit–cost ratio and other criteria.

On June 30, 1968, each student at the center was evaluated in terms of percentage of job readiness and general adjustment to training-center life. Numerical grades were given in each academic and vocational course taken. These reports are brutally frank. They indicate that 27 percent of the trainees have drinking problems, which have resulted in fighting and other disturbances at the center, and they make slower progress than those who do not drink. The typical trainee with a drinking problem was rated at 25 percent of job readiness, the typical nondrinker at 30 percent. Since both groups entered the center at the same time, drinking is apparently retarding the progress of many.[11] Drinkers are likely to take two to three months longer to complete training, if they complete it at all, resulting in higher training costs than for nondrinkers.[12]

Since the problem drinkers will be difficult to place, or, if placed, may soon leave their initial employment, the rate of return to training for this group will undoubtedly be low. Besides those with drinking problems, other trainees seem unlikely to profit by the training. The student evaluation reports reveal instances of refusal to attend classes, psychiatric problems, trainees disappearing for a week or more and then reappearing, and a lack of interest by some in the program.

[9] At first glance it appears that many of the occupations enumerated under "government services" are also a part of the adult vocational training curriculum (Appendix Table A-15) and that the Roswell program is, in this instance, merely duplicating an established program. However, this is not the case. The students entering the government services area at Roswell, while they may be high school graduates, are so academically retarded that they need these special educational facilities, which are not provided under the regular adult vocational training program.

[10] Interview with Joseph Lasalle, September 1968.

[11] One could argue that drinking was a consequence of slow progress and not a cause of it, but a detailed review of the reports indicates that the drinking is associated with other factors, such as social adjustment problems.

[12] Moreover, problem drinkers receive extra attention from staff counselors, which also increases the cost of training.

Despite many infractions of training center rules, only five were dismissed in the first six months of 1968.

Because there is a backlog of applicants awaiting training, it is not clear why more have not been separated from the program. It would seem more useful, given a limited budget, to allocate resources to a maximum number of persons who clearly have the potential for training, rather than to concentrate them on a limited number with problems that might be handled better elsewhere.

However, the greatest fault may lie not with the center staff but with the local employment assistance officer. Since there are more applicants than there are openings at the training center, an effective screening operation would eliminate many potential troublemakers. There is no excuse for sending chronic alcoholics, those with severe mental or physical problems, and uninterested individuals for training when there are many without those problems seeking admission to the program.[13]

The Madera Employment Training Center

The Education and Technical Services Division of the Philco-Ford Corporation, under a BIA contract, established a training center in Madera, California, in 1967. A graded vocational training program is offered which allows for varying entry levels based on trainee aptitudes and education, as well as various exit levels, ranging from a minimum employable skill to semiskilled employment. The center offers educational opportunities for all members of the family, including basic education for the spouse and all eligible wage earners, public school training for school-age children, and day care programs for preschoolers.

The training courses are divided into the following occupational areas: clerical; automotive and small engine repair; electronics assembly; appliance and radio-television maintenance; drafting; and supplementary occupations, such as culinary arts, health, and building trades.

As in the case of the Roswell program, basic education is provided and is related as closely as possible to vocational training. The follow-

[13] The chief of the Crow Indians, Edison Real Bird, indicated that the local employment assistance officer seemed to have no idea of the background of many of the applicants for employment assistance. Real Bird felt that had there been any communication between the tribe and the officer, scarce funds would not have been wasted on those who had virtually no chance of profiting from the various programs.

ing table shows that the educational achievement level of the trainees is similar to that of those in the Roswell training program:[14]

Test	Mean grade level
Arithmetic	5.1
Spelling	6.6
Reading	6.5
Composite	5.4
Formal schooling	8.0–9.0

The Madera trainees, like their Roswell counterparts, are two to three years behind grade level on the various achievement subtests.

The Bureau of Indian Affairs in August 1968 completed a statistical follow-up survey of 276 former Madera participants. Because the typical trainee surveyed had been separated from the program for only about six months, any conclusions drawn from the analysis presented below are tentative.

INTERNAL RATE OF RETURN AND BENEFIT-COST ANALYSIS

As in the case of other manpower programs, data are available on earnings before and after program participation. However, while income data for the programs described in Chapter 6 included earnings for three years before and after program participation, data for the Madera trainees refer to the year before training, and earnings for the six months after training are projected to predict earnings for the year after training.[15] The internal rate of return is 33 percent, the benefit–cost ratio at a 5 percent discount rate is 6.1 to 1, and at a 10 percent discount is 3.4 to 1, on the assumption that the differential in earnings before and after program participation is constant.[16]

The internal rate of return is about three-fifths of that calculated for the adult vocational training program (see Chapter 6). This is because the increment in earnings after training at Madera is lower, and the

[14] Bureau of Indian Affairs, "Followup Survey of Madera Employment Center Trainees" (August 1968; processed).

[15] Future surveys should obtain a more detailed earnings history.

[16] Rates of return are based on the following data: average income for year prior to training, $1,280; projected income for one year after training, $2,350 (includes zero income for participants who are unemployed and not in the labor force); average training and administrative cost per trainee, $2,820; forgone earnings for seven months of training, $675. Data computed from survey material in Bureau of Indian Affairs, "Followup Survey of Madera Employment Center Trainees."

costs (training and administration plus forgone earnings) are higher than those of the adult vocational training program.

LABOR FORCE STATUS

Because the Madera program is attempting to reach less educated families and individuals who are in greatest need of help, one would expect that the unemployment rate of the participants before training would be very high. This is borne out by the following table, which shows the labor force status in percentages of the 141 graduates before and after training:[17]

Labor force status	1967	1968
Employed	30	51
Unemployed	50	37
Not in labor force	20	12

The data are not encouraging. Only 51 percent of the graduates were employed. Perhaps six months is not long enough for the typical trainee to find a desirable position, and so some of the unemployment may be frictional (associated with job changing). However, the low level of labor force participation also reflects withdrawal of married women from the labor force.

Of the graduates who returned to the reservation, 83 percent were unemployed.[18] It appears that participants in this program have a much greater tendency to return to the reservation than those in other programs. Nearly half returned within six months of leaving the center.[19]

The follow-up survey indicates that of those employed six months after departing from Madera, 52 percent were in positions related to training, less than the 59 percent of 1963 participants in the standard adult vocational training program who in 1968 were in employment related to training (see Chapter 6). Thus five years after training, the proportion of standard program participants in training-related employment was larger than the proportion of Madera graduates six months after training.

[17] Figures for 1967, author's estimates; for 1968, computed from data in Bureau of Indian Affairs, "Followup Survey of Madera Employment Center Trainees."

[18] Bureau of Indian Affairs, "Followup Survey of Madera Employment Center Trainees."

[19] This may be due to the participants' limited formal schooling. Studies cited in Chapter 6 indicate that the lower the level of formal schooling of migrants (without training), the greater their tendency to return home.

APPENDIX C

Derivation of Benefit-Cost Estimates

Rates of return can be calculated in two ways. The internal-rate-of-return method consists of solving for the rate of discount that will equate costs with future returns. Symbolically, the internal rate is derived from the equation:

$$C = \sum_{i=1}^{n} \frac{R_i}{(1 + r)^i}$$

where:

C = relevant costs,
R_i = returns in the ith year,
r = unknown discount rate (that is, rate of return), and
n = number of years remaining until retirement.

The second method of evaluation is to calculate the benefit–cost ratio where the present value of the benefits is given by:

$$B = \sum_{i=1}^{n} \frac{B_i}{(1 + r_1)^i}, \quad \text{and the benefit–cost ratio is } B/C,$$

where:

B_i = benefit (income) in the ith year,
r_1 = selected discount rate, and
C = costs.

Since costs do not occur over time but are concentrated in the period when training and/or relocation takes place, there is no need to discount costs.

Costs

In determining the costs to be considered in this study, it was decided to include all resource costs, regardless of who pays them, and to exclude transfer payments (most of which are subsistence allowances given during training).[1] Thus, the principal costs used here are the training, relocation, and administrative costs (calculated on a per-trainee basis), and the opportunity costs, or forgone earnings, which are the private costs borne by the participant. These costs for three Indian manpower programs are shown in Appendix Table C-1. The data on relocation, training, and administrative costs are derived from

TABLE C-I

Resource Costs per Trainee, 1963 Indian Manpower Programs

(*In dollars*)

Type of cost	Direct relocation	On-the-job training[a]	Adult vocational training
Relocation, training, and administration	1,300	650	1,460
Opportunity cost[b]	40	0	1,280
Total	1,340	650	2,740

Sources: U.S. Bureau of Indian Affairs, "A Followup Study of 1963 Recipients of the Services of the Employment Assistance Program" (October 1966; processed), and author's estimates based on July 1968 revision of the "Followup Study"; and U.S. Bureau of the Census, *Census of Population: 1960, Subject Reports, Nonwhite Population by Race*, Final Report PC(2)-1C (1963), Tables 33 and 56, pp. 104, 234.

a. Includes initial transportation to facility, subsistence en route, and miscellaneous relocation costs.

b. Forgone earnings.

a follow-up survey made in 1966 of 1963 program participants, taking into account average length of courses and percentage of completions.[2]

Opportunity costs are determined on the basis of prior earnings (presented below) and length of time during which training and/or relocation took place. For example, average annual income for migrants participating in the direct relocation program was $1,040 before leaving the reservation. Since first job placement occurred two weeks after leaving the reservation, earnings forgone were approximately $40.

[1] For the logic of this position, see Thomas I. Ribich, *Education and Poverty* (Brookings Institution, 1968), Chap. 3.

[2] Since the earnings of dropouts are included in this study, their costs are also included.

Opportunity costs of on-the-job trainees are considered to be zero because, unlike many on-the-job training programs operated for non-Indians, incomes are above what could have been earned if the participant had not enrolled in the program.

Returns

Before-tax income gains accruing to participants in these programs are used as the measure of returns. This is done in the interest of simplicity, but it is doubtful that basing returns on after-tax income would change the results significantly. Appendix Table C-2 presents data on pretax income for three years before and three years after training. The data given for on reservation, near reservation, and field office cities refer to the place of employment in 1966 of the participants. As was indicated in Chapter 6, those who returned to the

TABLE C-2

Average Incomes for Three Years before and Three Years after Participation in 1963 Indian Manpower Programs

(In dollars)

Program	Average income, 1960–62	Average income, 1964–66
Direct relocation		
All	1,040	2,690
Men	1,101	2,700
Women	770	2,680
On reservation (men and women)	n.a.	2,030
Near reservation (men and women)	n.a.	1,980
Field office cities (men and women)	n.a.	3,430
On-the-job training		
All	1,260	2,320
Adult vocational training		
All	1,280	3,320
Men	1,320	3,580
Women	970	2,620
On reservation (men and women)	n.a.	2,710
Near reservation (men and women)	n.a.	3,610
Field office cities (men and women)	n.a.	3,630

Sources: Relocation program, 1960–62, Bureau of Indian Affairs, "A Followup Study of 1963 Recipients" (1968, rev.); other figures, author's estimates based on *ibid.* (1966 and 1968, rev.). n.a. Not available.

reservation had much lower incomes, on the average, than those who remained in the urban centers where they were placed.

Before benefits are determined, several assumptions must be made, some of them arbitrary. First, it is assumed that returns or benefits will accrue for the remaining working life of the trainee and/or relocatee. While it might be argued that job mobility and worker obsolescence call for a shorter period of accrued returns, it is felt that any shorter period would be equally arbitrary. Moreover, it is possible that some of the work skills and habits acquired in training could be useful for the trainee's entire working life.

Second, it is assumed that there is no increase in earnings differentials between participants and nonparticipants over time; that is, "a tendency for some trainees to improve upon their short-run gains is assumed to be exactly counterbalanced by a tendency for others to lose at least part of their initial earnings advantage as their occupations undergo 'obsolescence' in future periods."[3]

There seems to be little agreement among economists on the appropriate rate of discount.[4] Consequently, both a 5 percent rate (the approximate federal bond rate in 1968) and a 10 percent rate (an approximation to the rate of return on corporate capital) are used.

No vital statistics are maintained for Indians living off the reservation; however, such data are available for reservation Indians and for non-Indians. In adjusting benefits for mortality, it was assumed that relocated Indians would have the same mortality patterns as non-Indians.[5]

Some benefit-cost analyses of training programs examine data on earnings only of those who complete the program.[6] However, since even partial completion of a training program may make a man employable, and since the industrial discipline acquired as a result

---

[3] Ribich, *Education and Poverty*, p. 49.

[4] For some alternative views, see Otto Eckstein, "A Survey of the Theory of Public Expenditure Criteria" (plus comments and reply) in *Public Finances: Needs, Sources, and Utilization* (Princeton University Press for National Bureau of Economic Research, 1961), pp. 439–504, and Burton A. Weisbrod, "Preventing High School Dropouts" (plus comments and concluding statement) in Robert Dorfman (ed.), *Measuring Benefits of Government Investments* (Brookings Institution, 1965), pp. 117–71.

[5] This is because health and housing conditions are more similar to those of non-Indians than of reservation Indians. Benefits to on-the-job trainees are adjusted for mortality using the vital statistics of non-Indians. This was done for consistency and also because higher incomes should allow the trainees to live better and longer than Indians remaining on the reservation.

[6] For example, see David A. Page, "Retraining Under the Manpower Development Act: A Cost-Benefit Analysis," *Public Policy*, Vol. 13 (1964), pp. 257–67.

of participation in an Indian manpower program could increase productivity, it seemed more reasonable to include the earnings of all participants.

In lieu of a control group, age-earnings profiles taken from the 1960 census of population were used to estimate what incomes would have been had the men not participated in the program. Thus, it was assumed that, due to age alone, men's incomes would have increased $75 a year from 1964 to 1966 without the program, and women's incomes would have increased $50. In addition, men's incomes would have risen $60 and women's incomes $50 a year as a result of the rise in income on the reservation due to economic growth.[7]

As an example, let us derive the earnings differential for 1964 through 1966 between male participants in the direct relocation program and nonparticipants. The average annual income of male participants in the program was $2,700 (see Appendix Table C-2). The income of nonparticipants was estimated to be $1,365 in 1964, $1,530 in 1965, and $1,695 in 1966, or an average of $1,530 annually for 1964 through 1966. Thus, the earnings differential (assumed to be constant over the working life of the participant) would be $1,170.

Appendix Table C-3 presents data on the present value of benefits, calculated at 5 percent and 10 percent discount rates, for the various programs.

In Chapter 6, it was argued that the returns to adult vocational training are overstated, since they include a return to migration and not merely to training per se. To adjust for this, the "extra" costs connected with the program (that is, the costs involved in actually training the participant, which equals total cost minus the cost of relocation) may be compared with the "extra" benefits, that is, the additional income resulting from training as distinct from the extra income earned because one is in an urban area. To estimate these "extra" costs roughly, the cost per migrant from the direct relocation program is subtracted from the cost per trainee under the adult vocational training program ($2,740 − $1,340 = $1,400).[8] The extra income resulting from training may be measured approximately by the earnings differential between male direct migrants (without training)

[7] This estimate is based on the growth of income between 1949 and 1959 as given in U.S. Bureau of the Census, *Census of Population: 1950*, Vol. 4, *Special Reports*, Pt. 3, Chap. B, *Nonwhite Population by Race* (1953), and *Census of Population: 1960, Subject Reports, Nonwhite Population by Race*, Final Report PC(2)-1C (1963).

[8] This understates the extra cost, because part of the $1,340 cost per migrant (without training) is for the staffs (see Appendix Table C-1), which must work harder to place a direct migrant (without training) than a trainee.

TABLE C-3

Present Value of Benefits, 1963 Indian Manpower Programs,
at 5 and 10 Percent Discount Rates

Program	5 percent discount rate	10 percent discount rate
Direct relocation		
All	21,220	12,500
Men	20,180	11,990
Women	29,250	16,700
On reservation (men and women)	9,950	5,510
Near reservation (men and women)	8,750	4,970
Field office cities (men and women)	33,600	19,100
On-the-job training		
All	14,700	8,360
Adult vocational training		
All	27,100	15,450
Men	29,400	16,800
Women	21,200	12,200
On reservation (men and women)	17,190	10,100
Near reservation (men and women)	33,000	18,800
Field office cities (men and women)	33,500	19,000

Sources: Derived from income data in Appendix Table C-2; and age-income profiles from Bureau of the Census, *1950 Census, Nonwhite Population by Race*, and *1960 Census, Nonwhite Population by Race*.

and adult male vocational trainees. For 1964 through 1966, this was $880 annually ($3,580–$2,700). The internal rate of return and benefit–cost ratios for the vocational training program after adjustments for these extra benefits and extra costs is presented in Appendix Table C-4.

Costs and Benefits Not Included

Because of a lack of data some items are not included in the calculation of the benefit–cost ratios. First, the moving costs (and earnings forgone) of returnees from urban metropolitan areas are not included, causing a slight overestimate in the benefit–cost ratios of participants who have left the cities where they were originally placed. Second, no attempt has been made to adjust benefits by taking account of variations in cost-of-living differentials between the reservation and urban areas. These variations may not be large, but lack of information

TABLE C-4

*Adjusted Internal Rate of Return and Benefit–Cost Ratios, Participants
in 1963 Indian Adult Vocational Training Program*

Internal rate of return (in percent)	48
Benefit–cost ratio at 5 percent discount rate	7.3:1
Benefit–cost ratio at 10 percent discount rate	4.1:1

Source: Calculated as described in the text.

makes it impossible to determine in which location the cost would
be lower for the Indian.

Medical care is furnished free of charge to most reservation Indians
by the U.S. Public Health Service. While free care can be obtained
off the reservation, it is presumably more difficult to obtain. The cost
of food and clothing is higher on reservations than in most urban
areas, since reservation stores and trading posts are usually small (and
thus unable to purchase in quantity) and may, because of their isolation, be in a near-monopoly position. Many reservation Indians have
built their own homes on allocated or tribal land and have little
housing expense, but in a city this is not the case. However, the
housing off the reservation is generally of higher quality. Thus, it
is impossible to determine whether housing costs, per unit of quality,
are higher off than on the reservation. Factors such as these make a
cost comparison impossible.

Selected References

Ablon, Joan. "American Indian Relocation: Problems of Dependency and Management in the City," *Phylon*, Vol. 26 (Winter 1965).

Adams, Evelyn C. *American Indian Education: Government Schools and Economic Progress*. New York: Columbia University Press, 1946.

Anderson, Kenneth E., E. Gordon Collister, and Carl E. Ladd. *The Educational Achievement of Indian Children*. U.S. Bureau of Indian Affairs. Lawrence, Kansas: Haskell Press, 1953.

Bass, Willard P. "An Analysis of Academic Achievement of Indian High School Students in Federal and Public Schools, 1966–67." Processed. Albuquerque, N.Mex.: Southwestern Cooperative Educational Laboratory, Inc., January 1968.

Brazziel, William F. "Effects of General Education in Manpower Programs," *Journal of Human Resources*, Vol. 1 (Summer 1966).

Bryde, John F. *The Sioux Indian Student: A Study of Scholastic Failure and Personality Conflict*. Published by author, 1966.

Cain, Glen G. "Benefit/Cost Estimates for Job Corps." Processed. Madison: University of Wisconsin, Institute for Research on Poverty, 1967.

Carroll, Adger B., and Loren A. Ihnen. "Costs and Returns for Two Years of Postsecondary Technical Schooling: A Pilot Study," *Journal of Political Economy*, Vol. 75 (December 1967).

Coleman, James S., and others. *Equality of Educational Opportunity*. U.S. Department of Health, Education, and Welfare, Office of Education. Washington: Government Printing Office, 1966.

Corazzini, Arthur J. "The Decision to Invest in Vocational Education: An Analysis of Costs and Benefits," *Journal of Human Resources*, Supplement, Vol. 3 (1968).

———. "When Should Vocational Education Begin?" *Journal of Human Resources*, Vol. 2 (Winter 1967).

ENKI Corporation. "Evaluation Report, Bureau of Indian Affairs Title I Programs, Elementary and Secondary Education Act." Processed. San Fernando, Calif.: ENKI, 1967.

Graves, Theodore D., and Minor Van Arsdale. "Values, Expectations and Relocation: The Navaho Migrant to Denver," *Human Organization*, Vol. 25 (Winter 1966).

Haas, Theodore H. "The Legal Aspects of Indian Affairs from 1887 to 1957," in George E. Simpson and J. Milton Yinger (eds.), *American Indians and American Life, Annals of the American Academy of Political and Social Science,* Vol. 311 (May 1957).

Hamel, Harvey R. "Educational Attainment of Workers, March 1966," U.S. Bureau of Labor Statistics, Special Labor Force Report No. 83. Washington: BLS, 1967.

Hough, Henry W. *Development of Indian Resources.* Denver: World Press, 1967.

Human Sciences Research, Inc. "A Comprehensive Evaluation of OEO Community Action Programs on Six Selected American Indian Reservations." Processed. McLean, Va.: HSR, September 1966.

Institute for Government Research. *The Problem of Indian Administration.* Baltimore: Johns Hopkins Press, 1928.

La Farge, Oliver. "Termination of Federal Supervision: Disintegration and the American Indians," in George E. Simpson and J. Milton Yinger (eds.), *American Indians and American Life, Annals of the American Academy of Political and Social Science,* Vol. 311 (May 1957).

Leupp, Francis E. *The Indian and His Problem.* New York: Charles Scribner's Sons, 1910.

Levitan, Sar A. *Antipoverty Work and Training Efforts: Goals and Reality.* Joint publication of Institute of Labor and Industrial Relations and National Manpower Policy Task Force. Ann Arbor and Washington, 1967.

Martin, Harry W. "Correlates of Adjustment Among American Indians in an Urban Environment," *Human Organization,* Vol. 23 (Winter 1964).

Mincer, Jacob. "On-the-Job Training: Costs, Returns, and Some Implications," *Journal of Political Economy,* Supplement, Vol. 70, Pt. 2 (October 1962).

Orshansky, Mollie. "Counting the Poor: Another Look at the Poverty Profile," *Social Security Bulletin,* Vol. 28 (January 1965).

——. "The Shape of Poverty in 1966," *Social Security Bulletin,* Vol. 31 (March 1968).

Philco-Ford Corporation. "Quarterly Report, Madera Employment Training Center." Processed. April 1968.

RCA Corporation. "Quarterly Progress Report." Processed. July 1968.

Ribich, Thomas I. *Education and Poverty.* Washington: Brookings Institution, 1968.

Sasaki, Tom. "Sources of Mental Stress in Indian Acculturation," in J. Cobb (ed.), "Emotional Problems of Indian Students in Boarding Schools and Related Public Schools." Processed. U.S. Bureau of Indian Affairs, 1960.

Saslow, Harry L., and May J. Harrover. "Research on Psychosocial Adjustment of Indian Youth," *American Journal of Psychiatry,* Vol. 125 (August 1968).

Schmeckebier, Laurence F. *The Office of Indian Affairs: Its History, Activities and Organization.* Baltimore: Johns Hopkins Press for Institute for Government Research, 1927.

Selinger, Alphonse D. *The American Indian High School Dropout: The*

Magnitude of the Problem. Portland, Oreg.: Northwest Regional Educational Laboratory, September 1968.

Sjaastad, Larry A. "The Costs and Returns of Human Migration," *Journal of Political Economy,* Supplement, Vol. 70, Pt. 2 (October 1962).

Stewart, Omer. "Questions Regarding American Indian Criminality," *Human Organization,* Vol. 23 (Spring 1964).

Striner, Herbert E. "Toward a Fundamental Program for the Training, Employment and Economic Equality of the American Indian," in *Federal Programs for the Development of Human Resources,* A Compendium of Papers Submitted to the Subcommittee on Economic Progress of the Joint Economic Committee. 90 Cong. 2 sess. Washington: Government Printing Office, 1968.

Taussig, Michael K. "An Economic Analysis of Vocational Education in the New York City High Schools," *Journal of Human Resources,* Supplement, Vol. 3 (1968).

U.S. Congress. House Committee on Interior and Insular Affairs. *Indian Unemployment Survey,* A Memorandum and Accompanying Information from the Chairman. 88 Cong. 1 sess. Washington: Government Printing Office, 1963.

————. Senate Committee on Labor and Public Welfare. *Indian Education,* Hearings before the Special Subcommittee on Indian Education, Pts. 1–5. 90 Cong. 1 and 2 sess. Washington: Government Printing Office, 1969.

U.S. Department of Health, Education, and Welfare, Public Health Service. *Indian Health Highlights.* Washington: Government Printing Office, various years.

U.S. Department of the Interior, Bureau of Indian Affairs. "The Osage People and Their Trust Property." Processed. Pawhuska, Okla.: Anadarko Area Office, Osage Agency, 1953.

U.S. Department of Labor. *Manpower Report of the President.* Washington: Government Printing Office, various years.

Watkins, Arthur V. "Termination of Federal Supervision: The Removal of Restrictions over Indian Property and Person," in George E. Simpson and J. Milton Yinger (eds.), *American Indians and American Life, Annals of the American Academy of Political and Social Science,* Vol. 311 (May 1957).

Wax, Murray L., Rosalie H. Wax, and Robert V. Dumont, Jr. *Formal Education in an American Indian Community,* Supplement to *Social Problems,* Vol. 11 (Spring 1964).

Wax, Rosalie H., and Murray L. Wax. "Dropout of American Indians at the Secondary Level," in *Indian Education,* Hearings before the Special Subcommittee on Indian Education of the Senate Committee on Labor and Public Welfare, Pt. 4. 90 Cong. 1 and 2 sess. Washington: Government Printing Office, 1969.

Young, Robert W., compiler. *The Navajo Yearbook.* Window Rock, Ariz.: Navajo Agency, 1961.

Zintz, M. V. "The Indian Research Study, Final Report." Processed. Albuquerque: University of New Mexico, College of Education, 1960.

Index

Aberle, Sophie D., 51n, 67n, 70n, 71n, 158n, 160n
Ablon, Joan, 121
Adult education (see also Adult vocational training): BIA administration, 38-40; budget, 39-40; need, 38-39, 129n; RCA Corporation project, 207-09; recommendations, 179-80; scope, 39 (table); teachers, 40, 178
Adult vocational training (see also Adult education): alcoholism, 208-11; behavioral effects, 129-30; benefit–cost ratio, 113-15, 208, 212-13; cost-participant, 106 (table); dropouts, 127; education factor, 114n-15n, 128-29, 208-09, 212; eligibility, 33, 36; employment level after, 118-20, 213; income levels after, 114-16; language, 209; Madera Employment Training Center, 211-13; RCA Corporation Training Center, 207-09; women, 133, 187
Agriculture: BIA administration of, 68-70, 75-77; capital equipment, 70, 77; Dawes Act, 6, 68; decline, 78-79; development projects, 75-76; education factor, 69-70; extension program agents, 68-69, 79n; financing, 68-70, 77; interest in, 18, 68, 77-79, 182; land use, 66 (table); leasing, 66-67, 149; livestock industry, 68, 70-71, 73-74; management ability, 67-70, 74-75, 77, 79; Navajo-Hopi Rehabilitation Act of 1950, 77; Navajo Training Farm, 147; ownership, 71-72, 182; productivity factors, 67-72; recommendations, 182-83; seasonal nature, 14; size of holdings, 70-71, 79; tribal corporations, 72-74; vocational training, 74-75, 182; wage levels, 95
Airlines. See Transportation
Alabama Indians, 158
Alaska: education, 38, 47; mineral resources, 90-91; population, 4, 32
Albuquerque Indian School, 41, 47n
Alcoholism: research need, 65, 182, 191; returnee factor, 122n; training programs' effect on, 130, 208-10

Alcohol, restriction of, 8
Aleuts, 4, 32
Allen, Thomas, 82n
Amizuñi Corporation, 132
Anderson, Kenneth E., 23n
Apker, Wesley, 26n
Area Redevelopment Administration (ARA), 80, 91-92, 114
Arizona, 3-5, 10-11, 14, 73, 83, 90, 105, 123, 147, 160, 166
Arizona State University, 185
Artichoker, John, 96n
Assimilation. See Dawes Act; Termination

Babyline Furniture Company, 147
Bass, Willard P., 24n
Becker, Gary S., 32
Behavior (see also Mental health): generation gap, 2-3; industrialization factor, 95-96, 125-26; manpower programs' effect on, 129-30; sensitivity, 125-26
Bennett, Robert L., 142, 155n
Birth control, 63-64
Birthrate, 13, 14n, 134n
Blackfeet Irrigation Project, 67
Blackfeet Reservation: agriculture, 76 (table); birth control, 64; claim settlements, 137, 144; employment level, 14 (table); industry, 93; medical care, 58
Brands, Allen J., 61n
Brazziel, William F., 134n
Brophy, William A., 51n, 67n, 70n, 71n, 158n, 160n
Brule tribe, 141
Bryde, John F., 23n, 26n, 30, 95n
Burckell, Christian E., 27n
Bureau of Indian Affairs (BIA): administration, 5; adult education programs, 38-40; agricultural development role, 68-70, 75-77, 182; budget, 7, 39; census distinctions, 4; creation of, 5; education, problems in, 28, 33, 39, 44, 46, 48-50; employment programs, 14, 119-21; general assistance program, 162-63; housing programs, 172, 174; individual bank account supervision, 151-56;